Casebook in
Abnormal Psychology
Second Edition

Casebook in Abnormal Psychology

SECOND EDITION

John Vitkus

Barnard College

McGRAW-HILL, INC.

New York   St. Louis   San Francisco   Auckland   Bogotá   Caracas   Lisbon
London   Madrid   Mexico   Milan   Montreal   New Delhi   Paris
San Juan   Singapore   Sydney   Tokyo   Toronto

For Allison Rebecca and Ian Kendall

234567890 DOC DOC 909876543

ISBN 0-07-006546-2

The editors were Jane Vaicunas and Beth Kaufman;
the production supervisor was Annette Mayeski.
R. R. Donnelley & Sons Company was printer and binder.

Library of Congress Cataloging-in-Publication Data

Vitkus, John.
    Casebook in abnormal psychology / John Vitkus. —2nd ed.
        p.   cm.
    Includes bibliographical references.
    ISBN 0-07-911168-8 (set)
    1. Psychiatry—Case studies.   I. Title.
    [DNLM: 1. Mental Disorders—case studies.
2. Psychopathology—case studies.   WM 40 V844c]
RC465.V58   1993
616.89'09—dc20
DNLM/DLC
for Library of Congress   92-49349

INTRODUCTION

The *Casebook in Abnormal Psychology, Second Edition* consists of a selection of 16 different psychiatric case histories representing several major areas of abnormal psychology, including anxiety disorders, mood disorders, personality disorders, substance use disorders, psychotic disorders, organic mental disorders, sexual disorders, and disorders usually first evident in infancy, childhood, and adolescence. The diagnoses follow the conventions of the *Diagnostic and Statistical Manual of Mental Disorders, Third Edition-Revised* (American Psychiatric Association, 1987), commonly abbreviated simply as *DSM-III-R*. Any exceptions are noted with the particular case.

Each case is presented with a particular treatment. The treatments represent basic approaches to abnormal psychology: psychodynamic, cognitive-behavioral, sociocultural, biomedical, and eclectic. Some cases present somewhat atheoretical treatments, such as residential therapy and supportive therapy. The *Casebook in Abnormal Psychology, Second Edition* is meant to be used as a supplement for any textbook in abnormal psychology. Consequently, the therapy descriptions presented are only a general description of the processes involved in psychotherapy. For a more detailed discussion of the theoretical foundations and therapeutic techniques of any particular approach to therapy, readers should refer to their texts, practitioner's guides, or therapy handbooks.

The cases in this book are based on actual material provided by practicing psychiatric professionals. The presenting symptoms described in this casebook were actually observed, and the therapeutic techniques utilized in treatment were actually administered. However, because of the need to maintain confidentiality, details such as names, sex, occupations, and places that may identify particular individuals have been changed. Any resemblance to real persons is purely coincidental.

CASE ORGANIZATION

Each case is organized into five sections: presenting complaint, personal history, conceptualization and treatment, prognosis, and discussion. These categories reflect, in a general way, how psychiatric professionals organize their cases and describe them to each other.

The **presenting complaint** refers to the various symptoms and circumstances that prompted the person to seek psychiatric help. Most often this information is collected at the first therapy session, which usually involves an initial interview. In some instances, family members are relied upon as primary information sources because the individual is unable to provide an adequate account of his or her symptoms. An example of this might be a woman suffering from Alzheimer's disease or a child with autistic disorder.

The **personal history** section provides background information the therapist may find helpful in diagnosing and treating the person. Unlike a person's presenting complaint, the person's personal history is actively solicited by the therapist. As a result, these histories vary greatly from case to case, depending on the type of information the particular therapist may find useful. For example, traditional psychodynamic therapists often devote a great deal of time in therapy to obtaining a detailed account of the person's childhood in the hopes of uncovering the sources of unconscious conflicts. Since, according to this view, a person's symptoms are merely superficial manifestations of underlying unconscious dynamics, knowing the precise nature of these symptoms is important only to the extent that they can provide clues to the person's latent problems. More important are the various clues that may shed light on the person's unconscious (e.g., dreams, fears) In contrast, most behavior therapists are concerned primarily with the objective history of the disorder: the form of the symptoms, when and under what circumstances the symptoms first appeared, and so forth. For these therapists, a knowledge of the person's dreams or childhood memories is irrelevant and therefore unimportant. Medically oriented therapists tend to focus on organically relevant information, such as alcohol use, coronary disease, and the like. For them, the patient history primarily provides clues as to behaviors and habits that may have affected the person's physical health. A particularly interesting comparison can be found among the case histories of generalized anxiety disorder, dysthymic disorder, and Alzheimer's disease.

The differences between various theoretical approaches become most evident when one examines the way in which therapists formulate their treatment plans and implement them. The next section, **conceptualization and treatment**, focuses on these processes. The case conceptualization refers to the therapist's organization of the case as he or she attempts to makes sense of the person's symptoms. The therapist draws together different information from the person's complaints and history and pieces them together to form a coherent picture of the disorder. The therapist then uses these facts to determine an official diagnosis. To help clarify these diagnoses, a definition of the relevant *DSM-III-R* disorder also appears in this section.

The treatment section documents the exact methods used to implement the treatment plan. Specific therapy techniques are described in as much detail as possible. In some cases, segments of actual dialogues between the therapist and the person seeking treatment are included. When medication is prescribed, the actual dosage is provided. The aim of this section is to give the reader a concrete and vivid impression of what actually occurs in the therapy session.

Readers must keep in mind that the therapy approach presented with each case is not the only treatment available; virtually every disorder may be treated by a variety of different therapeutic programs. By presenting a particular treatment with each disorder, it is *not* intended to imply that the particular form of treatment presented is the most effective—or even the most common—treatment for that particular disorder. (However, in no case is a therapy inappropriate for its diagnosis.) Instead, the aim of providing specific treatments along with each case is to expose readers to the specific techniques commonly practiced by psychiatric professionals of different theoretical orientations. By describing specific therapeutic techniques, it is hoped that readers will gain a clearer concept of how different theoretical approaches are employed in the course of therapy.

The case **prognosis** refers to the therapist's prediction of how the person will function after therapy. In some cases, the person is expected to be more or less cured of the disorder. In other cases, the person is predicted to relapse. In the more chronic cases, the person is not expected to show a significant improvement in the foreseeable future and in all likelihood will continue to deteriorate until death. These prognoses are based on both the individual's response to therapy and the typical response most people with this disorder show. Keep in mind, however, that therapists will tend to present cases that have been treated successfully; consequently, the prognoses for these case histories may be more optimistic than population norms would suggest.

Finally, the **discussion** section describes general aspects of the case not directly tied to the person's treatment. General population norms and current research on the disorder are presented in this section. The discussion also notes any aspect of the case history that was atypical, such as any unusual treatment techniques or procedures. In some cases, other therapy techniques that are commonly used to treat the disorder are pointed out. This section also reviews the therapist's personal approach to the case.

THE PURPOSES OF THIS CASEBOOK

There are three main purposes of this casebook. The first is to provide readers with a detailed and vivid account of the symptoms that characterize various disorders. Many descriptions of psychiatric disorders employ general terms, such as describing an anxious man as being "paralyzed by irrational fears." Although this description is accurate, it does not provide the same impression as noting that this man "worries about finding the 'perfect' suit to such an extent that he has not bought any clothes at all in over two years." Similarly, this casebook aims to provide a concrete view of how therapy is conducted. Using the same example, saying that the anxious man was "given a task-oriented homework assignment" is not as informative as providing the actual dialogue in which the therapist gives the person direct instructions to go to two nearby clothing stores that afternoon. In short, the primary goal of this casebook is not to describe what different disorders and therapies are; it is to describe what these disorders and therapies are *like*.

It has been said that the psychotherapy a person receives depends more on the training of the therapist than on the presenting symptoms. Accordingly, a second goal of this casebook is to highlight the differences in how various therapies are conducted. Many of these differences are obvious. Some therapies last for weeks; others are lifelong. Some focus on immediate concerns, others focus on past issues, and still others rely almost exclusively on medications. In addition to these overt differences, various therapies contain more subtle discrepancies that nevertheless may affect a person's therapy in important ways. For example, some therapists refer to the people they treat as *clients*; others refer to them as *patients*. The difference between these two terms involves certain subtle yet clear implications for the person's role in the therapeutic process, specifically the person's status vis a vis the therapist. As another example, some therapists insist that the person seeking therapy define the goals of treatment for him- or herself; other therapists prefer to maintain their own agenda. This distinction will have a great impact on the course of therapy and its duration. Many people are ignorant to some extent or another of the many different options available to them when they seek therapy. By outlining the differences between various therapeutic approaches, it is hoped that this casebook will provide some idea of these various options. Of course, this is of particular pragmatic value should the reader, or someone he or she knows, decide to seek psychiatric help.

Although this casebook discusses different treatment approaches as though they were clearly distinct, in reality these differences tend to be blurred. Practicing psychiatric professionals rarely ally themselves solely with one theoretical orientation; to varying degrees most therapists employ a more or less eclectic approach. This trend has been increasingly prevalent over the past decade. Evidence of this spreading eclecticism can be seen throughout this casebook, from psychodynamic therapists who employ medications and situational manipulations to behavior therapists who interest themselves in the person's subjective thoughts and feelings. Although an argument can be made for calling every form of therapy in this casebook "eclectic," for clarity's sake the cases presented here are labeled with the theoretical approach that forms the primary basis of each particular treatment.

The third purpose of this casebook is to illustrate the limitations of the psychiatric professional in everyday practice. For example, therapy that aims at achieving a dynamic insight is limited to those people who are intellectually capable of this accomplishment. Therapy for young or more seriously disturbed people would require some fundamental alterations. As another example, behavior therapists find themselves at a loss with people who conceptualize their problems in nonspecific terms. When the person says, "I want to be fulfilled" or "I want to be happier," the behavior therapist must first translate these rather vague goals into more concrete terms before therapy can proceed. Of course, virtually every form of psychotherapy is limited in its ability to treat disorders involving psychosis or severe organic impairment. Most therapists would agree that pharmacological treatment, in some cases combined with supportive therapy for the person's family, is the only realistic approach for these disorders.

As a final note, it is hoped that this small, select sample of case studies will provide the reader with information on psychopathology and psychotherapy that is beyond the scope of general texts. More generally, it is hoped that readers will find this casebook interesting, stimulating, and thought-provoking.

ACKNOWLEDGMENTS

I am very grateful to the following consultants for their time, help, and expertise. Along with providing me with the basic information about various diagnoses and different forms of treatment, they gave me a fascinating behind-the-scenes view of the therapeutic enterprise.

Ellie Bragar, Psy.D.
private practice, New York, NY

Howard A. Crystal, M.D.
Albert Einstein College of Medicine
Yeshiva University, Bronx, NY

Zira DeFries, M.D.
private practice, New York, NY

Jennifer Egert, B.A.
Association for the Help of Retarded Children, New York, NY

John Fogelman, M.D.
St. Luke's/Roosevelt Hospital Center, New York, NY
private practice, Pomona, NY

Andrea Friedman, M.Ed.
Association for the Help of Retarded Children, New York, NY

Kevin MacColl, M.P.S., C.A.S.
Stuyvesant Square Program, Beth Israel Medical Center,
New York, NY

Acknowledgments

Harriet N. Mischel, Ph.D.
private practice, New York, NY

German Nino-Murcia, M.D.
Sleep Medicine and Neuroscience Institute, Palo Alto, CA

Pat Pantone, Ph.D.
St. Luke's/Roosevelt Hospital Center, New York, NY
private practice, New York, NY

Steve Rasmussen, M.D.
Butler Hospital
Brown University, Providence, RI

Sharon Silver-Regent, Ph.D.
private practice, New York, NY

David Spiegel, M.D.
Stanford University Medical Center
Stanford University, Stanford, CA

B. Timothy Walsh, M.D.
Columbia/Presbyterian Medical Center, New York, NY

At McGraw-Hill, I wish to thank Jane Vaicunas, Psychology Editor, for her guidance from the inception of this second edition through its completion. I am very grateful to Beth Kaufman, Assistant Editor, for her unflagging support throughout this project. Her encouragment and humor were invaluable. I also want to thank John Morris, Senior Editing Manager, whose thoroughness is matched only by his promptness.

I am also indebted to Eleanor Merczynski for her energetic and diligent assistance in compiling background information for the cases. Finally, I am grateful to Lisa Vitkus for her encouragement and enthusiasm.

CONTENTS

Contents

Casebook in
Abnormal Psychology
Second Edition

GENERALIZED ANXIETY DISORDER
Cognitive-Behavioral Therapy

PRESENTING COMPLAINT

Terry is a 31-year-old man living in Washington, D.C. At his initial interview, he was dressed in clean but rather shabby "college clothes" (a T-shirt, jeans, and an old, worn warm-up jacket). Terry's manner and posture revealed that he was very apprehensive about therapy; his eyes nervously scanned the interview room, he held himself stiffly rigid and stayed by the door, and his speech was barely audible and marked by hesitations and waverings. After some brief introductions, Terry and the therapist each took a seat. The therapist began the session, asking, "What is it that brings you here today?"

Terry's reply was very rapid and forced. He stated that his problems began during his hospital internship after he graduated from medical school. His internship was a high-pressure position that involved a great many demands and responsibilities. The schedule, involving 36-hour on-call periods, daily rounds, and constant emergencies, was grueling and exhausting. Gradually he began to notice that he and the other interns were making a number of small errors and oversights in the care they provided their patients. He found himself ruminating about these lapses, and he began to hesitate in making decisions and taking action for fear of making some catastrophic mistake. His anxieties about making a mistake worsened until he began calling in sick and avoiding particularly stressful situations at the hospital. As a result he was not completing many of the assignments given to him by the chief resident of his program, who threatened to report him to the department head. As the year wore on Terry's performance continued to decline, and by the end of the year he was threatened with dismissal from his program. He resigned at the end of the year.

Before his resignation he began making plans to be transferred to a less demanding program. With some help from his father (who is a physician) and some luck, he was accepted into a program in Washington, D.C. This internship was indeed less demanding than the first, and he felt that perhaps he could manage it. After a few months, though, Terry again felt overwhelmed by his recurrent anxieties of making a terrible mistake. He had to quit the second program after six months. He then began to work in a less stressful position as a research fellow for the Food and Drug Administration (FDA). Even in this relatively relaxed atmosphere, Terry found that he still had great difficulty carrying out his duties. He found that he could not handle any negative feelings at work, and he again began missing work to avoid trouble. Terry's contract with the FDA expired after six months and was not renewed. At this time even the prospect of having to apply for another position produced terrible anxieties, and Terry decided to live off a trust fund set up by his grandfather instead of working. For the last two years he has been supported by this trust fund and, in part at least, by his girlfriend, with whom he lives and who, according to Terry, pays "more than her share."

Terry's incapacitating anxieties have interfered with his relationships with his family and his girlfriend as well as with his career. For one thing, he has avoided visiting his parents for the last three years. He states that his parents' (particularly his father's) poor opinions of him make going home "out of the question." He also confesses that he avoids discussing any potentially controversial subject with his girlfriend for fear that he may cause an irreconcilable rift. As Terry puts it, "I stay away from anything touchy because I don't want to say something wrong and blow it [the relationship]. Then what'll I do?" Even routine tasks, such as washing his clothes, shopping for groceries, and writing letters to friends are impossible to accomplish for fear that some small step may be bungled or overlooked. Terry freely acknowledges that his fears are exaggerated and irrational. He admits (after some persuasion) that he is an intelligent, capable young man. Nevertheless, he feels utterly unable to overcome his anxieties, and he takes great pains to avoid situations that potentially may bring them on.

Along with these dysfunctional cognitions, Terry reports a number of somatic symptoms. He is very tense; he always feels nervous or "keyed up" and is easily distracted and irritated by minor problems. He complains of frequent throbbing headaches, annoying body aches and pains (especially in his back and neck), and an almost constant feeling of fatigue. He also admits to feeling worthless, and he describes himself as having low self-esteem and little motivation. Occasionally he also experiences brief periods of panic in which he suffers from a shortness of breath, a wildly racing heartbeat, profuse sweating, and mild dizziness. These feelings of panic tend to come on when some feared situation (e.g., having to make a decision or having to confront his girlfriend) cannot be avoided. He states that these symptoms first emerged during his first internship and have gradually intensified over the past few years.

Terry began dynamic psychotherapy soon after he lost his job with the FDA and stopped working. He reports that this therapy was very complex and involved. In particular, he says that his therapeutic experience gave him two important insights into the underlying causes of his paralyzing anxieties and his low self-esteem: (1) his parents expectations of him were too high, and he always felt a great pressure to be perfect in their eyes and (2) the teasing he received from his peers as a child has made him self-conscious of his weaknesses. Although Terry felt that these insights were valid, they did not seem to precipitate any significant change in his behavior, and they were becoming less useful to him. A friend suggested that Terry might benefit from a more direct form of psychotherapy and referred him to a cognitive-behavioral therapist.

PERSONAL HISTORY

Terry grew up in a small town in Ohio. His father is a general practitioner in town and is on the staff of the county hospital. Terry's mother is a teacher. She quit her job when his older sister was born. After his younger sister was diagnosed as mentally retarded, however, she returned to school to receive special training in teaching disabled children. She now teaches learning-disabled children as part of the county special education program. Terry's parents, particularly his father, always had high aspirations for him and were quite demanding.

Terry's older sister still lives with her parents and attends a small, little-known law school near home. Terry describes her as "not too bright." He states that his father is frustrated at being stuck in a small town and criticizes his daughter for not getting into a more prestigious law school. His younger sister is moderately mentally retarded. She, too, lives at home and works at a sheltered workshop run by the county special education program.

Terry always had the impression that he was looked upon as the "success" of the family. He had always gotten excellent grades in school; in fact, he won full scholarships that supported his undergraduate education and his training in medical school, both at highly prestigious universities. He had always considered himself to be a very good student. He enjoyed studying, even in the difficult atmosphere of medical school. He described his academic achievement as something he did for himself—for his own education and improvement. In contrast, during his internship he felt that he was toiling endlessly on what he considered to be "someone else's scum work." For the first time he began to fear his own fallibility and to avoid anxiety-provoking situations.

CONCEPTUALIZATION AND TREATMENT

Terry is a very intelligent and articulate young man who appears to be much more competent and capable than he describes himself to be. He shows no evidence of a psychotic disorder. He seems willing, even pressured, to discuss his problems, and he seems highly motivated toward reducing them. The therapist thought it reasonable, then, to take Terry's complaints at face value.

Terry's primary problem involves his excessive and unwarranted apprehension about his own fallibility and his need to perform every activity perfectly, no matter how trivial. This overriding fear has crippled his occupational and social functioning as well as his ability to perform—or even to attempt—a variety of routine, everyday tasks. This anxiety is also manifested by a number of physiological symptoms, including constant vigilance, distractibility, and irritability; pervasive muscle tension; and autonomic hyperactivity (as expressed by his occasional feelings of panic). Although he complains of periods of feeling depressed and worthless, his worries and anxieties are clearly not limited to these periods. Thus, it seems that his anxiety is his primary problem and not merely a response to his mild depression.

Terry's symptoms clearly fit the *DSM-III-R* criteria for generalized anxiety disorder. People with this disorder suffer from pervasive feelings of dread or worry that involve at least two or more major life areas (career, marriage, child care, etc.). The focus of these anxieties is much more broad and unspecified than is the case with more circumscribed anxiety disorders such as panic disorder or simple phobia. Furthermore, these feelings of anxiety are not solely associated with any other Axis I diagnosis. Thus, for example, although someone with generalized anxiety disorder may also experience a major depressive episode, his or her anxieties are not solely about being depressed. In addition, people with generalized anxiety disorder display somatic signs of their apprehension, including motor tension, autonomic hyperactivity, and defensive vigilance.

Terry's therapy can be organized as a process involving four general steps. The therapist's initial aim was to establish rapport with her client. To establish a better working relationship with Terry, she attempted to make him feel comfortable with her. The first step was to explain her approach. Since cognitive-behavioral therapy requires much more direct, active participation than many clients suppose (particularly those with a history of psychodynamic treatment), it is important that the client be fully aware of what to expect. The therapist also gave Terry encouragement that his disorder was treatable with cognitive-behavioral therapy. It is important to establish this basis of hope to foster the client's expectations for change.

The second step was to have Terry form goals for his therapy. Ideally these goals would involve some specific behavior or attitude. Concrete plans that address some specific feared situation, such as "I want to send my résumé to 50 prospective employers," are more effective than more general aims, such as "I want to work." Like most clients with generalized anxiety disorder, though, Terry's initial goals were quite vague and unfocused. He stated that he wanted to start working, to get along with his parents better, and to "not be so apprehensive about things." At first these general goals are adequate; the important point is to have the client formulate *some* goals. Overly general ones can always be specified and put into behavioral contexts as therapy progresses.

Third, relaxation training is suggested for clients who show a great deal of physical tension and seem amenable to this treatment. Therapists have developed relaxation techniques that specifically address a client's dysfunctional cognitions, muscular tension, and autonomic hyperactivity. When he began therapy, Terry showed a variety of physical manifestations of tension. Having been trained in medicine, he was especially attuned to the somatic aspects of healing and was very willing to try relaxation techniques that involved physiological elements.

The fourth step in therapy was a review by Terry and the therapist of the issues and goals Terry had targeted. By going over his initial complaints and plans, both the therapist and the client are assured that they understand each other fully. In addition, this review allows the client, with the aid of the therapist, to put vague initial goals into more specific and workable terms.

Therapy began by first discussing the specific issues that were of immediate concern to Terry. These topics were not necessarily a central part of Terry's goals, nor were they necessarily closely related. For example, Terry's first few sessions of therapy focused on a variety of distinct problems including, among other things, his inability to buy a suit, his anxiety concerning needed dental work, and his dread of an upcoming visit to his parents. These loosely related issues were dealt with on a problem-by-problem basis, a process the therapist referred to as "putting out fires." This troubleshooting approach is employed for several reasons. First, cognitive-behavioral therapy is most effective if therapeutic issues are specified and well defined; individual psychological "fires" are particularly suited to this. Second, the clients' enthusiasm for therapy and belief in the effectiveness of treatment is likely to be increased by initial success experiences, especially in immediate problem areas. Third, although these issues do not appear to be closely related, for the most part they share a common foundation: they are indications of Terry's tendency to avoid situations that carry a possibility of failure, however slight. Over time, clients are expected to integrate these isolated issues and generalize their therapeutic gains to other areas of their lives.

The first topic Terry wanted to discuss was his inability to buy himself a suit. It had been years since Terry had shopped for clothes; he contented himself with wearing worn jeans and T-shirts. Several months ago, Terry's girlfriend made plans for the two of them to take a vacation to Boston to visit her sister. As a part of the preparation for this trip, she asked him to buy some new clothes, including "at least one decent suit." He thought about buying a suit on several previous occasions, but every time, the prospect of having to pick one out overwhelmed him.   He would begin shaking and sweating even as he approached a clothing store.   Terry explained that he hated shopping for clothes, especially suits, because he was convinced that he would not be able to pick out the right suit and would waste his money.   To be at all acceptable, the suit had to be just the right color, just the right material, just the right cut, just the right price, etc.   It also had to be practical—appropriate for every possible occasion, from sightseeing to going to the symphony.   The threat of making a mistake and buying "the wrong suit" made him so anxious that he could not bring himself to even enter a clothing store.

The therapist began by having Terry clarify exactly what he was and was not capable of.   She then gave him clear assignments that she judged he would be able to accomplish successfully.   These assignments started off with small steps which Terry anticipated would be easy; gradually they became more and more complicated and difficult.   The following segment of a therapy session illustrates this process:

> **Terry:** You see, I just can't go through with it [buying a suit].
>
> **Therapist:** Do you mean you are unable to, or that you'd rather avoid the whole thing?
>
> **Terry:** What do you mean?
>
> **Therapist:** Well, if I held a gun to your head, would you be able to go to the clothing store?
>
> **Terry:** Well, yeah, I suppose so.
>
> **Therapist:** So you are physically able to walk into a clothing store, right?
>
> **Terry:** Yeah, I guess I am.
>
> **Therapist:** OK. I want you to go to at least two clothing stores on your way home today. Alright?
>
> **Terry:** The mall's too far away. I couldn't possibly make it today.
>
> **Therapist:** There's no need to go to the mall. There

are at least five good clothing stores right around here; three are on this street.

Terry: Well, they're too expensive.

Therapist: No, not really. I've shopped at most of them, and the prices are actually better than at the mall.

Terry: I really don't know if I'll have the time.

Therapist: It'll take a half an hour at most. Come on, Terry, no more excuses. I want you to go to two stores. Today.

Terry: But what if I buy the wrong suit?

Therapist: You don't need to buy anything. Just walk into two stores. That's it. If you feel comfortable with that, then start browsing. You might want to try one or two suits on. But for today, I just want you to take the first step and go to two stores. Agreed?

Terry: Alright.

At the next session Terry was noticeably excited and pleased. He had followed the therapist's directions and had gone to a store. After he got to the first one, he found that looking for a suit was not as difficult as he had expected. In fact, he actually went to three stores and even bought two suits. Unfortunately, Terry was not able to enjoy his success for long; his enthusiasm evaporated when he began to describe another problem. Several weeks ago Terry's driver's license expired. He felt very anxious about driving with his expired license, and he knew that he had to get his license renewed, which involved taking a simple written test of basic traffic regulations. He got a copy of the driver's manual and planned to go over it several times, but each time he was struck with a terrible fear that he might miss some vital piece of information and fail his test. Terry admitted that his worries were irrational. He had taken similar written tests three times before and had missed only one or two questions in total. He realized that the test was very basic and that the chances of his actually failing the test were very remote, even if he did not study the manual at all. Still, he could not bring himself to study the manual, and the thought of taking the test "cold" terrified him.

Again, the therapist approached the problem directly and made concrete suggestions. First, she reassured him that he was a very intelligent person who graduated from medical school; he would have no trouble passing a simple driving test. Next, she suggested different ways to get him to actually read the manual, such as skimming it or just reading every other page. She explained that failing the exam was not the end of the world; even on the slight chance that he did fail the exam, he would still have two other opportunities to retake it. Finally, she reminded him that it was worse to be stopped while driving with an expired license than to just go ahead and get his renewed. This last warning was meant to propel Terry to action; however, it could have been counterproductive in that it might have caused him to develop so much anxiety about driving that he might have given it up altogether. With this in mind, the therapist reassured Terry that driving with a license that expired only a few weeks ago would most likely get him only a warning. At worst, he would have to pay a small fine. As time wore on, however, trying to explain that he "just forgot" about his license would become less and less credible.

Again Terry followed the therapist's instructions. He read over the manual carefully and tried not to be too concerned if he did not remember every fact. Following her directions, if he felt that he could not remember some information from any particular page, he would consciously limit himself to skimming that page once. As expected, he passed his test. In fact, he didn't miss a question. Just like the previous week, however, his accomplishment was accompanied by another "emergency" that had occurred during the week.

Over the weekend Terry lost a filling in one of his teeth when he was eating some caramel candy. He realized that he needed his filling replaced, and his girlfriend suggested her dentist, whom she recommended highly. Terry had not been to a dentist for over three years, and he was very apprehensive about the possible injury and pain a dentist could inflict. His most horrible fear was that this dentist (or any dentist, for that matter) might inadvertently damage the nerve of the tooth, thus necessitating a root canal. In spite of this fear, Terry realized that he needed his filling replaced and called for an emergency appointment. He was able to make an appointment for Tuesday morning and went in for a consultation.

Although hesitant, Terry was able to make it to the dentist's office, accompanied by his girlfriend. Once in the dentist's chair, however, he became panicky and unmanageable. He clenched his mouth and made it impossible for the dentist to perform an examination. He repeatedly grabbed the dentist's hand and tried to jerk him away. Terry's girlfriend, who stayed with him throughout the appointment, told him that he made a high-pitched whistling sound resembling a drill whenever the dentist picked up one of his tools, even tools totally unrelated to the drill, such as the probing pick or the suction tube. She had never seen him this nervous before. At first the dentist refused to schedule another appointment, but Terry's girlfriend, who was a longtime patient, persuaded him to schedule an appointment for the next week.

Terry was depressed over this embarrassing experience. The worst part of it, he thought, was that his girlfriend would lose interest in him now that she saw how anxious he was about simple things like dental exams. But since she had been able to schedule the appointment, Terry felt that his first priority now was to learn to control his apprehensions about going to the dentist.

Terry's therapy that week focused on relaxation training. First, he was taught to begin by taking slow, deep breaths. After a few deep breaths, he was told to relax his body completely. He was instructed to focus on his bodily sensations. He was to move his focus slowly from head to toe, concentrating on relaxing each part of his body. He was to sense how his forehead felt, then his eyebrows, then his nose, and so on. If he noticed tension in any part of his body, he was instructed to relax it. (Many therapists have their clients consciously tense and then relax various parts of their bodies during this exercise. In her experience, however, Terry's therapist prefers to focus primarily on relaxing as she has noticed that most clients with anxiety disorders are already extremely tense. She prefers to avoid any suggestion that may exacerbate their muscular tension.) Terry was also told that if he found himself becoming distracted or had any stray thoughts, he was to "blow them away like puffy clouds" and replace them with soft, relaxing images. The therapist then asked Terry about the activities that were particularly pleasant to him. He replied that he loved the tranquility of lying in the sun on some tropical island. As a result, the therapist told him that he should try to replace any stressful thoughts with scenes of sunbathing on a Caribbean beach.

Terry was told to practice this relaxation technique two or three times a day. To get her clients to do this practice, Terry's therapist makes relaxation tapes that gently and calmly guide the clients in these exercises. The tapes are made individually, with the client's name and special instructions tailored for him or her. To help ensure that her clients do not lose interest in these relaxation exercises, the tapes are short, from 10 to 15 minutes long. Because of his impending dental appointment, Terry's therapist made his tape right after their session. She also wrote out the rationale for not continuing to avoid the various things that he needs to accomplish and the role of relaxation in reducing his anxiety so that entering into these situations would be possible. He expressed gratitude for her effort and her personal concern when he picked these up the next morning.

Terry began the next session by proudly exclaiming, "I survived!" He reported that he used the relaxation training to divert his focus throughout the appointment, and this was very successful. (In fact, he reported that he focused on his feet.) Terry's therapist, who herself had a filling replaced just two months before, acknowledged that it was a stressful and difficult procedure and that he should be congratulated on his accomplishment. During the session Terry reported that he had also used the relaxation training in a completely different situation. While he was having lunch with some friends, Terry began to feel that his friends were ignoring him. He became upset and irritated at them and began worrying that his companions were no longer interested in maintaining their friendship with him. Instead of leaving the restaurant, however, he decided to use the relaxation training to relieve his tension and to replace these negative anxieties with more pleasant scenes. As a result he was able to remain calm during lunch, which turned out to be a pleasant experience after all.

The next several sessions focused on different individual topics. For example, Terry had not done any laundry in over a year. He avoided this chore because he could not bring himself to go through the effort of sorting the clothes properly, making sure each load of clothes had the correct amount of detergent and was run under the right cycle, and so forth. He also dreaded folding the laundry, lining up each crease exactly and folding the T-shirts just right to avoid any wrinkles. Nevertheless, he wanted to surprise his girlfriend by doing their laundry, and he asked the therapist for her help. First, the task of doing the laundry was broken down into manageable tasks (sorting, selecting the cycle, etc.). Terry was then instructed to approach each task separately and to proceed to the next only if he felt calm and relaxed. He was also told that most people find that their first instincts are best, so once he made a decision about sorting or folding, he was to go through with it. Prior to starting, Terry wrote out careful instructions on exactly how to wash the clothes and put them away. It took Terry quite a while to accomplish this job, but he was able to control his anxieties and move steadily from task to task. When he reported completing the job at the next session, he was complimented and encouraged to attempt other avoided activities.

Another source of apprehension concerned writing a letter to an old roommate from college. They had exchanged correspondence for years, but Terry had not responded to this friend's last three or four letters for fear that he might make some mistake in his grammar or spelling. He worried that the friend, who was a journalist, would see this mistake and lose respect for him. Terry's anxieties were heightened after his friend's last letter. In it, the friend jokingly wondered whether Terry had forgotten how to write. This comment made Terry wonder if he had indeed lost his ability to compose a letter that would be acceptable to his friend. Like everything else, his therapist had Terry approach this problem in gradual steps. First, he was to make a brief outline of what he would put in a letter. Next, he was to write a letter that they could go over during the next session. As was the case with shopping for a suit, renewing his license, and doing the laundry, Terry found that just starting an avoided activity greatly diminished his apprehensions, and he finished and sent the letter without ever showing it to the therapist.

Terry found that after each "fire" was put out, he felt much less anxiety about that topic the next time he attempted it. It also required fewer steps to complete these tasks. After several sessions of "putting out fires," Terry's therapy began to focus on more global interpersonal issues. At one session Terry discussed his fears that his girlfriend was planning to leave him. During the previous week she said that a special project came up at work (she worked in an architectural firm) and that they would have to postpone their vacation to Boston for a month. Terry, who constantly harbored fears that she would end their relationship, took this as a sign that she was ready to leave. He asked the therapist what he could do to make her stay. The therapist told him that no one could guarantee that their relationship would last forever and began to discuss whether it was likely that Terry's fears were accurate. Initially Terry refused to discuss this possibility, saying "Don't tell me anything about her leaving. I don't want to hear it." His therapist persisted, however, and reminded him of the importance of not avoiding important topics. Over the next two sessions he gradually became able to discuss the possibility of her leaving him. He even made some plans if indeed this occurred. (As it turned out, she had been honest with him, and they went to Boston on the postponed date.)

While they were away, Terry's mother fell and broke her hip. This became the topic of discussion when he returned. Terry knew he was expected to visit her, but he dreaded going home and interacting with his parents, particularly his father. He said that his father was very demanding and would undoubtedly ask him about what he has been doing over the past few years. He pleaded with his therapist, "Tell me what to say."

The therapist engaged Terry in a role-playing exercise. First, she instructed him to enact his father while she modeled effective responses to the father's comments and criticisms. Terry was told to pay close attention to her while she modeled these behaviors; he was to remember her posture, the color of her blouse, etc. Mostly these details were meant to give Terry a clear, visual reference that would help him remember the gist of the modeled responses. After going over several responses, the roles were changed. Now the therapist enacted the role of Terry's parents, and Terry discussed possible responses from his own viewpoint. Since it was felt that maintaining a good interaction with his parents was just as important as dealing with a bad one, Terry practiced responding to many different types of comments, both positive and negative.

When Terry returned from Ohio, he reported that his father was indeed as critical as he had suspected. His father was very disappointed that he had "thrown away" a career in medicine, and he kept asking Terry what he had been doing for the past three years. His father felt that every man should at least support himself by the time he was finished with his education. Although these interactions made Terry very anxious, he was able to stay in the family home for the entire visit (10 days). Terry stated that his interactions with his mother and older sister were generally positive. He found, somewhat to his surprise, that he really enjoyed their company. Although he still felt nervous about visiting his parents, he felt that he could have an adequate interaction with them and decided not to wait so long before visiting them again. (Although Terry was more comfortable about discussing his parents after six months of therapy, by this time he still had not actually visited them again.)

The next focus of therapy was for Terry to apply for jobs. Initially Terry seemed perfectly happy to keep on living off of the trust fund, even though he reported "getting back to work" as a goal of therapy. He also admitted that his father had a point: he was 31, and he should begin to support himself. In addition, his therapist reminded him that the trust fund provided a fixed income that would not keep pace with inflation. She also noted that the longer he waited before he started working again, the harder it would be to explain the ever-increasing gap in his résumé.

Like every other aspect of therapy, Terry and his therapist approached this task one step at a time. First, they discussed the sorts of jobs that he would be interested in and capable of performing. Terry's estimations of his own abilities were consistently lower than his therapist's. He also wanted to avoid any job that involved pressure and responsibility. At first, he thought of becoming a library researcher for some government agency. His therapist, who also thought it wise to avoid any high-pressure positions, told him that he could probably do better, perhaps something that would enable him to use his medical training. They finally decided that he should seek employment that involved medical issues but was outside a hospital or clinic setting. The therapist's instructions were concrete and firm: by the next week he was to have his résumé compiled, and one week later he was to have it printed. She then directed him to send out at least 10 applications per week until he heard something. During this time they rehearsed possible interview questions through role-playing. After eight weeks (and by making use of a few old contacts), he was offered a part-time position at the Food and Drug Administration as a research assistant. He found that he enjoyed working and could do his job well. After six months he was offered a full-time staff position.

Terry discontinued therapy at about the time that he was hired full-time. His therapy had involved an eight-month process of directly approaching various psychological "fires" and learning to cope with his fears. With these success experiences, he was able to slowly develop a sense of himself that was more in line with his actual abilities. Over the past few months he reported that his self-esteem had gradually improved and that his risk-avoidance habits were starting to decline. He still worried about performing various tasks and duties well, but he was now able to attempt these activities in spite of his apprehensions. Only rarely did his fears cause him to avoid these situations. He was able to discuss possible negative consequences of his own and other people's actions. In short, although he stated that he still felt anxious about some situations, he felt that he was learning to control his fears. He felt better about himself and his work. Most noticeably, he was working steadily and routinely engaging in a wide variety of activities that he would not have even attempted just six months before.

PROGNOSIS

Terry's prognosis is excellent. When he began therapy, he had very low self-esteem and very little confidence in his abilities to perform even the most trivial task adequately. Consequently he avoided situations that involved any amount of pressure or responsibility. His constant fears of being embarrassed or rejected also interfered with his interpersonal relationships. Without treatment, it is possible that Terry would have become severely agoraphobic, that is, so overwhelmed by his anxieties that he would be unable to leave his home or interact with other people. At the very least, it is likely that his ability to carry out his day-to-day tasks and his ability to maintain his relationships with his family, friends, and girlfriend would have continued to deteriorate.

Terry has reversed this trend. His paralyzing anxieties are greatly diminished, and his avoidance behavior for the most part has ended. By encouraging him to face feared situations directly and in small increments, Terry's therapy seems to have gradually enabled him to approach a variety of previously avoided situations. In addition, he is able to apply this step-by-step approach and the relaxation training he received to problem areas that were never directly discussed in therapy. He also seems to have been able to integrate the therapeutic gains of these isolated tasks and make progress in his more global problems involving his interpersonal relationships and his career. In addition to his behavioral gains, Terry has also built up his self-esteem and self-confidence, as evidenced by a shift in his therapy goals. Initially Terry's aim in therapy was to avoid any pain, rejection, or pressure in his career or his interpersonal relationships. Now, however, his goal is to attempt to work through difficult tasks and to avoid situations only if they may be unduly stressful. This shift appears to be a good indication that Terry will maintain his therapeutic gains.

DISCUSSION

Terry's presenting complaints suggest the presence of a number of different anxiety disorders. For example, his refusal to engage in everyday tasks for fear of being ridiculed may be taken as evidence of a social phobia (a strict avoidance of potentially embarrassing or humiliating situations). However, he also fears a variety of situations that have no obvious evaluative component (e.g., washing his clothes), and he seems to be more apprehensive about his own and others' possible failures than about the negative evaluations of these failures. Similarly, Terry's panicky feelings and obsessive thoughts about his fallibility may indicate the presence of either panic disorder or obsessive compulsive disorder, respectively. However, these symptoms are not sufficiently marked to fulfill the *DSM-III-R* criteria for these diagnoses.

Terry is not unique. Researchers have noted an overlap between generalized anxiety disorder (GAD) and other anxiety disorders and mood disorders (Brown, Golding, & Smith, 1990; Shekim, Asarnow, Hess, & Zaucha, 1990; Weissman, 1990; Weissman & Merikangas, 1986). Gorman (1987) suggests that GAD is often used as a residual category; that is, it provides a diagnosis for people who show symptoms of other anxiety disorders but who don't fulfill the *DSM-III-R* criteria for any particular one. In any case, the therapist must take care to determine the appropriate diagnosis for each case.

In addition to his anxiety disorder, Terry's attitudes seem to reflect an underlying compulsive personality disorder. His perfectionism, his preoccupation with details, his indecisiveness, and his conviction that other people are incompetent all indicate the presence of this personality disorder. In fact, it could be said that Terry's anxiety disorder first emerged when he became overwhelmed by these compulsive characteristics.

There are two atypical features in Terry's case. First, most people diagnosed with GAD suffer from diffuse, vaguely formed anxiety; rarely are they able to identify the exact source of their pervasive worries. Terry's fears, on the other hand, seem to be organized around issues clearly associated with his compulsive traits. In fact, this type of compulsive thinking occurs in only a small minority of the cases.

Second, GAD rarely becomes so thoroughly crippling. Most clients with this disorder report feeling "unhappy" or "uncomfortable" with their lives, and some suffer some minor disruption of their occupational and/or interpersonal functioning (for example, they may be passed over for promotion because of their tendency to hesitate, or their spouses may become irritated by their constant fears and worries). However, most people with GAD are usually quite productive. In fact, it is estimated that over half of those who suffer from GAD never seek treatment (Weissman & Merikangas, 1986; Whitaker et al., 1990). In contrast, in the course of a few years Terry had stopped working completely and was on the verge of becoming a total recluse. He was unable to complete even the simplest everyday tasks. In his therapist's words, "Terry didn't just suffer from severe anxiety, he really wasn't living a life."

Research on Generalized Anxiety Disorder

Epidemiologic surveys from a variety of nations and cultures have found that GAD is a commonly observed anxiety disorder with prevalence rates ranging from 5.7 to 10.0 percent

(Faravelli, Degl'Innocenti, & Giardinelli, 1989; Hollifield, Katon, Spain, & Pule, 1990; S. Jacobs et al., 1990; Karno et al., 1989; Stephansson, Lindal, Bjornsson, & Gudmundsdottir, 1991; Whitaker et al., 1990).

Researchers have suggested a variety of biological causes for GAD, including genetic factors (Kendler et al., 1991; Weissman, 1990), blunted hormone response (Abelson et al., 1991), and neurological abnormalities (Wu et al., 1991). Other researchers have suggested that GAD may be triggered by an environmental trauma such as rape (Frank & Anderson, 1987) or the death of a spouse (S. Jacobs & Kim, 1990). To date, the origins of GAD are unclear.

Generally speaking, three approaches are commonly used to treat GAD: cognitive-behavioral treatment, psychodynamic treatment, and pharmacological treatment. A variety of antianxiety medications have been found to be effective in reducing the anxiety of GAD patients, including chlorprothixene (trade name Taractan) and bromazepam[1] (Kragh-Sorensen et al., 1990); clorazepate (Tranxene) and buspirone (BuSpar) (Rickels, Schweizer, Csanalosi, Case, & Chung, 1988); and diazepam (Valium) (Downing & Rickels, 1985).

Among the two psychological treatments, cognitive-behavioral therapy is quite different from more traditional psychodynamic therapy. Cognitive-behavioral therapists have little interest in their clients' family histories or in their interpretations of past events, and consequently the histories they obtain tend to be limited to objective, factual information such as the chronology of the person's symptoms and the situations that seem to exacerbate these symptoms. Instead of investigating the clients' early traumas and dynamic interpretations of events, they take a more active role in directly modifying their clients' actual behaviors. That is, a client's specific complaints are not considered superficial or defensive but are usually taken at face value; seemingly minor, specific problems ("I can't buy myself a suit") are considered part of the "real problem" and addressed directly. Eventually the treatment of these individual concerns will be generalized to other life situations.

Often this direct perspective is exactly what the clients are seeking. In other cases, though, they become very uncomfortable with this approach. They feel that direct therapy is too "trivial" or "superficial," and they fear that they will never get to the "real problem." Most therapists feel strongly that a client's beliefs about the effectiveness of therapy is an important part of the treatment. At the present time, there is little evidence that any particular treatment approach is more efficacious than any other (Gorman, 1987).

[1] Bromazepam is not listed in the most current edition of the *Physician's Desk Reference* (1992).

OBSESSIVE COMPULSIVE DISORDER
Pharmacological Therapy with Behavioral Therapy

PRESENTING COMPLAINT

Mary is a 68-year-old married homemaker in a middle-class suburb of Pittsburgh. She and her husband have been married for 46 years and have four children (three sons and a younger daughter) and 10 grandchildren; three children and eight grandchildren live in the same town. Mary and her husband are both the children of Polish immigrants and were raised in strict religious homes. They have continued this tradition in their own family, and Mary describes herself and her family as devout Catholics.

Throughout her life Mary has been neat and orderly. She has always valued cleanliness and has quite a disdain for dirt and clutter. She put great effort into keeping her house clean and tidy (which was quite a job with three sons), and she has always been very careful in her personal habits. In the course of a typical day Mary would brush her teeth three or four times and wash her hands perhaps six to eight times.

Mary has also been very careful in her religious practices. For example, she often worried about whether she had confessed completely or whether she had performed various rituals correctly. Over the past few years, however, her religious obsessions have become markedly more severe, leading her to perform compulsions that occupy several hours every day. Her increased anxiety seems to focus primarily on one issue: the taking of the wafer during holy communion.

The worship service of most Christian denominations includes some form of communion, a ritual where the congregation members partake of the body of Christ (usually symbolized by a small piece of bread or a wafer) and the blood of Christ (usually symbolized by wine or juice). According to traditional Catholic doctrine, the wafer and wine are not merely symbolic but are actually part of the Host and are themselves holy. As a result, only someone who is absolved of sin (the priest) can touch the sacramental elements without contaminating them, and he must place the wafer directly into the mouth of the parishioner. Then in 1969, Pope Paul VI declared that this procedure was no longer necessary. This pronouncement caused great anxiety for Mary, since she considered herself unclean and feared that she would contaminate the Host by touching the wafer. Much to her relief, her priest was very conservative in his practices and continued to place the wafers into the mouths of his parishioners.

But about 10 years ago this priest retired and was replaced by a younger man who encouraged his parishioners to take their wafers directly. Mary, along with a few others, insisted that he continue to feed her the wafer, and he honored her request. However, Mary's husband, children, and friends now took their wafers directly. Interestingly, Mary did not see her family members as contaminating the Host; rather, their contact with the Holy Spirit allowed the Host to be transferred to everything they touched. This idea began with their drive home from mass. The steering wheel, the door handles, and eventually the entire car was now holy and could not be contaminated. Any object at home that was touched, be it a chair, a table, the kitchen sink, and even the toilet, was imbued with the Holy Spirit and had to be avoided. At first Mary tried to keep track of what was touched and what wasn't, but she couldn't keep up. She also realized that her family could touch many things without her knowing it. She eventually became agoraphobic. She spent most of her time shut up in her room and would not allow others to enter.

Mary began to equate her fate with that of King Midas: she was trapped in a house where she couldn't touch anything or anyone. When the extreme anxiety generated by this situation became too much to bear, Mary settled on a compromise that entailed two types of responses. One response was to make herself as clean as possible before she touched the Holy Spirit, thus minimizing her contamination of the Host. Her handwashing became more frequent until she was at the point of washing her hands for six to eight *hours* every day until they were cracked, raw, and bleeding. The other response was to try to rid an object of the Host before it could be contaminated with her touch. Mary's washing compulsions gradually escalated to the point where she would spend hours busily scrubbing fixtures that were already gleaming and wiping furniture that had no visible signs of dust. Mary mentioned that the most baffling problem was the faucet, which left her with a catch-22: she couldn't touch the faucet handles without first washing her hands, but she couldn't wash her hands without touching the faucet handles.

Perhaps the most tragic aspect of Mary's illness concerned her relationship with her family. She had to limit her contact with her loved ones, since they themselves were holy and would carry the Holy Spirit to other objects. When Mary insisted that they constantly wash their hands and take frequent showers (which was her attempt to rid the Host from their bodies), they responded with annoyance and resentment. It has been three years since she last kissed or hugged her husband or any of her children and grandchildren, and she has had no contact at all with her grandchildren for the past several months.

Mary was well aware of the illogical nature of her obsessions and the compulsive behavior needed to reduce her level of anxiety, but out of embarrassment she kept her religious anxieties to herself. Along with her anxieties, Mary suffered from intermittent periods of depression as a result of the uncontrollable nature of her compulsions and the increasingly limited contact with her family. Mary had always been in fairly good health, and she was always wary of doctors. Consequently, she had no primary-care physician, and her raw hands and depressed affect went undiagnosed and untreated. Eventually her anxieties and depression became overwhelming, and Mary began to have persistent suicidal thoughts. She finally confided in her husband. After hearing her concerns over contaminating the Holy Spirit, he urged her to discuss this problem with their priest. On the priest's recommendation, Mary decided to seek help at a clinic.

PERSONAL HISTORY

Mary's childhood appears to be unremarkable. She is the second of five children, with an older brother, two younger brothers, and a younger sister. Her older brother served in World War II and one younger brother served in Korea, but neither was injured or seems to have been noticeably affected by their wartime experiences. This same younger brother died of a heart attack eight years before her admission to the clinic. Her other siblings are alive and keep in regular communication.

Although Mary described her upbringing as strict, she denies any cruelty or abuse, or even that it was oppressive. In Mary's words, "When I said a 'strict' upbringing, I meant disciplined, not mean or vindictive or anything like that." Mary could not think of any particularly upsetting event in her childhood or adolescence; instead, she said she had "the usual ups and downs of childhood."

As noted in her presenting complaint, Mary has a history of mild obsessions and rituals. For example, she frequently had notions that some numbers were good and others were bad, which would lead her to perform minor compulsions such as turning light switches off or on a certain number of times or buying a certain number of items at a store or inviting a certain number of guests to a party. Mary is an avid gardener and enjoys growing many types of flowers. But after seeing petunias at a friend's funeral, she stopped growing them because "they would bring bad luck." (It is interesting that Mary had no fear of dirt or germs, particularly since her obsessions involve themes of contamination.) Mary also admits to having several minor phobias, including spiders, snakes, and electricity. Mary's problems with her anxieties have waxed and waned over the course of her lifetime but have generally not interfered with her duties as wife and mother. The one exception occurred when she was 22, when her first child was 15 months old and she was pregnant with her second. At that time she began having obsessional ideas about harming her son and did not want to be left in charge of him. Mary's mother moved in and took care of her son for about three months. Mary's obsessions gradually diminished as her pregnancy progressed, and she had no further obsessions after the birth of her second son.

Mary's family history shows no evidence of any mental illness. Mary's daughter, however, has been in therapy for depression and continues to take antidepressant medication. In addition, Mary's oldest son has intermittently suffered from periods of anxiety. From Mary's description, he seems to suffer from panic disorder, but because he has never sought treatment, this cannot be confirmed.

CONCEPTUALIZATION AND TREATMENT

DSM-III-R defines obsessive compulsive disorder (OCD) as the existence of recurrent obsessions or compulsions (or both) of such severity that they cause distress or interfere with everyday activities and relationships.

Obsessions are unwanted, intrusive thoughts, ideas, or impulses, usually of a disturbing or senseless nature. Initially the person tries to ignore the obsession or mask it with some other thought, but the obsession persists. Obsessions take many forms (J. G. Henderson & Pollard, 1988; Rasmussen, 1990); some of the more common obsessions are contamination (fear of dirt, germs, infection), doubt (wondering if one has completed simple tasks or has violated a law), somatic illness (fear that one will become ill), need for symmetry, violence (fear of harming a spouse, killing a child), and promiscuity (fear that one may not control one's sexual behavior). About 60 percent suffer from multiple obsessions. Obsessions are almost always greatly anxiety-provoking, both because of their inherently upsetting nature and because in most cases they lead more or less directly to specific compulsions. The person understands that the obsessional thoughts are illogical but is unable to control them.

Compulsions are ritualized, repetitive behaviors performed to reduce anxiety, most often as a result of obsessional thoughts. Sometimes, though, compulsions are performed in a stereotyped way or simply because the person somehow feels that the behavior must be performed. The most common compulsions are checking, washing, counting, asking advice and/or confessing, needing symmetry and precision, and hoarding (J. G. Henderson & Pollard, 1988; Rasmussen, 1990). About half suffer from multiple compulsions. Not all compulsions are expressed in observable behavior, though. Some people engage in covert rituals, such as silently reciting stereotyped statements or counting to themselves. Covert compulsions are harder to recognize, but once they are identified they can be treated in the same manner as overt rituals. For a small group of patients, such as those who suffer from obsessional perfectionism, obsessions do not lead to identifiable rituals. These cases are the most resistant to behavior therapy.

As they are with their obsessions, most people are greatly distressed by their compulsive behavior. The person recognizes that the compulsive behavior serves little practical function and is usually excessive. Usually the person attempts to resist the compulsion, at least initially, but anxiety increases to the point where the compulsion must be performed. People with OCD do not enjoy the compulsive behavior. Behavior patterns that are initially enjoyable but become uncontrollable, such as compulsive gambling, are not true compulsions and are probably better thought of as addictions.

Mary's deep-seated and persistent fear of contaminating the Holy Spirit, whom her family members transmitted from their holy wafers to her car, home, and themselves, followed the pattern of a classic contamination obsession, but with one unusual twist: Mary wasn't afraid of being contaminated; instead, she was afraid of contaminating her home with her own impure nature. This obsession led her to perform the typical washing compulsions of excessive handwashing and persistent washing and wiping of everything (and everyone) in her home.

Recently Goodman and his associates (Goodman, Price, Rasmussen, Mazure, Fleischman, et al., 1989; Goodman, Price, Rasmussen, Mazure, Delgado, et al., 1989) developed the Yale-Brown Obsessive Compulsive Scale (Y-BOCS), which provides an objective measure of the severity of OCD that is independent of the content of the obsessions and compulsions and is not affected by other disorders the person may suffer concurrently. The Y-BOCS is administered by the therapist and consists of 10 questions, 5 concerning the severity of obsessions and 5 concerning the severity of compulsions. The therapist scores each item from 0 (no pathology) to 4 (extreme pathology). Thus, total scores can range from 0 to 40.

During Mary's initial interview she detailed the intrusiveness of her obsessions and compulsions and the anxiety they provoked. She scored a 32 on the Y-BOCS, indicating severe to extreme problems with virtually every aspect of her obsessions and compulsions. Of more immediate concern, however, was Mary's severe depression, as indicated by her depressed mood, lethargy, and suicidal ideas. Her score of 34 on the Hamilton Rating Scale for Depression (HRSD) indicated severely depressed mood. At this point it was important to determine whether Mary suffered from a concurrent major depressive episode or whether her depression was secondary to her OCD. Because Mary had no history of previous depressed episodes, and because her depression appeared to result from her inability to control her compulsions and from her consequent estrangement from her family, her therapist concluded that her depression was most likely secondary to her OCD.

The majority of OCD patients are treated on a five- to eight-week outpatient treatment program. However, the severity of Mary's depressed mood, including her inability to care for herself and her suicidal thoughts, indicated that she be admitted as an inpatient.

The initial goal of therapy was to relieve Mary's depression. She was prescribed clomipramine hydrochloride (known by the trade name Anafranil). Anafranil is one of the family of drugs known as tricylic antidepressants and is especially indicated for patients suffering from obsessional ideas. As is true with most cases involving pharmacological treatment, care must be taken to avoid or at least minimize the side effects of medication. This is particularly important with elderly patients. Mary's dose was gradually increased until she was taking 150 milligrams per day, which is a moderate dose. Fluvoxamine (Prozac) is also commonly prescribed for OCD. Both are roughly equal in their efficaciousness (Rasmussen, 1990); use is determined primarily by the consideration of side effects.

During her stay at the hospital, Mary participated in milieu therapy, which consisted of general supportive care, group discussion sessions, and education as to the nature of OCD. At the same time, Mary's husband and her children still living nearby were also provided with education explaining OCD as a disorder and suggestions for supportive care at home, including information on the action and possible side effects of Mary's medication.

Mary's depression began to lift after about four weeks, and at this time behavior therapy began. (With severely depressed patients, behavior therapy is usually delayed until their depression begins to abate.) Mary's behavior therapy consisted of two elements: exposure therapy and behavioral contracting.

As the name suggests, exposure therapy calls for the patient to be exposed to the object of the obsessions and then prevented from performing the compulsion. Gradually the patient's anxiety will begin to decrease without having resorted to the compulsion, and through extinction the connection between the obsession and the compulsion will be weakened and eventually broken. Most OCD patients with contamination obsessions find the hospital to be a generally relaxing place, since the usual contaminants are kept to a minimum. Contaminants, then, must be imported into the hospital.

In Mary's case the object of the obsession was the Holy Spirit, so her therapist arranged for a priest to come to the hospital and begin imbuing objects with the Holy Spirit. Since Mary's obsessions began with the holy wafer, this was used in her therapy. At first the priest handled a wafer and then placed his hands on a table in Mary's room. She was not allowed to wash the table beforehand, nor was she allowed to wipe the Host away. Before her admission to the hospital, this would have caused excruciating anxiety for Mary. But she was able to tolerate this situation surprisingly easily, perhaps because of her four weeks on Anafranil. As she became accustomed to the Host on the table, the therapist then had Mary touch the table herself. Again, Mary was not allowed to wash her hands or the table. At first Mary showed moderate levels of anxiety to this procedure, but gradually her fears subsided. Finally Mary was asked to hold a wafer herself. When she was able to do this with little anxiety, the exposure portion of her treatment was considered complete.

The second stage of Mary's behavior therapy was behavior contracting. Mary was instructed to make specific agreements that would limit her compulsive behavior. These contracts were to be in writing and signed by Mary, her husband, and her therapist. One of her initial contracts was that she would wash her hands no more than 10 times a day. Soon this agreement was amended to allow only five daily handwashings. Another contract was to plant petunias in her garden. Generally these behavior contracts provide the patient with a formal way to resist the need to perform compulsions and with support from others to aid in this resistance.

After one week of behavior therapy, Mary's obsessional thoughts and compulsive behaviors were reduced dramatically. She washed her hands fewer than five times a day, and she made no attempt to clean objects around her room. Most importantly, she no longer felt the need to avoid her family members. Her scores on both the Y-BOCS and the HRSD were 9, showing mild, subclinical levels of disturbance on both measures. Her medication dose was reduced to a maintenance level of 50 milligrams per day, and she was discharged.

PROGNOSIS

Mary was seen for follow-up one year after treatment. She reported relatively little disturbance from her obsessional thoughts and a virtual absence of compulsive behavior. She had little difficulty fulfilling her various behavioral contracts during the year. In fact, she proudly described the petunias she had planted the previous spring. Her contracting was discontinued. Mary was most pleased with her relationships with her family, which she described as close and supportive. Mary's second follow-up revealed no substantial changes in the intervening year. Both times she scored below 10 on both the Y-BOCS and the HRSD.

Mary died of a massive heart attack about five years after her treatment. In those five years there was little evidence of any remission of her OCD symptoms. Her husband reported that she continued to have mild obsessional thoughts, mostly related to doubt, particularly concerning her participation in religious rituals. However, he stated that as far as he could tell, Mary's obsessions had become less severe and less frequent over time. He could not think of clear instance of a compulsion in the past few years.

DISCUSSION

OCD has long been thought of as a very rare disorder, but recent evidence indicates that it is much more common than previously believed (Flamert et al., 1988; J. G. Henderson & Pollard, 1988; Rapoport, 1986; Rasmussen & Eisen, 1990; Regier, Narrow, & Rae, 1990). Community surveys have reported prevalence rates ranging from 2.2 percent (Kramer, German, Anthony, von Kopff, & Skinner, 1986) to 2.8 percent (J. G. Henderson & Pollard, 1988) in the general population. Rasmussen and Eisen (1990) outlined four reasons why OCD might have been underdiagnosed in the past. First, as was true with Mary, patients realize how "crazy" their obsessions and compulsions would sound to others and therefore hesitate to discuss their symptoms. Second, many professionals have a narrow view of OCD as including only certain types of obsessions and compulsions and thus fail to recognize OCD in some of their patients. Third, many OCD cases are simply misdiagnosed, usually as schizophrenia. An associated problem is that OCD is often overlooked in the presence of other psychiatric disorders. For example, Rasmussen and Eisen (1989) and Weissman and Merikangus (1986) report high rates of concurrent anxiety and mood disorders in their OCD patients. Baer et al. (1990) found that over half of their sample of OCD patients also suffered from at least one personality disorder. Interestingly, the most common personality disorders were borderline and histrionic; only 7 percent of their sample were diagnosed as having compulsive personalities. Finally, because OCD was believed to be so rare, most professionals did not routinely screen for it in their initial patient evaluations. Weissman and Merikangus add that many family members of patients with anxiety disorders may also suffer from an anxiety disorder but go untreated. They recommend that professionals routinely inquire as to the status of the family members of patients with anxiety disorders. Zetin (1990) predicts that as the characteristics of OCD become more clearly defined and the efficacy of treatment for OCD becomes more widely understood, a "hidden epidemic of silent sufferers" will begin to seek therapy. Consequently, the prevalence rates for OCD will continue to rise.

OCD prevalence rates do not vary significantly between the sexes (Karno, Golding, Sorenson, & Burnam, 1988) or across different cultures and nationalities (Marks, 1986). OCD also remains stable over time, with roughly equal prevalence rates being reported among adolescents (Berg, Whitaker, Davies, Flament, & Rapoport, 1988; Flamert et al. 1988; Weissman & Merikangus, 1986) and the elderly (Kramer, German, Anthony, von Kopff, & Skinner, 1986).

Research on OCD shows that Mary's case was typical in many ways. She first developed obsessional thoughts and compulsive behaviors in adolescence, and these patterns continued off and on for the rest of her life. Although it is somewhat unusual for someone to first seek treatment at such an advanced age, historical events provide an explanation. Like many people with mild to moderate obsessional thoughts, Mary was able to remain in control, though undoubtedly she suffered persistent anxiety. But this control was built on the relatively fragile foundation of strictly observing numerous small rules and rituals; it did not survive the seemingly minor change in the communion service.

Mary's case was typical in other ways. She suffered from a secondary depression, which is quite common among OCD patients, affecting perhaps 60 percent (Rasmussen, 1990). Mary received a combined treatment involving medication and exposure therapy, which is quite typical. At Mary's clinic, between 80 to 85 percent of OCD patients receive both medications and behavior therapy (S. A. Rasmussen, personal communication, May, 1992). As is true with many OCD patients, other family members showed signs of mental illness. Although there was no evidence of mental illness in Mary's family history, her daughter and one of her sons showed signs of depression and panic disorder, respectively. Finally, Mary suffered from a contamination obsession and washing compulsions, which are very common among OCD patients.

One aspect of Mary's case was very unusual: she was treated as a hospital inpatient. The vast majority of OCD patients are treated on an outpatient basis. Since they spend less time per day in treatment, however, the usual course of therapy is somewhat longer for outpatients. A typical program would consist of four weeks of education, two weeks of family discussion, and two weeks of exposure therapy and behavior contracting.

Mary's case was also unique in that her contamination obsession took a curious form: she saw herself as the source of the contamination and was afraid of desecrating the objects and people around her. Thus her handwashing ritual was aimed at preventing her from infecting others instead of vice versa. On the other hand, Mary developed a compromise compulsion of wiping and washing all affected surfaces, which ironically resulted in washing the sacred Host down the drain. This behavior takes the form of a classical washing compulsion.

Religiousness and OCD

Cases where the person is reacting to religious beliefs and ideals naturally raise the following question: To what extent does religion contribute to psychopathology? This is an interesting and important question that merits examination.

In his work with OCD patients, S. A. Rasmussen (personal communication, May, 1992) has found that religious beliefs tend to influence the types of obsessions a person may develop. Deeply religious patients are more likely than other patients to report obsessional thoughts involving religious blasphemies, sexual promiscuity, and uncontrolled violence. However, these patients do not differ from other patients in the overall severity of their symptoms. D. Greenberg (1984) has found that for a number of different forms of psychopathology, religiousness affects the content of a person's disturbance more than its severity.

MULTIPLE PERSONALITY DISORDER
Psychotherapy with Hypnosis

PRESENTING COMPLAINT

Sherry is a 31-year-old nurse's aide who has received in-patient psychiatric care off and on for the past five years. Approximately two weeks after her most recent readmission, she became very confused about her surroundings and complained that "everything had changed." She demanded to know who had rearranged the hospital and the grounds, and she repeatedly asked to see people who didn't exist, both patients and staff members. When staff members attempted to calm her, she became verbally and physically abusive, shouting obscenities and swinging her fists.

Sherry had been admitted with a diagnosis of schizophrenia, disorganized type. She had a history of previous hospitalizations, and her strange and irrational behavior seemed to be clear evidence of a yet another psychotic episode. Other therapists, however, believed that Sherry's behavior might be evidence of a dissociative state, a state of consciousness where one part of her awareness is split off from another. Sherry was given the Hypnotic Induction Profile (HIP) and was found to be highly hypnotizable, scoring a 4 out of a possible 5. While in a hypnotic trance, she gave the present date as being eight months earlier than it in fact was and stated that she was at a hospital over a thousand miles away. The date she gave and her description of the hospital corresponded to a clinic she attended just prior to her most recent admission. The therapist who hypnotized her found that she had no memory of anything after leaving this clinic; it was as if she had lost the last eight months of her life. Through hypnosis, Sherry was able to experience age regression (a reliving of the past as though it were the present) to the time of her earlier hospitalization. After the session involving age regression, she was able to reorient herself to her present time and location, and her "psychotic" behavior diminished.

Amnesic periods were not new to Sherry; she frequently complained of episodes for which she had no memory. Sherry is a quiet, demur, and conscientious person, but her behavior often changes during her amnesic episodes. According to the reports of her friends, family, and past therapists, her behavior during these blackouts was often hostile, angry, and self-destructive. Although Sherry could not remember what she did during these episodes, she would often find physical evidence of odd behavior. Sometimes she would notice new cuts and bruises after a blackout, and on several occasions she woke up to find herself in bed with a strange man. For Sherry, the knowledge that she could not control her own behavior was positively frightening.

A recent blackout period occurred about three weeks earlier. Under hypnosis Sherry experienced age regression back three weeks to the time of this amnesic episode. Sherry was put into a deep hypnotic trance. After a minute or so, she suddenly looked up at the therapist and yelled, "What the hell do you want?" Her voice and tone had changed completely from the shy woman who had gone into the hypnotic trance; she was now hostile, angry, and sarcastic. The therapist was somewhat startled by Sherry's sudden change in tone, but he remained calm and asked Sherry who she was. She responded, "Why should I answer you; I don't owe you anything. But what the hell; it doesn't make any difference. You can call me Karla."

The therapist then asked "Karla" what had happened just now (that is, during the amnesic episode Sherry experienced three weeks ago). Karla made it clear that she was irritated at the intrusion on her time and gruffly explained what happened. She had just picked up a man at a bar with the intention of going back to his apartment. But Sherry had spoiled her fun by crying at the bar, causing the man to lose interest. Determined to punish Sherry, Karla threatened to inflict a deep cut on Sherry's leg. With intense hatred and bitterness, Karla ran an imaginary knife over a recently healed cut on her leg, shouting, "I'll show her; I'll really cut her this time! I'll go to sleep and let her find it!" She then closed her eyes. When her eyes reopened, her voice and manner were those of Sherry. Sherry gently touched the wound and sobbed quietly. When the therapist asked her how she got this cut, she appeared to be confused and hesitantly replied, "Well, I . . . I don't know. I guess I ran into something."

PERSONAL HISTORY

Sherry has a twin sister. They both had suffered numerous episodes of physical abuse and neglect throughout their childhoods. At one time their mother bloodied Sherry's nose, and on another occasion she broke Sherry's tooth with her fist. Both of these events occurred before the age of 4. Once Sherry's mother also threw a pot of boiling water at her in a fit of rage, leaving her with second-degree burns on her arms and chest. Sherry's parents divorced after a bitter marriage lasting five years. Two years later her mother remarried. Unfortunately for the twins, their new stepfather was also violent; as his primary form of punishment he would beat the twins using a board studded with nails. After three or four years Sherry and her sister moved in with their biological father. Although he was more caring than the mother and stepfather, he nevertheless was capable of abuse, particularly during his not infrequent alcoholic binges. On these occasions he would beat the twin girls with a belt buckle. After several years Sherry's mother obtained a court order that gave her custody of the children. Immediately after winning their custody, however, the mother sent the twins off to live at a strict military boarding school. After graduation Sherry joined the Army and was separated from her sister.

For most of her life, Sherry reduced the anxiety of this abuse and neglect by dissociating the traumas onto her sister. That is, she frequently experienced her physical and psychological pain as having happened to her twin sister instead of to herself. For example, Sherry stated that her mother once threw boiling water on her sister. However, her mother's and sister's testimony, as well as her medical records, show that in actuality Sherry was the one who was scalded as a child. It was not until she was separated from her sister, however, that she began to experience uncontrollable amnesic periods.

When Sherry joined the Army, she had hopes of being trained as a nurse, but her Army career had barely begun when trouble arose. During basic training she began to notice long periods of time that she could not remember. Her behavior during these periods was reported to be wild and unpredictable; she would often begin violent arguments with other recruits, and on several occasions she had sexual relations with male soldiers on the base or with strange men she would pick up at one of the local bars. Sherry had no recollection of these actions. She also made several suicidal gestures during her amnesic episodes, usually in the form of cutting herself on the forearms and/or taking overdoses of tranquilizers. In addition, she had gone to the camp infirmary on several occasions and complained of auditory hallucinations and depression. As a result of her bizarre and disruptive behavior, Sherry received a psychiatric discharge and was hospitalized with a diagnosis of schizophrenia, disorganized type. While in the hospital she was given antipsychotic medication, which did little to relieve her symptoms.

Over the next five years Sherry was admitted to several different psychiatric institutions and received several different diagnoses, including bipolar disorder, major depression, schizophrenia, and borderline personality disorder. As a result she has been treated with lithium, antidepressants, and antipsychotic medication. All of these efforts, however, had little lasting effect.

CONCEPTUALIZATION AND TREATMENT

Three aspects of Sherry's history were fundamental in the conceptualization of her case. First, Sherry has a strong dissociative capacity, as evidenced by her high hypnotizability. Second, she suffered relatively severe and persistent abuse and neglect as a child. Third, and most crucial, consciousness was split between two very different personalities ("Sherry" and "Karla"). These characteristics are the hallmarks of someone suffering from multiple personality disorder (MPD).

People with strong dissociative capacities, even those who have suffered significant childhood traumas, do not necessarily develop alter personalities. Generally they will utilize their dissociation skill as a defense against particularly painful experiences, a sort of emotional buffer. In some cases, however, the dissociation processes themselves become involuntary and uncontrollable. "Blackout" periods and reports of uncharacteristic behavior that cannot be remembered are indications of these involuntary dissociations. Finding themselves unable to control their behavior, these people are then compelled to seek psychological help (either by their own fears or by the insistence of other people). This seems to be the case with Sherry. Based on this conceptualization, the therapist established a diagnosis of MPD with hysterical, psychotic, and depressive features and discontinued her antipsychotic medication, which in any event did not seem to be effective.

Sherry's therapy was organized into five stages. The first stage of therapy was aimed at recognizing and eventually controlling her dissociations. Using Sherry's hypnotizability as a therapeutic tool, the therapist attempted to provide structure to her spontaneous dissociative states through formal hypnosis. The therapist regularly contacted Karla during hypnotic trances.

As therapy progressed, Sherry was gradually trained in self-hypnosis techniques, which gave her a measure of control over her dissociative states.

The second stage of psychotherapy involved setting limits on her self-destructive tendencies. Using self-hypnosis, she was taught to reexperience her past psychological traumas and learn not to blame herself for her past punishments. Sherry was also taught to express her emotions more openly in an attempt to prevent her hostility from being expressed through her dissociative states. On a more behavioral level, Sherry was frequently hospitalized for short periods to prevent her from carrying out her suicidal threats. In addition, antidepressant medication was administered to counteract her depressive symptoms.

The third stage of therapy focused on the transference between the patient and the therapist. Given Sherry's history of almost continuous abuse and neglect, one would not expect her to trust her therapist fully and to believe that he truly cared for her welfare. Indeed, initially she suspected that the therapist was interested in her only because she was a fascinating case that would lend him prestige if he could cure her. In this light her frequent suicidal gestures were seen as tests of his commitment. Would he remain concerned for her welfare even at the risk of professional failure? At this stage it was essential for the therapist to face the possibility of failure as well as to convey a genuine interest in her well-being in spite of her suicidal gestures and her resistance to therapy.

The fourth—and perhaps the most crucial—stage of therapy involved integrating the two personalities into one being. To accomplish this, Sherry first had to be convinced that the hostile and disruptive aspects of her subconscious were valuable and should not be suppressed. Indeed, the assertiveness and self-confidence expressed by Karla were assets that should be incorporated into a more well-rounded personality. One technique that promoted this integration was giving "equal time" to both "Sherry" and "Karla." In this way, Sherry learned to tolerate Karla's more aggressive emotions, thus reducing the need for Karla to rebel and undermine Sherry. Similarly, Karla was taught that Sherry's good-natured attributes could be quite useful in forming and maintaining relationships with others. Over a period of years, both personalities gradually incorporated elements of the other, and the shifts between them became smoother and less disruptive. After approximately three years of therapy, Sherry reported that she was aware of Karla for the first time. She described this realization as "opening a door in myself." Karla then added, "I'm in here too. We're both here. It's not one or the other; we're together."

Another important aspect of this integration was to have the patient understand the traumatic memories and events that caused the dissociations in the first place. However, the therapist must be cautious in this endeavor. On the one hand, pushing a patient to relive early traumas too quickly may exacerbate the dissociations. On the other hand, failing to deal with repressed traumas may perpetuate the need for dissociations in the future. In general, these patients are encouraged to confront and accept their painful memories, to gain control over these memories, and to restructure these memories in a way that is consistent with their emerging unified self-image.

In Sherry's case, her mother's persistent manipulation and neglect engendered extreme emotional dependence, which led to persistent feelings of guilt and obligation. One example of Sherry's obligation toward her mother is that she pays her mother's bills and provides her mother with a rent-free room in her apartment, this in spite of the fact that her mother is financially secure. (In fact, since Sherry has spent a great deal of the past 10 years in psychiatric hospitals, her mother is much better off than she is.) To add insult to injury, Sherry's mother does not appreciate this help. The mother rarely attends family therapy sessions, and when she does, she usually shows much more concern for her own interests (e.g., vacation plans, clothing purchases) than for her daughter's improvement. Understandably, Sherry was very resentful of her mother's callous selfishness, yet she felt unable to challenge her directly. Instead she would criticize herself for being so weak and dependent. Often this self-derogation and repressed anger was expressed by Karla, who would cut Sherry's wrists or perform other acts of self-mutilation to punish Sherry for being so weak. Many times after paying her mother's bills, Sherry would emerge from the bathroom with her arms dripping blood. She was saying to her mother symbolically what she couldn't say directly: "You are bleeding me to death." To prevent Sherry from venting her frustration in self-destructive ways in the future, Sherry's therapist urged her to ask her mother to pay her own bills and move out of her apartment. This confrontation was not without some cost; Sherry entered a severe depression after this episode. However, she responded well to antidepressant medication and began to function better after her recovery.

Finally, the fifth stage of Sherry's therapy involved interaction management as a means of helping her to avoid the pathologic compliance and repressed resentment that characterized her previous relationships. Interaction management is a therapy technique used to teach the patient more effective ways of dealing with other people through the use of role-playing and modeling. As a part of this therapy, Sherry attended conjoint sessions with her mother, her sister, and, later, her boyfriend. The therapist then provided Sherry with ways to react to the various interpersonal demands of these people more assertively.

The course of Sherry's therapy was very gradual. For several months she received intensive treatment as an inpatient before she was released and continued psychotherapy on an outpatient basis. After three years both personalities had finally recognized each other, and shortly thereafter she began a relationship with a man. Her outpatient therapy, which took the form of frequent office consultations and occasional active interventions, continued for two more years. During this time Sherry broke up with her boyfriend and entered a severe depressive episode. However, she made no serious suicide attempts; she was given antidepressant medication and was able to remain an outpatient. Her outpatient therapy drew to a close about one year later. Approximately three years later Sherry was raped. At that time she was brought to the hospital in a confused and agitated state. Hypnotic regression enabled her to relive the painful events of the rape and to convince herself that she was not responsible for the trauma. She was released from the hospital after only two weeks. For the past few years Sherry has received supportive psychotherapy off and on at her own request.

PROGNOSIS

Sherry has made steady progress since the beginning of therapy. Over the course of several years, her uncontrolled bursts of anger and self-mutilating behaviors for the most part have ceased, she has developed a more equitable relationship with her mother, and her therapy has progressed from inpatient care to outpatient care to intermittent support sessions. However, she remains vulnerable to future dissociative episodes in response to severe stress, particularly if it involves sexual or financial exploitation. An example of this vulnerability was evidenced after her rape. Although Sherry had been in therapy for several years, she nevertheless suffered from uncontrollable dissociations as a result of this painful trauma.

Sherry's power to dissociate is a two-edged sword. While her ability to separate and repress the traumatic events of her life may insulate her from severely painful experiences, it may also leave her open to uncontrollable dissociations that frequently result in self-damaging acts or unacceptable behavior. Sherry's continued adjustment will depend on her ability to learn to use her powers of self-hypnosis to gain mastery over her intrapsychic processes. Although the prognosis for Sherry is generally good, her therapist remains cautious about her ability to cope with painful, traumatic experiences independently. It remains to be seen whether Sherry will be able to completely control her dissociations in the face of severe life pressures.

DISCUSSION

Multiple personality disorder is an exceedingly rare diagnosis. As a consequence, until recently little was known about this disorder aside from anecdotal clinical reports. However, some researchers have begun to specialize in treating MPD patients (often called "multiples"), and they are beginning to publish data based on their own samples (Bliss, 1984; Coons, Bowman, & Milstein, 1988; Coons & Milstein, 1986; Miller, Blackburn, Scholes, White, & Mamalis, 1991). Still, the number of multiples seen at any one clinic is usually relatively small, requiring much effort to collect usable samples. For example, Philip Coons (Coons et al., 1988) reported that it took 13 years to collect data on 50 multiples from his personal practice! To speed up data collection on samples large enough to generate reliable results, researchers have utilized some innovative techniques. One strategy is to survey many different therapists, each of whom may have treated only one or two multiples (Putnam, Guroff, Silberman, Barban, & Post, 1986; Ross, Norton, & Wozney, 1989). Another strategy is to combine data from different clinics that specialize in MPD. In this way Ross et al. (1990) collected a sample of 102 multiples across four sites.

Common Characteristics

Research findings from the six studies cited above have been remarkably consistent. A clear majority of multiples are women (from 75 to 92 percent). Most multiples are in their twenties and thirties (though their ages range from 11 to 67), and the majority recall first noticing instances of dissociation in childhood or early adolescence. Most multiples have a history of being abused as children, either sexually (55-90 percent), physically (60-90 percent), or both (46-68 percent). The vast majority (94-97 percent) have suffered some form of severe, longstanding trauma. Putnam et al. (1986) reported one particularly alarming finding: during childhood 45 percent of their sample personally witnessed the violent death of another person. Coons and Milstein (1986) recorded the following types of abuse:

Types of Abuse or Trauma in 20 Patients

Patient	Age	Sex	Abuse	Abuser(s)	Frequency
1	15	M	incest, beating	father	repeatedly
2	28	M	severe toileting	mother	repeatedly
3	47	M	beating	father	repeatedly
4	14	F	incest, beating	father	repeatedly
5	17	F	incest	father	repeatedly
6	19	F	incest	father	once
			beating	stepfather	repeatedly
7	21	F	incest	father, brothers	repeatedly
			beating	father	repeatedly
8	22	F	sexual fondling	grandmother's boyfriend	repeatedly
9	23	F	neglect	parents	repeatedly
			incest	uncle	once
10	23	F	incest	father, brother	repeatedly
				uncle	repeatedly
			beating	father, brothers	repeatedly
11	26	F	incest	stepfather	once
				uncle, cousin	once
12	29	F	verbal abuse	father	repeatedly
13	31	F	incest, beating	father, brother	repeatedly
14	32	F	incest	father	repeatedly
15	32	F	beating	mother	repeatedly
16	33	F	beating	husband	repeatedly
17	35	F	sexual fondling	father, brother	once
			watched sister burn to death		
18	42	F	incest	uncle	once
			beating	father	repeatedly
19	44	F	incest, burned	father	repeatedly
20	46	F	sexual fondling	stepfather	repeatedly
			pushed dn stairs	stepfather	once

From *The Journal of Clinical Psychiatry*, 47:3 (*March,1986*) 106-110
Copyright 1986, Physicians Postgraduate Press

Another common characteristic of multiples is that they are highly hypnotizable. This characteristic is shared by patients who suffer from other dissociative disorders such as amnesia (memory loss) and fugue (forgetting one's identity and assuming a new identity). Many therapists see the ability to be hypnotized as a fundamental marker for the ability to dissociate, and some have advocated its use in diagnostic screening (Spiegel, 1986). Others, however, argue that the concepts of hypnosis and dissociation are unclear and urge caution in the use of hypnotizability as a clinical tool (e.g., Frankel, 1990). A related point is that multiples typically developed elaborate fantasy worlds during childhood. These worlds often contained imaginary playmates that shard the child's pain. In Sherry's case, her twin sister may have fulfilled this role.

Drawing on the common characteristics he observed in multiples, Kluft (1984) developed a four-factor theory of MPD. First, children who have the ability to dissociate their experiences are particularly vulnerable to develop MPD. Second, traumatic events or circumstances can trigger these dissociative abilities into action as a way of escaping these painful experiences, or at least isolating them from conscious awareness. Third, children will use available psychological resources such as imaginary companions as models for their alter personalities. Finally, repeated abuse or a lack of healthy experiences with role models will fixate the pattern of dissociation. Initially, alter personalities serve to shield the child from painful trauma, but eventually they may take on lives of their own to the point where the person loses control over his or her behavior.

The Organization of Multiple Personalities

In MPD, consciousness is divided among two or more distinct and unique personalities, each with its own system of social relationships and behavior patterns. Different personalities have even shown differential responses in physiological functioning, including allergic reactions, food preferences, effects of drinking alcohol, and side effects from medication (Putnam et al., 1986).

48

In a particularly intriguing study, Miller et al. (1991) had an ophthalmologist conduct detailed eye examinations on the different personalities of 20 MPD patients. A matched group of 20 controls role-played different personalities during eye examinations. There was much more variation among the personalities of MPD patients than among the role-played personalities of the controls on a number of objective measurements and clinical assessments. Furthermore, these differences did not result from the expectations of the ophthalmologist. In the course of his examinations he was asked to guess whether each subject was a patient or a control; he could not reliably distinguish the two groups.

The number of alter personalities varies widely among multiples, ranging from 1 (as in Sherry's case) to 60 (Putnam et al., 1986). Although the average number of alter personalities is around 15, this figure is thrown off somewhat by a few patients with very many alter personalities. For example, Putnam et al. report an average of 13.3 alter personalities, but the most commonly reported number (the mode) was only 3. They also found an association between the number of reported childhood traumas and the number of reported personalities.

There is a wide variation in the characteristics of alter personalities. Most multiples (88-86 percent) report one or more personalities who are children under age 12, and over half (56-67 percent) have personalities of the opposite sex. At any one time only one personality tends to dominate the person's consciousness. As was true in Sherry's case, the shifts between these different personalities can be quite abrupt. Putnam et al. found that the switch between personalities often takes just seconds, and for over 90 percent of their sample the average duration of a personality switch is less than five minutes.

Generally speaking, alter personalities form three basic clusters: "core" personalities, aggressive personalities, and intermediary personalities. Core personalities contain the characteristics that describe the patient as he or she is generally known to most people. These personalities are usually meek, passive, and obedient, and they aim to please others and avoid pain.

A second cluster consists of one or more personalities that are self-confident, outgoing, and assertive. Often these personalities become aggressive, reckless, or promiscuous. Many times these personalities attack the people who have mistreated them in their lives (e.g., abusive or exploitive parents, spouses, or bosses), but usually their anger is directed toward the core personality. Sometimes they may attempt to "punish" the core personality through suicide attempts or by inflicting painful wounds. At other times these aggressive personalities may take advantage of the core personality in more subtle ways. In one case, a man's aggressive personality wrecked a car the core personality had borrowed from a friend. Subsequently, this second personality let the core personality "wake up" at the scene of the accident to explain the wreck to the police and the owner.

A third cluster includes personalities that act as intermediaries between the submissive and aggressive personalities. Often these intermediaries serve as referees to reconcile the different needs of the other personalities. They also seem to function as rational spokespersons who can sympathize with the meek core personalities and yet understand the wild and disruptive actions of the aggressive personalities. Therapists using hypnosis find it helpful to make use of these intermediary personalities at the beginning stages of therapy. These personalities tend to be fully aware of the actions of all other personalities, and they are relatively receptive to treatment.

The present case is somewhat unusual in that only two distinct personalities, "Sherry" and "Karla," emerged. In one sense, it was fortunate that Sherry had only one alter personality. Generally, the more complex and varied the personalities, the more difficult the therapy (Kluft, 1987). On the other hand, the absence of any intermediary personality may have impeded the initial reconciliation.

Interactions among different personalities have two common properties. First, these interactions are characterized by asymmetric amnesia, also called directional awareness. There are many patterns of asymmetric amnesia. Typically the core personality has no direct knowledge of the other personalities, whereas these other personalities have at least a limited knowledge of the core. In most cases at least one personality (typically an intermediary personality) is omniscient; this personality becomes the focus of therapeutic attempts at integration. Karla knew all about Sherry—her thoughts and feelings as well as her actions. In contrast, Sherry experienced amnesic periods when Karla took over and knew nothing about Karla's existence except for physical signs or reports from other people. Although Karla was a rather hostile personality who was somewhat difficult to work with, her omniscience provided the therapist with the best pathway toward integration.

A second characteristic of the interaction between personalities is trance logic, a suspension of the rules of logic and reason. Alter personalities often revert to trance logic to explain their attempts to harm the core personality. Putnam et al. (1986) found that 53 percent of the suicide attempts in their sample resulted from an alter personality's attempt to kill the core personality, a process these researchers refer to as "internal homicide." The alter personality seems unconcerned (or unaware) that a completed suicide will result in his or her own demise. For example, after Sherry made a suicide attempt, her therapist asked Karla whether she was worried about what would happen if Sherry actually died. Karla responded, "It doesn't matter. I could just float to some other body. But for now I've got to be with her."

Distinguishing MPD from Other Diagnoses
One difficulty in accurately diagnosing multiple personality disorder is that it shares many features with other diagnoses. The hostile, disruptive, and uncontrolled behaviors of the aggressive personality may indicate an oppositional disorder, an antisocial personality disorder, or a borderline personality disorder. The frequently observed depressed behavior and suicidal attempts lead many therapists to a diagnosis of major depression. In some cases, the aggressive personality is so uncontrolled and delusional that a diagnosis of schizophrenia or psychotic paranoia is indicated. In fact, establishing these

psychotic and depressive symptoms as resulting from a dissociation is no easy task. Researchers (Coons et al., 1988; Putnam et al., 1986; Ross et al., 1990) have found that, on average, multiples experience six to seven years of therapy and receive two or three other diagnoses before they are finally diagnosed with MPD. Among the most common prior diagnoses are depression, personality disorder, anxiety, substance abuse, and schizophrenia. Although multiples may concurrently suffer from other psychiatric disorders, these are usually secondary to their problems with multiple personalities. Generally, a diagnosis of MPD is greatly facilitated by a therapist who is experienced in recognizing and treating dissociative disorders. Many therapists have found that special training in techniques involving hypnosis has greatly enhanced their ability to identify this rare condition.

In the past, many professionals have been skeptical of hypnosis as a legitimate diagnostic and treatment tool. For example, Spanos, Weekes, and Bertrand (1985) argue that the use of hypnosis in the evaluation interview leads many patients to enact symptoms that mimic MPD in an effort to fulfill the therapist's expectations. Although this hypothesis is intriguing, research has not supported it. Putnam et al. (1986) found no differences between patients whose therapists used hypnosis at any point during diagnosis or treatment and patients whose therapists did not. Although the use of hypnosis in the diagnosis and treatment of MPD remains controversial—as does the validity of MPD as a useful diagnostic category—a growing number of therapists are diagnosing MPD and employing hypnosis in their treatment strategies. At the present time it is unclear whether this growth merely reflects an increased awareness of MPD or an actual increase in its incidence.

BIPOLAR DISORDER WITH MOOD-CONGRUENT PSYCHOTIC FEATURES
Eclectic Therapy

PRESENTING COMPLAINT

Julie is a 20-year-old sophomore at a small midwestern college. For the last five days she has gone without any sleep whatsoever; she has spent this time in a heightened state of activity which she describes as "out of control." For the most part, her behavior is characterized by strange and grandiose ideas that often take on a mystical or sexual tone. For example, recently she proclaimed to a group of friends that she did not menstruate because she was "of a third sex, a gender above the two human sexes." When they asked her what she meant, she explained that she is a "superwoman" who can avoid human sexuality and still give birth. That is, she is a woman who does not require sex to fulfill her place on earth.

Some of Julie's bizarre ideation took on a political tone. One instance of this political theme involved global disarmament. She felt that she had somehow switched souls with the senior senator from her state. From his thoughts and memories, she developed six theories of government that would allow her to save the world from nuclear destruction single-handedly. She went around campus explaining these six theories to friends and even to professors, and she began to campaign for an elected position in the United States government (even though no elections were scheduled at that time). Nevertheless, she felt that her recent experiences made her particularly well suited for a position high in the government, perhaps even President.

During this time Julie was worried that she would forget some of her thoughts, and she began writing these thoughts everywhere: in her notebooks, on her personal computer, and even on the walls of her dormitory room. Julie's family and friends, who had always known her to be extremely tidy and organized, were shocked to find her room in total disarray with hundreds of frantic and often incoherent messages written all over the walls and furniture. By and large these messages reflected her disorganized, grandiose thinking about spiritual and sexual themes.

By the end of the week Julie was beginning to feel increasingly irritated and fatigued. She began having difficulty walking, claiming that her right leg was numb. At this point her dormitory resident assistant brought her to the college health service, and she was seen by the therapist on call.

Julie spoke very rapidly in a rambling, loose style. Finally, when Julie's delusions (strange systems of thought based on false or bizarre foundations) were clarified to her, she realized that she was in need of help and did not resist the therapist's recommendation that she be hospitalized immediately.

> **Therapist:** Well, Julie, what brings you here?
>
> **Julie:** I have a lot of trouble walking and I need to walk because I have so many things to do before the election like make up posters and TV spots and interviews and all that stuff.
>
> **Therapist:** What did you say about your leg? You said something's wrong with it, didn't you?

Julie: Oh, yeah. Well, sometimes I can't feel it because it's really another person's leg and I can't always control it.

Therapist: You just said that your leg is really another person's leg. It that right?

Julie: I did? You know, this has happened to me before, the leg thing, I mean. I had a lot of strange thoughts then, too. I had to go to the hospital.

Therapist: I think this may be the same sort of thing, and you may need to go to the hospital again, OK?.

Julie: Alright.

Previous Episodes

In the course of therapy, Julie described two earlier episodes of wild and bizarre behavior. These manic episodes alternated with periods of intense depression.

Julie's first manic episode appeared during high school. In the summer between her junior and senior years, Julie went to a tennis summer camp with several other boys and girls her own age. During the trip she began to develop a strong attraction toward one of the boys. She had never had these feelings before, and they frightened her. She became extremely self-conscious of her sexual thoughts, and she became convinced that everyone else was constantly watching her and could read her mind. Although she never developed a relationship with the boy, she felt that she could not stand to be so near to him and had to leave and return home. She felt "safe" at home, and her agitation quickly subsided. She did not date during the remainder of the summer or during her senior year, which passed with no further incidents.

At the end of the summer, Julie went off to a private university in the east. After being away at college for 10 days, she developed a severe depression as a result of not coping with being on her own. She could not bring herself to attend classes or any campus activities. She suffered from a number of somatic difficulties characteristic of depression, including poor appetite, insomnia, an inability to concentrate, and psychomotor retardation. After two weeks Julie left school and was admitted to a psychiatric hospital near her parents' home. While in the hospital she was given an antipsychotic medication, halperadol (which is known by the trade name Haldol). She also attended psychodynamically oriented group and individual therapy. Gradually her depressed symptoms dissipated, and she was discharged after seven weeks.

At the beginning of the next school term, Julie enrolled in a private university in the midwest. Her past anxious and depressed episodes made her feel as though she had missed many social opportunities commonly experienced by people her age, and she decided to make a change and to have a "real college experience." Julie made friends with a group of students who smoked, drank, used recreational drugs, and engaged in casual sex. Over the next several weeks she became increasingly irritable and restless, and she had difficulty sleeping and concentrating. Her use of marijuana and cocaine increased, as did her reckless behavior. Her most disturbing memory was of the morning when she awoke and found herself in the bed of a male student whom she didn't know.

After half a semester she entered her second, and most severe, manic episode. She developed clearly bizarre thoughts and behaviors that revolved around themes of responsibility, sexuality, and religion. First she acquired several compulsive rituals. For example, she washed her hands whenever she thought about sex, and she found herself compelled to hold her hands together for most of the time. She believed that everyone was watching her and knew about her experiences with drugs and sex. She was deathly afraid that someone would somehow expose her. Paradoxically, she often felt as if she could control the world; at times she felt that she could prevent nuclear war, and at other times she felt personally responsible for nuclear explosions that she believed had occurred already. She also suffered from what she described as a "Jesus Christ delirium." She felt a special empathy with Christ, and she had what she later believed to be auditory hallucinations of Christ's talking directly to her. She wanted to "merge with the higher spirits," and at times she felt her body "floating up to heaven." Her delusions often included ideas about the special significance of parts of her body. For example, she felt that the follicles on the left side of her head were "sensitized" to receive thought messages from Christ. Many times she also attempted to include other people in these delusions. Once her boyfriend saw her pressing her legs together and caressing her breasts with her hand. When he teased her about how "sexy" she looked, she tried to convince him that her right leg and hand were actually his, and thus it was he who was really stroking her body.

As she gradually lost control over her psychotic behaviors, she began to get the attention of university officials. For instance, several students complained to her resident assistant after they watched her chanting "work . . . work . . . work" over and over. Finally she was hospitalized as a result of her gross delusions. One day she began babbling about finding the biblical garden during a lecture she was attending. At first she only muttered to herself, but eventually her incoherent babbling became audible to the entire class. Suddenly she ran out of the classroom, and campus security found her wandering around the campus.

Julie was admitted to the university hospital where she was put on antipsychotic medication and lithium. She was again enrolled in psychodynamically oriented group and individual therapy, where she developed a good relationship with her psychotherapist. After about a month of intensive group and individual therapy, her bizarre ideation gradually diminished, and she was released and returned to school. Although she was told to continue taking lithium, she complained of the nausea and diarrhea it caused and soon discontinued taking it.

Approximately a month after leaving the hospital, Julie began to feel depressed. Again, she experienced difficulty with eating, sleeping, and concentrating. She discontinued her favorite pastime, painting, and stopped going to classes. Finally, she withdrew from the university and returned home. She was not treated for her depression, which gradually lifted during the summer. At the insistence of her parents, Julie then enrolled in a small college near her midwestern home.

PERSONAL HISTORY

Julie grew up in a "traditional Catholic-Irish home," and she described her parents as overprotective and demanding. Of the five children, she was the one who always obeyed her parents and played the role of the good girl of the family, a role she describes as "being the Little Miss Perfect." Julie described herself as being quite dependent on her parents, who treated her as if she were much younger than she actually was. It seems that Julie also adopted this view; she states that she sees herself as much younger than her peers in college. In contrast, Julie describes her siblings as rebellious. Her older brother openly defied the Catholic church by announcing his atheism, and her older sister made it known to her parents that she was sexually active in high school. Julie also describes her two younger sisters as defiant, but to a lesser extent.

Julie describes her parents as exceptionally strict with respect to sexual matters; they never discussed issues related to sex except to make it clear that their children are to remain virgins until they are married. Throughout high school her mother forbade her to wear makeup. Julie describes herself as a "tomboy who played with trucks, fished, and always wore pants." She detested wearing dresses because they somehow made her feel a lack of control. She remembers being shocked and frightened when she began menstruating; she was especially distressed at the loss of control this entailed. Julie did not date during high school, and until recently has not had a steady boyfriend in college.

Julie's family history shows evidence of mood disorders: her maternal grandfather received electro-convulsive therapy

(ECT) for depression and her father's aunt was diagnosed as depressed at menopause.

CONCEPTUALIZATION AND TREATMENT

Julie suffers from episodes of wild and reckless manic behavior alternating with episodes of moderate to severe depression. This pattern is a prime indication of manic-depressive illness, which *DSM-III-R* terms *bipolar disorder*. To some therapists her grandiose and bizarre delusions could be taken as signs of a psychotic disorder. However, her history of alternating manic and depressed episodes, and the manner in which her psychotic symptoms seem to correspond to her disordered mood (i.e., the delusions that appear during her manic episodes are primarily grandiose and/or mystical) point toward a diagnosis of bipolar disorder with mood-congruent psychotic features, or, as it is more commonly known, manic-depressive psychosis.

Eclectic therapy draws on the assumptions of many different theoretical approaches and makes use of a variety of therapeutic techniques. Aspects of the biomedical, psychoanalytic, humanistic, and behavioral schools, among others, may be employed. Typically, eclectic therapists are trained in one of the prevailing theoretical approaches and later combine elements and techniques from different schools in ways that they feel provide the best explanation for the etiology of a particular case and the most effective treatment for that patient. By and large, eclectic therapists focus initially on their patients' presenting complaints and on ways to control these problems. Once these immediate issues are addressed, therapy can begin to explore possible underlying causes. Typically, a patient's personal history is investigated to help the patient delineate important events that may have shaped his or her life. Next, the ways in which these events may contribute to the patient's present problems are discussed in individual or group therapy (or both). Finally, the therapist and the patient discuss how these insights may help the patient's long-term functioning. Thus, the aim of eclectic therapy is to provide patients with a pragmatic and flexible approach to their problems.

In Julie's case, the initial consideration of her therapist is to control and, in time, eliminate her florid psychotic symptoms. Her initial treatment consisted of psychopharmacological therapy in a controlled environment. Once Julie's therapist became aware of her history of past manic and depressed episodes, she decided to hospitalize Julie and prescribe a combination of antipsychotic medication (in this case halperodol, since it had been shown to be effective previously) and lithium carbonate. Antipsychotics work to diminish a patient's psychotic behaviors; lithium carbonate, usually referred to simply as "lithium," has been shown to be especially effective in reducing the wild mood swings of bipolar patients. Once the bizarre psychotic features abate, Julie will gradually be taken off halperodol. However, she must remain on lithium treatment indefinitely to prevent the reoccurrence of her wild mood swings. Julie's therapist maintains her lithium level at approximately 0.5 milliequivalent per liter of blood. For Julie, this amounts to a dose of 1200 milligrams per day.

The next stage for Julie's therapy is to examine her past experiences to identify some potential causes of her disorder. In all likelihood it appears that Julie's problems, at least in part, may stem from her overprotective and strict upbringing. Julie describes her father not only as having strict values but also as being overbearing and demanding; she describes her mother as having perfectionist standards bordering on compulsiveness. One interpretation of Julie's behavior is that over time Julie developed a series of compulsive defenses to help her reduce the anxiety caused by her parents' high expectations. For example, in an attempt to attain her parents' high standards of sexual purity (a task made even more difficult by the more open sexual mores of her sister), Julie denied her own sexual urges and feelings. An unfortunate result of this strategy is that she developed a great confusion about her own sexuality and to some extent her gender identity. As was seen above, these themes pervade her psychotic delusions.

To fulfill her parents' other strict expectations, Julie attempted to be the perfect daughter, or as she describes it, "Little Miss Perfect." She has always been a very conscientious daughter. She received straight A's throughout school, she has very neat personal habits, and she has always had a willingness to take on duty and responsibility. Her psychotic compulsions, the most striking of which was her chanting "work . . . work . . . work" around campus, are further indications of this defense. Her grandiose delusions of being able to single-handedly bring about world peace are symbolic expressions of her need to fulfill her responsibilities. These compulsive defenses were also prevalent during her recent hospitalization. For example, despite the fact that she had already withdrawn from school, Julie insisted on having her books with her in the hospital so that she could keep up in her classes.

The term "Little Miss Perfect" also implies a repression of the sexual component of Julie's subconscious, and describing herself with this term is another of her compulsive defenses. Her attempts to deny her sexuality began early on with her "tomboy" stage. It is significant that wearing dresses made her feel a "lack of control" as a child. At age 13 she was understandably shocked and frightened when she began to menstruate, probably because it conflicted so directly with her desire to deny her emerging sexuality. In fact, her first manic episode, which appeared during her summer tennis camp experience, apparently resulted from her first strong feelings of sexual attraction. Later, when she was away at college, she was determined to rebel against her parents' strict expectations. Unfortunately, her experiments with drugs and sex seemed to overwhelm her compulsive defenses, resulting in a severe episode of manic psychosis. The themes of her psychotic delusions clearly illustrate her ambivalent feelings toward her own sexuality. On the one hand, her delusions about being a third gender convey her continued attempts to deny her sexuality, especially the physical symbol of her sexuality, her menstruation. On the other hand, many of her other thoughts express some attempt to reconcile her sexual feelings with her strict upbringing. Most notable among these is her explanation to her friends that she was a superwoman who could fulfill traditional sex roles without having to degrade herself with sex.

In addition to her problems in coping with her sexuality, Julie's psychotic ideation about spiritual themes seems to reflect her anxiety over trying to meet the relatively strict demands of the Catholic church while at the same time coping with the social pressures of modern college life. For many patients it is not uncommon for psychotic manifestations to incorporate a spiritual component, particularly for people with traditional religious backgrounds.

Often patients have a difficult time accepting the fact that they have repressed conflicts over their beliefs. Many firmly hold onto their (often unreasonable) principles and ideals and fail to understand how their internal standards may have contributed to their problems. In contrast, Julie recognized that her parents were very strict and at some level realized that her values were not the same as theirs. However, Julie did not understand the difficulty she had in defying the expectations of her upbringing. In a sense, Julie underestimated how strongly she still held her parents' values. Only gradually did she comprehend the extent of her own ambivalent feelings and how they might have an impact on her therapy.

Once the patients' underlying issues have been identified, the next step of therapy is to adjust their self-expectations in ways that reduce their anxiety while making sure that these adjustments are not so sweeping that they overwhelm their neurotic defenses. In Julie's case, her experimentation with drugs and sex was an attempt to change her self-image, but these experiences created neurotic conflicts that were too strong for her to cope with. Still, Julie seemed to have a need to free herself of at least some of the strict constraints imposed by her parents and her faith. With this in mind, Julie's therapist had her engage in a "mini-rebellion." After her hospitalization, Julie had to decide whether to stay at home for a while or to return to school. She was encouraged to return to school as a way of developing a sense of separation from her parents. This she did.

Julie was also told to think about the conflict between her wants and her duties and how she might resolve these problems. A question Julie kept in her mind was "When is Little Miss Perfect right, and when is she wrong?"

Julie's therapist also suggested concrete ways to diminish her neurotic defenses. For instance, Julie was told to try to become less concerned about her grades and to "loosen up" socially. At first, Julie had difficulty with this proscription. While she was still in the hospital, she had her parents bring her books so that she could study (even though it was already decided that she would not finish the semester). After she was released from the hospital, she refused to date and went out with her friends only rarely. The therapist frequently encouraged her to go out and enjoy life, to let herself be more relaxed. Only gradually did Julie's social activities increase. After about four months, Julie mentioned that she had a boyfriend. She was urged to continue seeing him, provided he understood her needs and was supportive of her. In fact, the therapist saw the boyfriend with Julie for two sessions so that he could get a better understanding of exactly what her needs were.

In addition to her individual therapy, Julie was also involved in a depression therapy group. Julie found the supportive atmosphere of the group to be extremely helpful in letting her overcome her shyness about telling people about her illness. Since Julie was the only bipolar in the group and had by far the most unusual experiences, the other group members treated her with respect and, in some cases, awe. Julie told her therapist that it felt good being able to help other people just by being open and friendly.

The focus of therapy then shifted to altering Julie's impressions of the demands of her parents and the church. For this the therapist employed a process of cognitive restructuring. One issue involved Julie's perception of sex. In therapy Julie frequently admonished herself for having sexual fantasies and for her past sexual behavior. Her therapist tried to convince her that sex was not evil and that having sexual thoughts, and even engaging in sexual behavior, did not mean that she would automatically be sent to hell. The therapist emphasized that sexual feelings are common to everyone, particularly young people her age, and that having sexual feelings was not something to be ashamed or afraid of. A second issue was Julie's dependence on her parents' approval. Julie often refrained from doing something she would have enjoyed for fear that her parents might disapprove. To counter these thoughts, Julie was told that her mother was old-fashioned and had different ideas about life. In all likelihood, her mother's standards were not as high as Julie guessed. But even if they were, it was probable that her mother did not fully understand Julie's feelings, thus creating standards that were impossible for Julie to meet. It was emphasized that Julie should not deny her mother's values; rather she was encouraged to accept them for what they are: another person's ideas which are different from her own.

The final stage of Julie's therapy involved support and maintenance. Julie's weekly visits now dealt primarily with supporting her sense of autonomy from her parents, especially in the areas in which they disagree. Just as important as her psychological support, these visits helped her maintain a proper level of lithium in her system. Once per month she has the lithium level of her blood analyzed to ensure that she maintains an effective yet safe lithium blood level.

PROGNOSIS

As is the case with the majority of patients with bipolar disorder, Julie responded well to lithium treatment. At the present time (13 months after her most recent manic episode), Julie appears to be doing well. She is still in supportive therapy, which has now been reduced to a biweekly basis. Julie is still somewhat tense and anxious, but she has had no psychotic symptoms since her last episode. Julie is very bright (so far she has earned a 3.9 GPA in college in spite of the disruptions caused by her illness) and has a great deal of insight into the causes of her problems. She describes her boyfriend as supportive and undemanding, and her relationship with him seems to be going well. Julie describes their sexual behavior as "a lot of necking and heavy petting"; they have not engaged in intercourse. Although Julie wants to keep sex at bay for the time being, she has begun to think about her future plans with her boyfriend and the possibility of getting married. Her main concern does not seem to be with her moral standards but rather with the possibility of a future pregnancy. Since lithium is contraindicated for pregnant women, she will need to interrupt her lithium therapy if she decides to become pregnant, and she fears that she may relapse into another manic episode when she interrupts her therapy. This is a legitimate concern. However, at the same time it shows the progress Julie has made in coming to terms with her own sexuality and reconciling her underlying gender confusion.

In general the early onset of Julie's disease and the severity of the psychotic symptoms Julie manifested would lead one to be rather pessimistic about her long-term prognosis (Cohen, Khan, & Cox, 1989). However, Julie's rapid response to lithium, her complete lack of residual psychotic features between episodes, her abstention from illicit drugs, and her keen insight into the causes of her disorder all argue against a diagnosis of an underlying psychotic pathology. Thus, the prognosis for Julie seems quite good provided she continues her lithium treatments and remains in a supportive relationship.

DISCUSSION

Julie's case was typical in many ways. Most people with bipolar disorder begin to experience symptoms in late adolescence; the average age of onset is about 20, a figure that has remained stable over the past century (Baptista & Novua, 1989; Burke, Burke, Rae, & Regier, 1991; Dwyer & DeLong, 1987, Weissman et al., 1988). Julie's age of onset was a bit younger, but not unusually so. In addition, Julie responded well to lithium, as do about 80 percent of bipolar patients (O'Connell, Mayo, Flatow, Cuthbertson, & O'Brien, 1991). Finally, Julie has a family history of affective disorders. Compared with the general population, bipolar patients are much more likely to have first- and second-degree relatives with a history of mood disorders (Klein, Depue, & Slater, 1985). The rate of mood disorders among these relatives ranges from 8 percent to 29 percent in different studies (Dwyer & DeLong, 1987; Gershon et al., 1982; Fieve, Go, Dunner, & Elston, 1984), and this rate triples or quadruples in children whose parents both suffer from an affective disturbance (Dwyer & DeLong; Gershon et al.). These figures lead many researchers to believe that bipolar disorder is transmitted genetically (Fieve et al.; Pardes, Kaufman, Pincus, & West, 1989). However, the genetic link is not direct; relatives of bipolar patients have increased rates of *some* mood disorder, but not necessarily bipolar disorder. Thus, bipolar disorder is thought of as a "spectrum disease" (Fieve et al.) inherited through multiple genetic factors that have not been identified.

Compared with the incidence of other mood disorders, the incidence of bipolar disorder in the general population is low; the reported lifetime prevalence rates range from 0.4 to 1.2 percent (Myers, Weissman, & Tischler, 1984; Robins et al., 1984; Weissman et al, 1988) and is equally common in males and females (Myers et al.; Weissman et al.; Winokur & Crowe, 1983). This rate has been slowly increasing over the past few decades, but it is unclear whether this rise reflects a true increase in the prevalence rate or merely an improvement in the diagnostic standards and procedures employed in epidemiologic research (Marquez, Taintor, & Schwartz, 1985). The latter may be particularly applicable to cases like Julie's. In the past, psychotic features of bipolar disorder where often seen as evidence of a purely psychotic disorder such as schizophrenia, delusional (paranoid) disorder, or schizoaffective disorder. These categories are difficult to tease apart unless the diagnostician has a reliable patient history and a clear indication that the psychotic features are congruent with the manic mood.

Finally, it should be noted that manic-depressives must be handled with special care. As a group they have a higher mortality rate than patients who suffer from other mood disorders (Weeke & Vaeth, 1986). Their impulsive and often irrational manic behaviors put them at particular risk for committing crimes (Kunjukrishnan & Bradford, 1988), having accidents (J. Jacobs & Glasser, 1984), and committing suicide (Barner-Rassmussen, 1986; Goldring & Fieve, 1984; Rihmer, Barsi, Arato, & Demeter, 1990). For these reasons special efforts should be made to bring these people to treatment, especially since they tend to be resistant to the idea of therapy.

However, the problems are not over once treatment begins. Although the majority of bipolar patients tend to respond very well to lithium treatment, this treatment is not effective in all cases (O'Connell et al., 1991). Furthermore, lithium carbonate is a strong psychoactive agent that has many potentially serious side effects. Gastrointestinal difficulties such as nausea and diarrhea are common. Worse, prolonged elevated levels of lithium could result in irreversible kidney and/or thyroid damage. For these reasons lithium treatment must be closely regulated. Finally, manic-depressives tend to have a very difficult adjustment after treatment (Turner, Dossetor, & Bates, 1986). Psychiatric professionals, family members, and friends should make special attempts to provide the patient with a supportive atmosphere and gently persist in encouraging him or her to seek appropriate help.

DYSTHYMIC DISORDER, PRIMARY TYPE
Psychodynamic Therapy

PRESENTING COMPLAINT

Marilyn is a 23-year-old M.B.A. student at the business school of a large midwestern university. For years she has been frustrated and dissatisfied with her life. She has always done well academically, but lately she has had little interest in doing her schoolwork and little confidence that she can do it well. She describes herself as a person with "big plans," who ultimately "won't cut it." She also fears that she will never be satisfied with life, even if she does succeed. She frequently feels irritable, despondent, and helpless. Marilyn said, "It's as if my entire life has been laid out for me. I don't feel like I have any choice about what I do. Worst of all, I think that it may all be a total waste." Lately her persistent negative cognitions have interfered with her ability to work on her thesis and to fulfill her duties as a teaching assistant. She is easily distracted from her work and usually puts it off until weeks after it is due. She says that sometimes she hesitates because she fears that her adviser will reject the work as substandard (although this has never actually happened), and sometimes she puts it off because she "doesn't really care about it anymore."

Marilyn describes herself not only as having problems with her academic work but also as having trouble establishing relationships with men. She describes a long-standing habit of picking up men (either at bars or at parties on campus) and quickly pressuring them to have sex with her. Within a week she then "dumps" them without an explanation, understandably engendering a good deal of hostility. Marilyn describes a recent example. Several weeks ago she met a man in one of her classes and asked him to come over for dinner. They slept together that night, despite his initial hesitancy. Marilyn described their sex as "boring and routine." Two days later they saw a movie. When his reactions to the movie differed from hers, she decided to stop seeing him because he was uninteresting and a relationship with him would be "a pointless waste."

Marilyn began drinking heavily during the past year. She usually drinks socially at campus bars and parties, especially when she is trying to pick up someone. She has found that her drinking often makes her pass out after sex or after "cruising" the local bars. She complains that her drinking is also interfering with her academic work by making her tired and easily distractible.

Marilyn complained about her problems to a fellow student, who recommended a psychodynamically oriented therapist he knew. At first Marilyn was put off by this suggestion, but she eventually came to the conclusion that it might be a good idea. After an initial interview, the therapist decided that Marilyn should be seen for individual therapy three times a week. Marilyn agreed.

PERSONAL HISTORY

Marilyn is the oldest of four children. Her father is a dermatologist. Her mother has a bachelor's degree in advertising, but she did not pursue a career after graduation. Both grandfathers died young, leaving both parents to grow up in single-parent homes. Marilyn's overall impression of her parents is that they were generally attentive and supportive, although paradoxically they seemed somewhat neglectful of her true needs. For example, when Marilyn had difficulty learning to read, her parents' response was to push her to try harder. They became frustrated at her slow progress. It was not until after several months that her need for corrective eyeglasses was finally noticed.

After medical school, Marilyn's father did his residency in Chicago, where both parents' families were located. However, he had always wanted to live in a rural area, so after his residency the family moved to a small town in Colorado. Marilyn, who had become a vociferous reader after she got her glasses, felt very unpopular in this small town, mostly because education and intelligence were not highly valued. After high school she applied to her father's alma mater but was rejected, partly, she believes, because of her substandard education. She grudgingly settled for the state university, which she felt was far below her intellectual capabilities.

Marilyn described her first two years of college as unremarkable. She spent her junior year of college in Europe, where she initiated her pattern of sleeping with men and then quickly breaking up with them. This pattern has persisted for the past three and a half years. When her therapist asked her how she felt about her relationships, Marilyn stated that she felt compelled to sleep with a man for him to really accept her. After a only a week or so, however, she would begin to feel bored and would look for someone new.

Upon her graduation Marilyn applied to several M.B.A. programs. She was bitterly disappointed when her first two choices turned her down, and she began worrying about whether she would ever be successful. In particular, she complained about having to miss out on the best schools and the most interesting cities, saying, "In my entire life I could never get anywhere that really mattered."

CONCEPTUALIZATION AND TREATMENT

When Marilyn entered therapy, she had experienced a chronic depressed mood since early adolescence. She complained of a lack of energy, low self-esteem, poor concentration, and persistent feelings of hopelessness. Her depressed symptoms were chronic, but they were never of the severity associated with a major depressive episode. Furthermore, although Marilyn complained that her depression disrupted her schoolwork, she nevertheless appeared to have been completing her assignments adequately. This constellation of symptoms clearly indicated the existence of a persistent, low-level depression, which *DSM-III-R* terms a *dysthymic disorder*, although many therapists informally refer to this pattern as a "depressive personality." Since Marilyn's symptoms began before age 21 and did not appear to be related to any preexisting, chronic psychiatric disorder, her dysthymia would be categorized as "early onset, primary type." In addition to her dysthymic disorder, Marilyn's intense emotional reactions to relatively minor events, her seemingly superficial attitude toward men, and her self-centeredness indicated an underlying histrionic personality disorder. Many therapists might take Marilyn's extreme dependence on others, primarily her mother and later her therapist, as indications of an underlying dependent personality. However, in most aspects of her life Marilyn functioned quite independently, and the majority of her life decisions were entirely her own. Thus a diagnosis of an underlying dependent personality disorder would appear to be unwarranted. Marilyn's admittedly heavy drinking is a cause for concern. However, she does not fulfill the *DSM-III-R* criteria for alcohol abuse or dependence.

Marilyn's therapy began by identifying underlying dynamics that contributed to her symptoms. Because these issues could be identified only gradually as therapy progressed, the initial sessions were rather unstructured. Marilyn was quite expansive in her initial sessions. She talked quickly yet carefully about a number of different global topics, including her dissatisfaction with her life, her need to be accepted, and the chances that she would be successful. Marilyn tended to focus on the "big picture"—that is, she worried about being successful and being loved, but she did not seem to think about just how she could go about becoming a success or how she could develop more satisfying relationships. She also appeared to feel a strong need to tell someone about her life, and apparently she saw therapy as a perfect opportunity. Initially Marilyn's therapist felt flooded by material, and she described Marilyn's self-descriptions as being like "water released from a pent-up dam." The first goal of therapy was for Marilyn to slow down and focus on specific topics and memories. She was also urged to apply the intellectual skills she possessed to the tasks at hand and not to get lost in the big picture.

In the third week of therapy, Marilyn discussed a series of dreams she had been having for the past few months. These dreams involved fears of being attacked by wild animals, a topic she had not thought about since she was a small girl. When Marilyn was 3 or 4 years old, she developed a terrible fear of the animals around their rural home. She was terrified that the "wild monsters," as she referred to them, would crawl up the side of their house and enter her window. Now she was dreaming virtually nightly about these monsters coming into her room. She reported feeling constantly worried by these thoughts, even though she realized that it was exceedingly unlikely that wild animals could ever get in through the window of her apartment.

The therapist suggested that these monsters might represent some person or force that Marilyn feared during her childhood. She and the therapist then began linking the monsters with her father, the person in her childhood who could potentially hurt her the most. The notion of "getting in through the window" was symbolic of her father's ability to see into her, that is, to gain an understanding of Marilyn's inner thoughts and fears.

At about this time the therapist began to discuss the transference process with Marilyn. By the way Marilyn eagerly described her problems, it was obvious that she felt a strong need to tell her thoughts and feelings to someone who would trust and protect her—someone like a father. Perhaps Marilyn saw the therapist as "another kind of father" (although the therapist was a woman), one who could better understand her. By pouring out her feelings to the therapist, Marilyn was in effect talking to her "father" about her father. Marilyn agreed that her father had been distant for much of her life, and she thought that the therapist might have had a valid point. But before they could pursue this idea further, Marilyn returned home for the summer break. Therapy resumed on her return to school approximately three months later.

Marilyn reported that she had been fighting with her mother quite frequently over the summer and that she "couldn't stand to be in the same house with her." In light of this information, the therapist wondered whether she had correctly interpreted Marilyn's recurring dream. Initially her therapist assumed that the monsters represented Marilyn's father because he had been the dominant force in her childhood. But now she suggested to Marilyn that her images of wild monsters may represent hostility that was directed toward her mother, not her father. (In hindsight, the therapist now realized that this was why her being a woman did not seem to impede the initial transference process.) This possibility came as somewhat of a surprise to Marilyn, especially since her initial descriptions (or, as they are often called, her "first layer of presentation") of her mother were always very positive. She described her as a loving and devoted parent who always put her family before herself. Now she had quite a different picture of her—a "smart lady who got robbed out of a good career because Dad had to live in the middle of nowhere." Analysis now focused on her mother's frustrations and bitterness at being trapped in a small town in Colorado, feelings that Marilyn did not understand as a child.

This revelation changed the therapist's initial conception of Marilyn's childhood. At first it was assumed that Marilyn had the standard Oedipal constellation of a stern, threatening father and a nurturing but ultimately unavailable mother. Instead, it appeared that Marilyn's father was the parent who was actually nurturing and undemanding, whereas her mother was strict and constantly pushed her to achieve. Marilyn found the weakness of her father and the assertiveness of her mother to be inappropriate qualities; each possessed the characteristics usually found in the opposite sex. It was now clear that Marilyn organized her world around her parents' interpersonal characteristics instead of their gender, but this left her in quite a dilemma with respect to her psychosexual identification. On the one hand, she could be like her dominant, assertive mother. That is, she could identify with her female parent only by adopting what she felt were masculine characteristics. On the other hand, she could side with her passive, nurturing father. She found herself unconsciously attracted to each, but she could not fit with either. Since she could not fully identify with either parent, her self-identity remained in a constant state of flux.

This confusion was clearly illustrated in Marilyn's inexplicable interest in a minor news story about Great Britain's Prince Charles and Princess Diana. She became very involved in this story and frequently discussed Diana's role as the "power behind the throne." Several aspects of Marilyn's current behavior also reflected this issue of sexual ambiguity. In particular, her persistent pattern of sleeping with men and then breaking up with them seemed to indicate her strong need for affection and caring combined with her intense fear of becoming dominated.

This ambivalence also emerged in the therapeutic relationship itself. During the first year of therapy Marilyn gradually became more and more dependent on the therapist. When the therapist went on vacation for a week, Marilyn panicked because she would have to miss three sessions. As Marilyn discussed these feelings, she began to realize that maybe she was becoming *too* dependent on therapy. She felt as though she was "being controlled from behind the scenes by a powerful female." At the first session after her therapist returned from vacation, Marilyn suddenly announced that she was cutting therapy back to one session per week and refused to discuss the matter any further. At the next session she angrily stated that she was quitting therapy altogether and left the session after only 20 minutes.

One month later Marilyn phoned the therapist and asked if she could continue therapy. The therapist was not surprised by this call and set up a session for later that week. During the session Marilyn stated that she was sorry for leaving. She was also scared. In the weeks after she left therapy, her recent boyfriend had broken up with her, complaining that she was trying to use him as a therapist. Realizing that she needed to work out the issue of her dependence on others, she wanted to continue therapy "starting from scratch."

Now the therapist had the impression that Marilyn was moving beyond her superficial level and was becoming more deeply involved in the therapeutic process. Marilyn developed a "questioning attitude" in which she was willing to discuss an important topic and analyze it. A prime issue for Marilyn was her need to be close to other people. In Marilyn's mind there were boundaries between herself and others that she needed to maintain to stay independent. Yet she needed to break these boundaries to feel close. She admitted that this need constantly to maintain and relax boundaries might be behind her ambivalent feelings about men. She also talked about her dependence on therapy. She described a dream she had had in which the therapist was coaching her in an important race. During the middle of the race, the therapist stopped coaching her and told her to finish the race on her own. This dream frightened Marilyn, and she said she felt scared at the extent to which she trusted and needed someone else. She said she felt upset at her dependence and that she wanted to quit therapy, but she had decided that she should stay.

Therapy now focused on Marilyn's childhood. Her first memory was of an incident when she was 3 years old. Her parents had bought a cat, and Marilyn had become quite attached to it. Marilyn's father had tried to housebreak the cat for several months, but without success. Finally he gave the cat away. Marilyn was afraid that she, like the cat, would be rejected or abandoned if she were sick or messy. For the next year or so she did everything she could think of to show her parents that she was strong and healthy; she remembers downplaying her sicknesses and hiding her dirty clothes. Despite her frantic efforts, Marilyn felt that her parents were losing interest in her. Her mother was now busy with the birth of her brother, and her father (who was a resident at the time) had little time to be with the family. Generally Marilyn got the impression that he was more inclined to get rid of his problems than to try to fix them. In the midst of describing these memories during a therapy session, Marilyn began crying and sobbing. She wailed, "They took away my kitty, and no one cares!" The therapist asked her why this episode made her so upset now, over 20 years later. Marilyn replied that she was afraid that the therapist would not be willing to "fix" her and would abandon her instead. Marilyn then became afraid that therapy would not work and that it would all be for nothing. At the next session Marilyn admitted that she had she cried during her entire drive home.

Another clear childhood memory was of an event that occurred when Marilyn was about 7 years old. She remembered needing to be around her mother constantly, and that she could not stand being away from her even for a short time. Often her mother had to order her to play outside with her friends. Once Marilyn became so upset at being ordered away that she threw a tantrum and broke a picture window. One night a few days later her parents went out for the evening. Afraid that her mother would never return, Marilyn turned to the babysitter and asked her, "Would *you* be my mother?" This shocked even her little brother (who was then 4). Marilyn says that her mother always made her feel special. Her mother always expected great things of her, and she pushed her to do her best at all times. She prized her relationship with her mother and had a difficult time accepting even short-lived separations. Gradually Marilyn recognized that her parents really did love her and that they were not going to abandon her because of her weaknesses. In fact, they (especially the mother) pushed her to achieve specifically because they had faith that she could succeed.

These insights did not occur quickly or easily. Marilyn and her therapist would grapple with certain issues for weeks or even months on end. First, important memories and themes

77

from her life had to be identified. Next, the importance of these issues in terms of Marilyn's life had to be determined. Often, important issues involving the transference between Marilyn and her therapist had to be discussed and reconciled. All the while, other practical concerns relating to current issues in Marilyn's life needed to be discussed.

Marilyn had been in therapy for almost three years when she was ready to graduate from her M.B.A. program. She was offered several jobs around the country, and she decided to accept a position as an investment manager for a medium-sized firm where her chances for advancement were good. This firm was located in suburban New Jersey, about 1000 miles away. Initially Marilyn found it difficult to leave therapy, but she also felt that moving would give her a chance to gain some independence. After her move, Marilyn began to write her therapist a long letter every week. In her letters she discussed the issues she found to be important in her life, particularly her difficulties in forming new relationships and the need to get reassurance while she set herself up in her new position. After several months Marilyn realized that writing letters was not a particularly effective way of dealing with these issues, and she finally asked to be referred to a local therapist in New Jersey, and she has since begun to see him for one session a week.

PROGNOSIS

Marilyn appears to be doing quite well. She has been at her present job for approximately two years. In that time she received an early promotion to a highly visible position and is getting a good deal of exposure with top management. She has maintained a therapeutic relationship with the male therapist. The fact that she is able to remain committed to a long-term, nonsexual relationship with a man is encouraging. Marilyn also seems to be experiencing more adequate relationships with other men, and for the past year she has had a steady boyfriend. However, she still appears to have some problems in making emotional commitments.   She admits to having frequent flirtatious experiences with men (she describes herself as "peeking over the edge but not jumping off"), but so far she has refrained from her earlier pattern of short-lived, casual sexual encounters.   In short, Marilyn reports feeling much more optimistic about her career and her social relationships than when she entered therapy.   She also reports experiencing negative moods less frequently in everyday events.   Furthermore, she seems to have developed a sense of autonomy and emotional maturity in her relationships, which makes it more likely that she will be able to maintain these improvements in the future.

DISCUSSION

Dysthymia is a common complaint. Surveys (Bland, Orn, & Newman, 1988; Boyd & Weissman, 1981; Escobar, Karno, Burnam, Hough, & Golding, 1988; Regier et al., 1988; Weissman, Leaf, Bruce, & Florio, 1988; Weissman, Leaf, Tischler et al., 1988) report consistently that approximately 4 percent of the adult population will suffers from the disorder at some point in their lives.

The distribution of dysthymia shows effects for both sex and age. Generally, the prevalence of dysthymia decreases with age. Children and adolescents suffer about twice the rate as do adults (Lewinsohn, Rhode, Seely, & Hops, 1991). Young and middle-aged adults, in turn, suffer about twice the rate as do older adults and the elderly (Blazer, Hughes, & George, 1987; Weissman, Leaf, Bruce, & Florio, 1988). At any age, dysthymia is approximately twice as common among females as males (Bland et al., 1988; Weissman, Leaf, Bruce, & Florio, 1988).

Although dysthymia is marked by persistent and unpleasant depressed mood, by itself it is a relatively mild pathology. However, it is often associated with other disorders. The most common comorbid complaint is major depression—so-called double depression (Klein, Taylor, Dickstein, & Harding, 1988b; Klein, Taylor, Harding, & Dickstein, 1988; Lewinsohn et al.,

1991; Scott, 1988). Dysthymia has also been thought to lead to other pathologies, including anxiety, conduct, and substance use disorders (Block, Gjerde, & Block, 1991; Kashani et al., 1987; Kovacs, Paulauskas, Gastonis, & Richards, 1988). Generally, an underlying dysthymia leads to more severe and more persistent symptoms in co-occurring disorders. Those with early onset dysthymia are particularly at risk (Klein, Taylor, Dickstein, & Harding, 1988a; Kocsis & Frances, 1987). In fact, Kocsis and Frances argue that the term *dysthymia* be reserved for those who suffered an early onset of the disease.

In many ways Marilyn presents as a typical case of dysthymia: she is young and female, developed an early onset, suffers from concurrent personality disturbance, and has problems with alcohol. All told, she presents as a relatively difficult case. But several factors work in Marilyn's favor. She is intelligent, articulate, and open to dynamic interpretations. Furthermore, the fact that she has no family history of depression bodes well for her chances of recovery (Klein, Clark, Dansky, & Margolis, 1988).

The Psychodynamic Process

As is typical for most psychodynamic therapies, the symptoms involved in the presenting complaint are not dealt with directly but are taken as symbolic representations of longstanding underlying pathologies. The development of a transference relationship with the therapist is the primary tool employed to uncover these underlying problems and bring them into focus. As the client achieves insight into these unconscious traumas, the neurotic defenses that guard against them will no longer be necessary and will begin to dissipate. In Marilyn's case, her extremely dependent transference relationship with the therapist uncovered two underlying dynamic issues: her difficulties in forming an identification with her mother and her early fears of abandonment. As she relived these traumas, Marilyn experienced a cathartic release. Gradually her ambivalent attitudes toward her career and toward men (the superficial manifestations of these unresolved issues) diminished.

Marilyn's therapist was concerned that perhaps therapy was being ended prematurely. Although Marilyn seemed to have made a good deal of progress during her three years in therapy, she still had some issues left to resolve, particularly those relating to her relationships with men. Whereas many therapists would have encouraged Marilyn to put off moving and "fight for therapy," her therapist felt instead that Marilyn's increasing sense of autonomy (itself a therapeutic goal) made it important for her to pursue her career. Although their work together was not finished (as evidenced by Marilyn's letters to the therapist), in the therapist's opinion Marilyn had made enough progress to move on to another therapist without jeopardizing the gains she had already made.

Several aspects of Marilyn's therapy were somewhat unusual. First, it is rare for a patient to become so intensely involved in the emotions of his or her childhood memories. In contrast, it is much more common for patients to isolate their emotions from the content of their stories and describe them with calm objectivity. Although Marilyn's intense affect may have aided her in fully reexperiencing her childhood traumas, at the same time it may have interfered with her ability to analyze their meaning rationally and thus achieve insight.

A second unusual feature of this case was the great sensitivity with which Marilyn was able to articulate the extreme dependence she felt on her mother and on the therapist. Again it should be noted that these insights did not occur quickly; Marilyn's recognition of this issue was well hidden and surfaced only after 18 months of therapy. On the whole, though, Marilyn was an unusually sensitive and motivated patient who was responsive to the psychodynamic approach to therapy and made significant gains as a result of it.

Finally, although many psychoanalyzes are seen through to completion, it is not uncommon for some patients to interrupt therapy at some point. As the transference process begins to uncover repressed conflicts, patients become very committed to their analysts as well as the work of therapy. But at the same time, the identification of underlying dynamic issues poses a threat. Unconscious resistance is omnipresent in the therapeutic process and evokes a variety of defensive reactions (S. Freud, 1912/1958); W. Reich (1949) terms this resistance "character armor." These defenses lead to a variety of responses. Some patients develop a dependency on their therapists, whereas others may discontinue treatment for months or years, or even permanently. In contrast, Marilyn appeared to have a short "panic reaction" to the realization of her extreme emotional dependence on others, and her willingness to return to therapy indicates an awareness of her need to address this issue. Consistent with traditional psychodynamic thought (Strean, 1985), Marilyn's therapist thought it wise to be patient and not force her to confront her defenses. Others (Davanloo, 1988) advocate a more active, confrontive role for the therapist. This issue remains controversial among psychodynamic theorists (Dewald, 1982; Greenson, 1967).

DEPENDENT PERSONALITY DISORDER
Sociocultural-Humanistic Therapy

PRESENTING COMPLAINT

Kathy telephoned the outpatient psychiatry clinic desperate for help. Over the last few years she had become increasingly frustrated with her life. She was dissatisfied with her physical appearance, which she summarized as "an ugly face and a fat body." She felt slighted and unappreciated at work. But the most of all, she had become convinced that her three-year-old marriage was falling apart. Her primary complaints about her marriage focused on three interrelated issues: (1) her husband's failure to pay adequate attention to her, (2) her perception that her husband was constantly attempting to seduce other women, and (3) her own jealous and bitter reactions to his behavior. Since Kathy's complaints centered around her relationship with her husband, Tom, she was encouraged to enlist his cooperation in couple therapy. Tom reluctantly agreed, saying that he did so "for Kathy's sake."

At their first session Kathy and Tom presented themselves as a successful young professional couple in their late 20s. Both partners appeared to be highly intelligent, friendly, and socially active. However, both partners seemed somewhat superficial, being overly preoccupied with their physical appearance and social activities. Contrary to her rather derogatory self-descriptions during her initial telephone call, Kathy was quite attractive and clearly intelligent. She held a master's degree in ecological science and worked as a consultant for the Florida State Water Commission. In addition, she taught aerobics at a local health club and occasionally modeled for an agency in Tampa.

It was obvious from just a brief description of Kathy's activities that she was successful in a scientific career and in modeling, yet she persistently described herself in critical terms. For instance, when she made minor mistakes, such as forgetting an item on a grocery list, she would demean herself by calling herself "spacey" or "airhead." Often Tom would reinforce this negative self-concept by pointing out her faults and describing her as "cute but slow" to his friends. Although he usually did this in a joking manner, Kathy nevertheless felt hurt by his frequent slights.

Tom held a master's degree in electrical engineering and worked for a large computer firm. He had great pride in his mathematical and analytical abilities and was quite confident, even vain, about his physical appearance and his popularity. He spent five or six nights a week (as well as most of the weekend) exercising and/or meeting his friends at local nightspots, usually without Kathy. Kathy described Tom as extremely good-looking and very intelligent.

During the first two therapy sessions both partners acted as if Kathy were the only one with a problem. Tom often portrayed her as a jealous neurotic who continually suspected her innocent husband. For the most part, Kathy seemed to go along with his interpretation of her behavior.

> **Therapist:** I'd like you to describe what goes on when you argue. Perhaps a concrete example would make it clear.

Tom: It happens all the time when I look at other women. Take Saturday night for example. Remember? The girl in the sports car?

Kathy: Oh, yeah.

Tom: I knew I couldn't say anything. I knew that if I looked at her, even glanced at her, I'd never hear the end of it.

Kathy: Well, you see, he's got this fetish about oriental girls. (Tom rolls his eyes, obviously restraining a comment.) And it's like I can't compete with them because I'm not one. It's kind of hard for me to deal with him looking at other women because I always have to wonder. I guess that's a typical jealousy reaction, but I think that's my major problem: I know I can't compete with what he's always looking at.

Therapist: You seem very worried about competing. What's at stake?

Kathy: Losing him. I guess that's what's at stake. Or his attention not focusing on me; instead it's on someone else.

Tom: Well, come on. My attention can't be on her 24 hours a day, can it?

At the third session Tom voiced his frustration at not being able to correct what he considered to be "Kathy's problem." He complained of feeling depressed after each session, saying he felt so bad that he couldn't have fun when he went out. He decided to discontinue therapy. Kathy felt that therapy was helping her and pleaded with Tom so that she could stay. Tom agreed that Kathy could continue, but he wanted no part of it himself.

During the first few sessions of her individual therapy, Kathy focused on the different expectations she and Tom had of each other and the different roles each of them enacted in their relationship. As Kathy discussed these issues, the extent of her dependence on her husband and his opinions became clear.

> **Therapist:** So, you're saying that you both want different things, is that right?
>
> **Kathy:** What Tom was saying is that he doesn't solely need me to be happy. He says that the only way I'll be happy is to spend 24 hours a day with him—and that's basically true.
>
> **Therapist:** Is it?
>
> **Kathy:** Yeah. I mean, I would give up everything just to spend time with him. Like if I had the day off, I'd putter around the house and the yard and then meet him for lunch. Now if *he* had the day off, he wouldn't bother to meet me. He'd go off on his own and have a great time.
>
> **Therapist:** And that's the problem.
>
> **Kathy:** Right.

PERSONAL HISTORY

Kathy described her family as tightly knit and "typically Greek." When asked to elaborate on this term, she stated that her family is very close and has traditional, conservative values. Kathy described her father as having a strong, dominant role as the head of the family. Her mother fulfills a nurturing role; she takes care of the domestic needs of the family (i.e., the housekeeping, food preparation, laundry) and works as a secretary for her husband. Her father's income also supports both of Kathy's grandmothers.

Kathy described her own role in her family as that of a good, obedient daughter. Throughout her life she had always looked to her parents for advice and had rarely made a decision independently, even as late as college. Her parents were also very strict with her throughout her college years. Kathy described several instances of her parents' control. Kathy's parents chose her college and graduate school for her. They gave her a midnight curfew when she was home on vacations, and they also imposed a curfew on her when she was at school. Kathy recalled the time when she was a junior at college and her parents wouldn't allow her to attend any sorority parties because they would "keep her out too late." Kathy continued to honor this curfew throughout college and graduate school.

Kathy remained dependent on her parents' approval after school. For example, Kathy began to develop ambivalent feelings about Tom in the months before their wedding; she decided to get married anyway because her parents had gone to a lot of trouble planning the wedding and she didn't want to disappoint them.

Kathy describes herself as being very submissive in her marriage. Her nights are very lonely because she spends most of her evenings alone watching television and waiting up for Tom. Although she hates to be alone, she feels that going out with friends "just wouldn't be right." Once in a while Tom would call and invite her to join him and his friends at a bar. Although she desperately wants to be with him, she usually finds these occasions more upsetting than staying home. Often she would arrive at the bar only to find him drunk and flirting with another woman. On several occasions he became intoxicated at the home of a female coworker and called Kathy to drive him home. When she asked him if he were having an affair, he accused her of neurotic jealousy. Tom did not deny that these events occur, but he stated that they were "nothing serious." Kathy felt both furious at Tom's insensitive attitude and foolish about her own willingness to put up with it. As a result of this sort of behavior, Kathy has become increasingly ambivalent about remaining in her marriage. Tom's behavior was causing more and more frustration, but she couldn't bear the thought of leaving him. Much to her surprise, her parents, who were very traditional and had always rejected the notion of divorce, suggested that she seek a legal separation from Tom. This suggestion has served to intensify her ambivalent feelings. On the one hand it compelled Kathy to defend Tom and their marriage, but on the other hand it made her look at her life with a more critical eye.

CONCEPTUALIZATION AND TREATMENT

Kathy has a long history of defining her identity in terms of important other people in her life, first her parents and now her husband. She has always obeyed her parents relatively strict rules for her behavior, even when she was away at college and graduate school. Kathy frequently accepts her husband's critical views of her appearance and intelligence, despite objective evidence to the contrary, and she always accepts his interpretation of events and his opinion as to what response is appropriate. In short, Kathy is extremely dependent on the opinions of her husband and her parents, she persistently considers other people's needs and wishes as more important—or at least more justified—than her own, and she is unable to make an independent decision or to form an identity independent of those close to her. Together these characteristics indicate a dependent personality disorder.

According to her therapist, Kathy's dependent characteristics in all likelihood are the result of her persistent adoption of a submissive, nurturing social role. Great pressure has been put on Kathy to assume this role, first by her traditional parents and later by her insensitive husband. Moreover, our society has a long history of emphasizing the importance of a woman's passive and nurturing characteristics while de-emphasizing the value of her independence and intellectual abilities. It is not surprising, then, to learn that Kathy's boss routinely assigns mundane tasks to her and her female coworkers while he entrusts projects entailing greater responsibility to male employees, even those with much less experience. Although injustices of this type have become less obvious over the past few decades, they nonetheless pervade many areas of our culture. It is possible that these subtle (and in some cases blatant) forces have induced her to channel her energies away from a career in science and instead to focus them on her modeling and aerobics, activities that our society considers more appropriate for attractive women.

A clear instance of this influence occurred when Kathy and Tom discussed the possibility of her changing jobs. When Kathy described how frustrated she was with her position at the water commission, Tom suggested that she quit and become a waitress at a bar he frequents. He said that she could meet many new people and that the tip money was good. At first she became despondent at the thought of becoming a waitress and constantly having to deal with strange men who were often drunk and verbally abusive. In spite of her reservations, though, Tom pushed the idea, and Kathy began to consider it seriously and brought it up in therapy.

As this example shows, Kathy was rarely encouraged to develop her own abilities; instead she was reinforced for conforming to other people's wishes and expectations. Perhaps as a result of this lifelong attempt to adopt roles that others have mapped out for her, Kathy has developed a rather superficial self-concept. The following incident illustrates how important her appearance (or more accurately, her husband's opinion of her appearance) was to her self-image.

> **Therapist:** You say that you're fat. Tell me, why do you consider yourself overweight? You look fine to me.
>
> **Kathy:** I could still lose a little in the hips. I used to be a lot thinner, you know. When I really started getting into aerobics, I pretty much stopped eating. I got down to 100 pounds. [Kathy is 5 feet, 7 inches tall.] I thought I still had a little ways to go, but Tom said I looked *too* thin. He said I looked skinny and not athletic. Boy, was I surprised at

that! Anyway, I guess he was right because I started having stomach problems then, and my doctor told me that I
was 25 pounds underweight. I don't
know what sort of standards they use,
but I don't want to be that heavy. I
gained a few pounds and Tom said he
liked me better that way. So now I try
to stay around 110.

Therapy for Kathy involved a two-stage process. The first
was to identify the interpersonal and social pressures that were
determining her choices. In particular, Kathy was made aware
of the ways in which her husband and her parents attempted,
perhaps unwittingly, to control her life. Second, Kathy was encouraged to explore her own wants, needs, and feelings and to
accept them as valid. The goal of this stage of therapy was for
Kathy to develop a more positive self-concept and a clearer sense
of her own identity. It was hoped that this would enable her to
become more self-confident and less dependent on the approval
of others.

Although Kathy recognized her frustration with her husband's behavior, at first she was unaware of the extent to which
his attitudes affected her. For example, Kathy described how
she would always check for Tom's approval whenever she got
dressed. If his response to a particular outfit was negative (or
even neutral), she would immediately change her clothes. If his
response was positive, she would wear the outfit, even if she dis-
liked it or felt uncomfortable wearing it. When Kathy was asked
why she would wear something she really didn't like, she simply responded that she wouldn't feel comfortable with him if he
thought she looked ugly or stupid. Vignettes like this were frustrating and demeaning for Kathy, but it never occurred to her
that her opinions were just as valid as his.

As therapy progressed, Kathy became less dependent on
the approval of others. However, she continued to describe her
life and her problems in terms of her husband and, to a lesser ex-

tent, her family. She also attempted to draw the therapist into a collusion where he would join Kathy in focusing on Tom's negative characteristics as the root of her troubles. Despite her increasingly negative attitude toward her husband, Tom still remained the central figure in her life and in her therapy. Her sense of her own identity was still vague and unclear, and she had great difficulty describing her own feelings and needs independent of her husband's or her parents'.

> **Therapist:** You said before that one of your goals is to be happy. Tell me, what do you think would make you truly happy? I guess what I mean to ask you is: What do you want out of life?
>
> **Kathy:** Well, Tom thought it would be great if we both started enjoying doing what we each like to do. He thinks that if I could enjoy what I like to do more, then he could enjoy what he likes to do more, and we'd both probably be a lot happier.
>
> **Therapist:** Um, that sounds like Tom's idea. What about you?
>
> **Kathy:** Well, I don't know. I guess I try to be a good wife. You know, I was always taught to be a good wife and have a good marriage. Those things were always really important. I guess that's what's expected of me.
>
> **Therapist:** Now this sounds like your parents talking. What about you, Kathy? What do *you* want out of life?
>
> **Kathy:** (pause) I have absolutely no idea.

By reinforcing her for making independent judgments and sincerely seeking out her emotions, the therapist supported Kathy's attempts to explore her own thoughts and feelings without relying on the opinions of others. Initially Kathy was hesitant to put forth her own views and would often try to change the subject of discussion. But by carefully prodding her, the therapist encouraged her to accept her ideas and emotions as being valid and worthwhile.

> **Kathy:** . . . and that's how it ended last night. (Her eyes begin to well up with tears.)
>
> **Therapist:** What's making you sad now?
>
> **Kathy:** (Openly sobbing) Look, you've really got me going now. I'm sorry about this.
>
> **Therapist:** You don't need to apologize to me.
>
> **Kathy:** (Wiping her eyes) Look at me. I bet my mascara looks really great, huh.
>
> **Therapist:** Do you think that's important?
>
> **Kathy:** No, I guess not.
>
> **Therapist:** Now tell me, what's making you sad?

By the tenth session, Kathy began to develop a greater sense of her own autonomy. She focused less on the wants and needs of her husband and her family and more on herself and her own expectations. However, she was still unconvinced as to the legitimacy of her own ideas.

> **Therapist:** Tell me if I'm right. I've noticed a change since you started coming here, and that is that at first you came to try to change Tom, like "What could I do to make him act a certain way?" Now it seems that your focus is on what you, yourself, could do. Do you see that or not?
>
> **Kathy:** Yeah, because when I first came here, I really wanted us to work out, and I wanted us to stay together. But I'm not so sure anymore. It's like, well, maybe

> I'm the one who has to change and not
> him . . . But will I be happy doing that?

As Kathy continued in therapy, her feelings of autonomy and self-reliance increased. For example, Tom was offered a job in Miami and had decided to accept. He did not ask her opinion or even consult her; he just assumed that she would quit her job and break her ties with the modeling agency and the health club and move to Miami with him. But Kathy didn't want to leave and decided that the separation offered her a good opportunity to test whether she should relocate with Tom or seek a divorce.

The separation proved to be an important event in Kathy and Tom's marriage. Kathy stayed with a friend in Tampa. Without having to spend her evenings waiting for Tom, she began to socialize more and got better acquainted with her friends. She also had more time to think about her job, which she found increasingly frustrating. After considering her occupational opportunities and her expectations of the success of her marriage, she decided to move to Miami to join Tom.

The two-month separation also affected Tom's behavior. He began sending Kathy cards and small surprises, and he made three weekend trips just to spend time with her. Kathy was surprised by the affection and respect he now showed her.

Kathy's changing professional ambitions provided a good illustration of her increasing independence and self-confidence. When he was offered the job in Miami, Tom again suggested that she take a job as a cocktail waitress. This time Kathy rejected the idea immediately. More importantly, she based this decision on what she wanted and what would benefit her. She felt that a waitress job was insulting to someone with her education and experience. When she decided to move to Miami, she applied for professional positions in the Miami area. She also asked her agents at the modeling agency to try to set up modeling assignments for her in Miami. She also applied to three Ph.D. programs in environmental science. Tom supported her professional ambitions and even used the few contacts he had made in Miami to help locate a job for her.

Therapy was concluded with Kathy's move to Miami. At the final session she reported that she had developed a better sense of her own identity and that she had acquired a more positive self-image and a greater sense of self-confidence. These changes were all gradual, resulting (presumably) from her therapist's frequent attempts to get her to accept her own views and wants. Interestingly, she also reported a greater satisfaction in her marriage, noting that Tom was much more considerate and saying that she had the impression of being "less trapped and having more options."

PROGNOSIS

In summary, Kathy appears to have made a number of significant changes in her thoughts and feelings that would lead to a lasting change in her personality. She began to depend less on the opinions of her husband and her family. As her sense of autonomy developed, so did her feelings of self-confidence and self-worth. In addition, these changes appeared to have affected her husband's behavior toward her; her increasing independence seemed to have fostered an increase in his affection and respect. In general, the prognosis for Kathy and her marriage with Tom is good.

However, the persistent nature typical of personality disorders would caution against an overly optimistic prognosis. It is likely that over time Tom's narcissistic characteristics (a grandiose sense of self-importance and a lack of regard for others) will reemerge. After he establishes new friends and new routines, his need for Kathy may decrease, and it is possible that she may find herself becoming increasingly dependent on his attention and approval. This is especially likely since she has relocated to an area where she must establish and develop a new social support network. But there are signs for optimism. Now, unlike before, Kathy has made concrete plans for the eventuality that she may need to separate from Tom, and it is likely that Kathy will be less tolerant of a poor marriage and more able to live independently. Another good sign is that dependent personality disorder tends to be associated with the best prognosis of all the personality disorders (Steketee, 1990). To a great extent, then, Kathy's prognosis depends on her ability to develop and maintain relationships (both with her husband and with new friends) that support her newfound sense of accomplishment and autonomy.

DISCUSSION

DSM-III-R describes a personality disorder as a long-standing condition characterized by relatively inflexible and maladaptive personality traits that cause either significant impairment in occupational or social functioning or subjective distress. In particular, a person would be diagnosed as having a dependent personality disorder if he or she (a) allows others to assume responsibilities for major areas of life (e.g., choice of job or home), (b) subordinates his or her own needs to those of others, and (c) lacks self-confidence.

As a class, personality disorders (or "character disorders," as they are sometimes called) have been difficult to diagnose reliably. One problem is that it is often difficult to distinguish the various personality disorders from each other. J. Reich (1990b) and Trull, Widiger, and Frances (1987) report a great deal of overlap between dependent personality disorder and other personality disorders, particularly avoidant personality disorder. In addition, clients often display traits that are characteristic of two or more different personality disorders, making it very difficult for therapists to agree on the appropriate diagnosis.

A second complication in the diagnosis of personality disorders is their frequent overlap with other types of medical and psychiatric problems. R. P. Greenberg and Bornstein (1988a, 1988b) found that people diagnosed with dependent personality disorder were more prone to a number of stomach-related physical symptoms (ulcers, stomach cancer, obesity) and psychiatric symptoms (addictions, eating disorders). Other researchers have noted associations between dependent personality disorder and depression (Mezzich, Fabrega, & Coffman, 1987) and phobias (J. Reich, Noyes, & Troughton, 1987).

A third problem is that the diagnostic criteria for personality disorders are rather loosely defined and leave room for a therapist's idiosyncratic interpretation. For example, researchers (Adler, Drake, & Teague, 1990; Ford & Widiger, 1989) found that therapists often rely on extraneous information, such as the sex of the patient, when diagnosing personality disorders. Furthermore, since personality disorders differ from personality traits only by degree, it is often a subjective decision as to where to draw that line. How severely must a client's work or social functioning be disrupted before he or she suffers "significant impairment"? How much "subjective distress" constitutes a personality disorder? These questions are difficult to evaluate objectively. Worse, these subjective criteria hold the potential for bias in psychiatric diagnosis. For example, M. Kaplan (1983) argued that the *DSM-III-R* criteria used to define personality disorders more commonly found in women (borderline, dependent, histrionic) contain many normal feminine behaviors, whereas the criteria used to define personality disorders more common to men (antisocial, compulsive, paranoid) contain few normal masculine behaviors. She claims that just by demonstrating sex-consistent stereotypical behavior, many women but few men would be labeled as having a personality disorder. Though this idea is intriguing, it has found little empirical support. Kass, Spitzer, and Williams (1983) responded to Kaplan by noting that women are no more likely than men to receive a diagnosis of personality disorder. And in two separate studies, J. Reich (1987, 1990a) found no sex difference in the diagnosis of dependent personality disorder. Nevertheless, this sort of debate has highlighted the need to carefully design and evaluate personality disorder criteria.

The Sociocultural Approach

When Kathy entered therapy, she and Tom agreed that she

was the one with the problem. However, Kathy did not develop her problems in a social vacuum; her overbearing parents, her sexist boss, and her insensitive husband contributed greatly to her behavior. Kathy's role in these relationships is to be the obedient daughter, the passive employee, and the neurotic wife, roles that make her vulnerable to receiving particular psychiatric diagnoses. Thus, Kathy's disorder lies not with her individual characteristics but instead with her dysfunctional social relationships. To use Minuchin's (1974) term, she is merely the "identified patient."

Generally speaking, the sociocultural perspective hypothesizes that many psychiatric disorders result not from people's inherent failings but rather from their adoption of dysfunctional social roles. Over time, these people become accustomed to their maladaptive roles and develop negative self-concepts. The way to treat people is by changing the structure of their relationships rather than by changing their individual characteristics.

Kathy's therapy involved two stages. In the first, Kathy and her therapist worked together to identify and analyze the social pressures that may have induced her to adopt an overly dependent role. The relatively strict expectations of her traditional upbringing, the dismissive attitude of her boss, the seemingly callous behavior of her husband, and society's role expectations for attractive women were all implicated as contributing factors. Once these different factors were identified, Kathy could be made more aware of exactly how they were affecting her behavior and what she could do about it.

Kathy would have little chance of countering these varied social pressures unless she first developed a clear sense of her own goals and a desire to obtain them. The second stage of therapy, then, was devoted primarily to having Kathy recognize and accept her own thoughts and feelings as valid and worthwhile. As Kathy incorporated these positive ideas into her emerging sense of self, her feelings of autonomy and positive self-regard increased, and she felt more capable of insisting that her goals and needs be respected.

This second stage of therapy utilized many of the techniques developed by humanistic psychologists. These techniques include providing clients with unconditional positive regard, at least to the extent that they are encouraged to explore and accept their ideas and feelings as valid and worthwhile; offering clients empathetic understanding and listening to them from their own perspective; and attempting to be genuine with them by establishing a close and sincere therapeutic relationships. As this case shows, the sociocultural and humanistic approaches are not necessarily exclusive. Here, aspects of both approaches are combined in an attempt to identify the ways in which others influence Kathy and the ways in which she can draw upon her own strengths to shape her own life.

BORDERLINE PERSONALITY DISORDER
Psychodynamic Therapy

PRESENTING COMPLAINT

Debbie is a 34-year-old married homemaker. Her husband, Mark, is a 37-year-old corporate lawyer who specializes in international law. Debbie and Mark met each other 11 years ago, shortly after he was hired by her father's firm. They have been married for seven years and have no children. They divide their time among three residences: a lavishly decorated townhouse in Boston, a 14-room summer home in New Hampshire, and a large condominium in Zurich, where Mark stays during his frequent business trips to Europe.

The therapist made first contact with Debbie one afternoon in February when she called in a panic about a "marital crisis." She was clearly agitated and sounded as if she had been sobbing. After briefly introducing herself, she described her crisis. She and Mark had gotten into an argument just as he finished packing for a business trip. She accused him of abandoning her and began to insult and berate him. In the heat of the fight she threw several porcelain figurines at him, each one costing several hundred dollars. None had struck him or even come close. As she continued to fight with him, he slapped her with enough force to knock her off balance. She then started sobbing. When he saw that she was not injured, he began to leave. Debbie threatened to kill herself if he left her alone, but he walked out the door. After a little while Debbie called a friend. The friend was a former patient of the therapist and suggested that Debbie call him.

The therapist was extremely concerned over the mention of suicide and asked Debbie if she really wanted to die. She seemed a little surprised by the urgency in his voice. No, she said, she didn't really want to die. But she often got so angry with Mark that she said things like that. The therapist continued. Did she have a concrete plan? Had she made any previous attempts? When her answers were again no, the therapist felt assured that she was in no immediate danger and did not require hospitalization. He then arranged an initial consultation during lunch the next day.

Debbie arrived right on time. She began by thanking the therapist for his concern the day before. His concerns were not over, though, and he began by asking her once again about her ideas of suicide and her feelings of depression. She repeated that suicide was a frequent threat, but that she had no real intention of dying. He then asked her about her mood. Had she been depressed? Irritable? Bored? She reacted to the latter, saying that for the last several years she has felt apathetic and lethargic. This was especially noticeable when Mark was away, but it persisted to some extent most of the time when he was home, too.

He then asked her whether she had spoken to Mark since their argument. She had called him in Switzerland to apologize and to say how important he was to her. Mostly she didn't want him to worry. According to Debbie, this switch from anger to concern was common.

> I have these 'lightning-fast' changes in my feelings for Mark. It's like there's a little switch inside me that moves from NICE to MEAN. I remember one time when we took an elevator to a

business party. I was feeling fond of him and proud of his success. But then, the moment he walked out of the elevator and into the hall, I suddenly hated him. I started saying that he only had his job because he married me, that he was living off my father's money. It's not true, you know. Anyway, I said that he was manipulative and controlling and arrogant. There we were in the hallway. I was yelling at him, and he was yelling back. We had to just turn around and leave. This happens all the time; I suddenly get mean and vindictive. I really worry that my hostility is driving him away.

The therapist asked Debbie about violence. Mark struck her yesterday; had he hit her before? She replied that he had slapped her once before. It was a slap like yesterday's. She has also slapped him on occasion, but usually she throws things at him. She claims that she doesn't really want to hit him. In fact, she never really aims. The violence has never escalated beyond this level. The therapist then asked her about other aspects of their relationship.

Therapist: How is your sexual relationship with Mark?

Debbie: What do you mean, how much or how good?

Therapist: Both.

Debbie: Well, it's pretty dismal. I guess we make love twice a month, on average. But remember, he's not home a lot.

Therapist: Do you enjoy it?

Debbie: He seems to, but I don't, really. I don't think I was meant to enjoy it. I used to get excited by sex, but I haven't for a long time now. I feel like I'm sexually dead.

101

Therapist: Do you have any plans for a family?

Debbie: God, no. We used to talk about it, but we usually ended up fighting. I'd get so angry at Mark that I'd swear I'd never have his children. I didn't think he deserved any. You know, I've had a couple abortions. I scheduled them for when he was away, and I don't think he knows. I mean really, why should I go through all that just for him? First of all, I don't know if I could take the pain of having children. But that's just the beginning. I don't think I could stand them always being around, needing me, depending on me. I suppose I would get a nanny, like my mother did for my brothers. But I'd still be their *mother*. They would always be needing things and wanting things. I don't want that. And then think of the money they'll cost.

Therapist: Would the money be a problem?

Debbie: Well, you can't just throw it away. Now Mark does that. His younger brother is always asking for a handout of one kind or another, and there's Mark, Mr. Generous, always shelling out. I feel robbed. You know, sometimes I think his brother is out to take us. I really do. But I try not to think about it. I have Mark's accountant look after all the money. I was never good with numbers myself.

The therapist scheduled Debbie for two sessions a week.

PERSONAL HISTORY

Debbie is the oldest of four children. She has three brothers who are 12, 15, and 17 years younger. Debbie had persistent problems with mathematics and writing throughout school. She graduated from high school without distinction and did not attend college. Debbie had a moderately successful career as a fashion model until her marriage to Mark.

Debbie's parents are from a poor manufacturing town in Connecticut. They were married in their teens when her mother became pregnant with Debbie. For the first few years of her life, Debbie lived in Cambridge, Massachusetts, where her father went to engineering school. Soon after graduating he founded a small company that designed and manufactured medical equipment. This business has grown into a large corporation with three plants in the United States and two in Europe. Debbie's mother has never been employed outside the home. Debbie describes her as a "professional hostess" who is very involved in entertaining clients and socializing at company events.

Debbie describes her father as a strict, demanding tyrant who gets his way through intimidation and reproach. She also describes him as opinionated and bigoted. He was very proud of his rags-to-riches rise in business, and he expected his children to show similar successes. Debbie recalls that he would stand over her while she did her homework and criticize her whenever she had any trouble. Countless times he asked, "Why can't you get it?" or "What's the matter with you?" Debbie describes her mother as a "non-entity" who passively submits to her husband's overpowering will. She rarely offered Debbie any encouragement or compassion; she seemed consumed with trying to perform to her husband's stringent expectations and by her growing dependence on alcohol and barbiturates. Over the years Debbie's parents spent less and less time with her, and by the time her brothers were born, they had little interest in child care. They hired professional sitters to care for the boys and saw them very little.

None of the four children is close to either parent. The oldest boy was always the nonconformist of the family. He is now a graduate student working toward his Ph.D. in history. At first his father was proud of his eldest son's academic accomplishments, but his pride turned to dismay when the son opted for a career as a history professor. His father would ask him, "Why don't you get a real job?" Two years ago this son married a Jewish woman. Not only did her parents refuse to attend the wedding, they disowned the son outright. The middle son has always had considerable difficulty in school. Like Debbie, he seems to have particular trouble with mathematics. Unlike his older brother, he felt intimidated by his father and constantly tried to please him. He is now attending a local junior college and plans to work in the company after he graduates. The youngest brother is a senior in high school. Debbie believes that he is the smartest of the three boys, but he has always gotten mediocre grades. She describes him as spoiled and apathetic. Debbie feels close to the eldest brother but not the younger two.

CONCEPTUALIZATION AND TREATMENT

Over the next several weeks, Debbie provided descriptions of events and feelings that reaffirmed and amplified her presenting complaints. For example, she mentioned that Mark is a highly successful corporate lawyer. He speaks fluent French, German, and Italian; is a wonderful negotiator; and was the key figure in establishing the overseas plants in Belgium and Switzerland. He is also a workaholic who is in the country less than half the time, and even then spends about 70 hours per week at the office. This information made Debbie's virulent suggestions of nepotism all the more dramatic, while also setting a context for their relationship and making her fears of abandonment more understandable.

Borderline personality disorder is defined as a longstanding character disturbance marked by sudden and dramatic shifts in mood, unstable and intense relationships, and inconsistencies in the evaluations of oneself and others. *DSM-III-R* lists eight specific criteria that define borderline personality disorder. A person must demonstrate at least five of the eight to warrant a diagnosis. Instances that fit each of these eight criteria can be found in Debbie's behavior. The eight criteria are:

1. unstable, intense interpersonal relationships
2. impulsiveness that is potentially self-damaging
3. unstable mood
4. inappropriate and/or uncontrolled anger
5. recurrent suicidal threats
6. persistent identity disturbance
7. feelings of emptiness and boredom
8. efforts to avoid abandonment

Consistent with traditional psychodynamic theory, the roots of Debbie's character disturbance lie in her relationship with her parents. According to self psychology (Kohut, 1977) and object relations theory (Mahler, 1968), children are utterly dependent on their parents early in life and require a certain degree of love, support, and encouragement from parents to form a healthy ego. Furthermore, the Oedipal drama that is central to Freud's theories requires an appealing opposite-sex parent and a threatening same-sex parent, or their symbolic equivalents. Without these elements, the Oedipal conflict will not be resolved, resulting in a disruption of ego identity and a failure to sublimate libidinal urges. Debbie's passive, uninvolved mother and her domineering, critical father possessed none of the qualities Debbie required for normal ego development. As a result Debbie's emotional and social development was severely impaired. Because her mother gave her no emotional support, she became overly dependent on others and was terrified of abandonment. At the same time, though, she was wary of this dependence and feared intimacy. Because of her father's abusive style, she never learned to channel her libidinal urges into sexual or career pursuits. Instead, she introjected her father's abusive style, which led to low self-esteem and prevented her from developing clear goals and ambitions. She also projects this hostility onto men, in particular her husband and her therapist. Her immature superego fails to control the expression of this rage, which often comes across as unpredictable.

It will take some time, perhaps several years, to overcome these deficiencies and develop an ego healthy enough to tolerate, let alone integrate, the positive and negative qualities she recognizes in herself and in others. In the meantime, Debbie's therapist set up a structured, goal-oriented treatment program to cope with her immediate concerns. The first and primary goal of this program was to develop a trusting, therapeutic alliance. But establishing this trusting relationship is easier said than done. Borderlines tend to be very difficult patients, and Debbie was no exception. However, once she developed a trusting alliance with her therapist, she was then able to focus on a goal-oriented program that directly addressed many problem areas in her life. Debbie's treatment program has five primary goals:

1. Improve impulse control
2. Increase self-esteem
3. Increase sexual contact with her husband
4. Reduce depressed mood
5. Diminish paranoid ideation

1. Improving impulse control. When Debbie began therapy, she had very little impulse control. This was expressed most dramatically in her sudden outbursts aimed at her husband, though it came out in other ways too, including spree shopping and reckless driving. One effective technique was to tap into Debbie's expressed interest in money. Once her therapist recognized this interest, he developed an economy metaphor. For each altercation with her husband, Debbie was to ask herself what it would cost her in terms of what she will gain from it in terms of pleasure, self-esteem, and security. When she felt the need to castigate Mark, she was to stop and first calculate the benefits and liabilities. Simply stopping to calculate this econometric helped Debbie avoid many of her impulsive behaviors.

2. Increasing self-esteem. Debbie's therapist found two ways to increase her self-esteem. The first involved focusing on Debbie's strengths, many of which had been glossed over. For example, Debbie works on many charity boards and organizations. She is very attractive and sophisticated, and she can be remarkably charming. As a result she is quite successful at fund-raising and dealing with corporate donors. However, she usually dismisses the value of her efforts by saying that it is "only" charity work. She was taught to recognize the value of her contributions.

A second approach to bolstering self-esteem was to diagnose conditions that might be interpreted as signs of general failure. Debbie's school history and her description of her middle brother's academic problems suggested the presence of an undiagnosed learning disability. The therapist arranged to have Debbie tested by a specialist in learning disabilities, and sure enough, she met the criteria for a diagnosis of developmental arithmetic disorder and developmental expressive language disorder. By explaining her limitations as diseases (which probably have genetic links), the therapist instructed her to no longer see herself as generally stupid but merely as someone who suffers from rather common, specific learning disabilities. She was also given some practical advice for how to live with these limitations, such as using a tape recorder instead of written notes to help organize her writing, and using a calculator to help with financial issues.

3. Increasing sexual contact. As therapy progressed, Debbie occasionally described elements of her sex life that she found particularly pleasing. It turned out that most of these experiences occurred with her husband. These pleasant memories were pointed out to her to highlight the positive aspects of her relationship with her husband, which were often forgotten when she went into a rage and focused only on his negative qualities. The approach to increasing her sexual behavior took much the same form as the treatment to control her impulses. She was asked to think of how much a pleasurable sexual encounter was worth to her. What would she get out of it? What would Mark get? How would it contribute to their sexual relationship as a whole?

Debbie was also encouraged to have open discussions with Mark about her problems with intimacy. In the beginning she was unable to tolerate more than a cursory exchange without feeling too threatened, but at least Mark was beginning to understand her somewhat hot-and-cold sexual behavior and not to take it personally.

Progress in this dimension was somewhat erratic. Certainly the quantity of her sexual activity with her husband increased, but often she felt threatened by the increased intimacy and recoiled. This would be expressed by her making preparations for a sexual encounter (making a special dinner, buying new lingerie) but then deciding not to engage in sex, leaving her husband confused and frustrated. Perhaps the biggest improvement came in the way she avoided intimacy. In the past she would attack Mark with a stream of hostile remarks when she felt threatened. More and more, she signaled her refusal to have sex by relatively benign behaviors, such as reading in a different room. Only when she began to make real progress in her ego integration did she really come to accept the intimacy that comes with sex and show a significant improvement in the quality of her sex life.

4. *Reducing depressed mood.* Aside from Debbie's rather alarming mention of suicidal threats during her initial telephone call, she showed few overt symptoms of depression. As therapy progressed, however, a consistent pattern of dysphoria began to reveal itself. Although Debbie remained fairly active socially, she regarded many of these activities as dull and monotonous. It became clear that most of her everyday activities were initiated by friends, relatives, or other external demands, such as a deadline for a charity drive. Much of her boredom and apathy stems from her identity disturbance: until she develops a coherent sense of self, the events in her life will tend to lack meaning.

Debbie was referred to a psychiatrist for medication evaluation, and he prescribed the antidepressant bupropion (known by the trade name Wellbutrin), which increased her general activity level and her interest in her outside activities. It also improved her willingness to complete some of the treatment recommendations suggested by her therapist.

5. Diminishing paranoid ideation. Sometimes Debbie's wariness of intimacy and her desperate need not to be abandoned combined to produce behaviors that had a paranoid quality. One indication of her deep mistrust is her extreme jealousy, expressed by her frequent accusations to Mark of his "screwing around" (to use one of her least vulgar terms). Although Mark's travel schedule and long hours provide him with ample opportunity for extramarital affairs, he has never given Debbie good cause to doubt his fidelity. Nevertheless, she frequently confronted him with jealous accusations. At a recent dinner dance, Debbie saw a coworker whom she suspected was one of Mark's lovers. Mark made no comment concerning this woman; in fact he hadn't even known she was at the dance before Debbie began sobbing quietly and making quiet (but noticeable) comments that she "knew all about that bitch." Mark quickly led Debbie out. A loud argument began in the hallway and lasted through the ride home. In therapy Debbie admitted that Mark had given her no reason to suspect this woman. Still, Debbie could not control herself.

Another sign of Debbie's paranoid ideation is her manner of holding grudges. Once Debbie called her therapist to reschedule an appointment she had to miss. He was seeing another patient at the time and asked her to hold. She hung up 30 seconds later. Knowing her inflated sense of entitlement, he was not particularly surprised by this. But he was surprised when she brought up this phone call four weeks later as evidence that he takes advantage of her.

The therapist's method for having Debbie gain control over her paranoid ideation had two steps. First, Debbie was asked to analyze the evidence that supports her suspicions as objectively as possible. Second, she was reminded that her accusations were not "free"; they carried certain costs, such as embarrassing and aggravating the accused as well as starting a hostile interaction. She was told to be responsible for her accusations. Together these suggestions had the effect of making Debbie think before pointing her finger, which greatly reduced the number of impulsive rages.

When Debbie began therapy, she was always prompt and attentive. Gradually, however, she began arriving late—first by a few minutes, but then by as much as half an hour. After three months she began skipping an appointment now and again, and then after four and a half months she discontinued therapy for a period of three weeks.

Up to this time Debbie and the therapist had made great gains toward establishing a therapeutic alliance; Debbie's comments became more open, revealing, and personal. At the same time, her level of hostility toward the therapist gradually increased. She never failed to question a bill he sent her, even though nothing had changed since the first one. But the most interesting expression of her hostility toward him was her grooming habits. It began when Debbie brushed her hair during a session. She brushed her hair again at the next session, but this time she pulled the hair out of the brush and let it fall on the couch. She quickly began to perform more and more of these grooming habits, and with each one the residue left behind wound up on the therapist's couch: used tissues, cotton balls, and even clipped toenails. The therapist became more and more annoyed, but he suppressed his anger and tried as best he could to remain cool and professional. Finally he decided to point out this behavior and discuss its underlying meaning.

Having been a fashion model, Debbie was careful to manage her appearance. She would be particularly careful with a male authority figure, whom she would naturally associate with her hypercritical father. By putting on makeup in front of the therapist, Debbie symbolically conveyed that she was willing to have him see the "real her" without her first needing to cover her faults. By leaving her litter behind her, she was also asking him to "clean up her garbage." Thus, she saw him as both savior and servant. As they developed a closer alliance, however, she felt threatened by the increasing intimacy and tried to drive him away, in this case with her rude, inconsiderate behavior. She was transferring her ambivalent feelings about her father, and to a lesser extent her husband, onto the therapist. She needed him to accept the "real" her, yet she feared that he might abandon her once he saw her faults. Her behavior was a test to see what he would put up with and how much he really cared.

When the therapist discussed this transference reaction with Debbie, she reacted with a blank look. She hadn't realized that she was performing her grooming behaviors at all, let alone understanding their underlying meaning. Though she had no immediate reaction to his interpretation, she seemed to think about it as she left. She arrived on time for the next session and has attended regularly ever since. At the next session she was very interested in the concept of transference and the way it revealed her underlying motives. Whether this experience will lead to a significant insight remains to be seen.

PROGNOSIS

Debbie has been in therapy for about eight months, and her prognosis is optimistic. She has many innate strengths, including a high IQ and a demonstrated capacity for ego integration. She was successful in establishing a therapeutic alliance, and she has begun to be more tolerant of intimacy with her husband. Her impulse control problems have diminished markedly, and they will most likely continue to recede. Most noticeably, her self-esteem has improved.

Still, personality disorders are notoriously persistent, and doubtless many problems will continue. It will take a number of years before she matures emotionally and is able to accept her hostile and libidinal urges. Until then, she will be dependent on a man, both financially and emotionally. In addition, she will be limited by her developmental disabilities (though she has learned to make allowances for them).

Whether Debbie continues to show ego integration depends on several factors, the primary one being how long she stays in her present therapy. If she stays for at least another year, she will probably continue to do well. If her present therapy is discontinued much earlier, most likely her still fragile ego could not take the stress of abandonment. After that, she could probably see another therapist without undue trauma. Her final termination from treatment will depend on life events as well as her therapeutic progress.

DISCUSSION

Borderline personality disorder is considered to be one of the most severe of all the personality disorders (Kroll, 1988), and treating borderline patients is not a task for the faint of heart. They are extremely demanding in terms of the therapist's time and energy. Two issues predominate treatment with borderlines. The first is establishing a therapeutic alliance. As we saw with Debbie, this can be a difficult process. In fact, Debbie's case was a relatively uncomplicated example. Many borderlines are treated for years without establishing a positive alliance; others switch from therapist to therapist (or from hospital to hospital) in their efforts to avoid emotional intimacy.

The second issue that predominates treatment involves transference and countertransference. Debbie's case provided a fairly clear example of the transference process. Because these transferences are often negative and persistent, therapists must be especially careful in managing their own countertransference reactions.

Debbie is quite a provocative person, both in her physical attractiveness and in her hostile rages. Although Debbie's therapist is generally a very easy-going and calm man, she often brought out the worst in him. On several occasions her therapist felt like he "wanted to sock her." At first he was distressed that

Mark had struck her, but after treating her for several months he understood Mark's frustration and believes that Mark is to be commended for showing such restraint and control over the past 11 years.

In addition to the demands of building a therapeutic alliance and managing transference and countertransference reactions, therapists who treat borderlines must contend with three additional problems. First, change tends to be slow and gradual, and therapeutic plateaus are frequent. Second, generally borderlines are unable to project their thoughts into the future, and thus they often fail to grasp their own improvement and how it might have an impact on their lives. Finally, most borderline patients have few inner resources in terms of ego strength and impulse control, and they have little reason to expect positive change.

Conducting research on borderline patients is also a fascinating but frustrating enterprise. There are two main difficulties: a failure of the field to settle on one set definition of borderline personality, and the overlap between borderline personality disorder and other forms of psychopathology.

Historically the concept of "borderline syndrome" was broader than the current *DSM-III-R* usage of the term. In addition to identity disturbances, unstable relationships, and mood shifts, borderline syndrome included an element of thought disturbance. Thus, a person was thought to be on the borderline between a neurotic and a psychotic disorder. With the advent of *DSM-III* in 1980, borderline syndrome was divided into two personality disorders: *borderline personality* described mainly problems in self-image and mood; *schizotypal personality* described thought disorder (Swartz et al., 1989). Many researchers (Edell, 1984; Kroll, 1988; Kullgren, 1987) disagreed with this decision.

Several measures for borderline personality have been developed based on these different notions, including the Borderline Syndrome Index (BSI) (Conte, Plutchik, Karasu, & Jerrett, 1980), the Diagnostic Index for Borderlines (DIB) (Gunderson, Kolb, & Austin, 1981) and the Diagnostic Interview Schedule/Borderline Index (DIS) (Robins, Helzer, Crougham, &

Ratcliff, 1981). Of these three, the DIS most closely adheres to the definition of borderline personality as described by *DSM-III-R*. The use of different diagnostic tools complicates research on this area because different results are often based on different methodologies (Akhtar, Byrne, & Doghramji, 1986).

A further complication is that people with borderline personalities are likely to suffer from a number of other psychiatric conditions, including substance use (Inman, Bascue, & Skoloda, 1985; Jonsdottir-Baldursson & Horvath, 1987; Nace, Saxon, & Shore, 1983), eating disorders (Esman, Dechillo, & Moughan, 1985; Pope & Hudson, 1989), and especially other personality disorders, particularly schizotypal personality disorder (Dahl, 1985; Edell, 1984; Gunderson & Zanarini, 1987; Spitzer, Endicott, & Gibbon, 1979). This overlap makes it difficult to estimate the prevalence rate accurately. One piece of good news is that the historical association between borderline personality and schizophrenia seems to have been severed successfully, and the two syndromes can be reliably distinguished (Gunderson & Zanarini, 1987; Kullgren, 1987).

Despite this complicated picture, some generalizations concerning the epidemiology and demographics of borderline personality disorder can be made. Using the DIS, Swartz, Blazer, George, and Winfield (1990) found that 1.8 percent of a community sample met the criteria for borderline personality. Other studies have shown similar rates (Gunderson & Zanarini, 1987). Generally, studies (Ahktar et al., 1986; Blazer et al., 1990) conclude that borderline personality is more common in women and in young people. Information on race, marital status, and socioeconomic status (SES) is inconsistent. More research is needed to better understand this fascinating but complicated disorder.

OPIOID DEPENDENCE
Residential Treatment

PRESENTING COMPLAINT

John is a 30-year-old mechanic who lives in a middle-class neighborhood in Philadelphia. He has been married for nine years and has two daughters, ages 8 and 5. For the past seven years John has worked as a heating-ventilation-air conditioning (HVAC) mechanic at a large city hospital.

John demonstrated superior job performance when he first began working at the hospital. He was known for doing a thorough and conscientious job, and he had a knack for motivating others. After only two years on the job, the manager of the maintenance department had decided to promote John to supervisor at the first available opening. Over the last few years, however, John's performance has gradually deteriorated. Starting in his third year at the hospital, John began arriving late for work and leaving early, first only once or twice a month, but then once or twice a week. Verbal reminders went unheeded. Eventually John's supervisor filed a written reprimand. At this point John asked to work the night shift, and his supervisor agreed, glad to have John be someone else's problem. For a while John's punctuality improved somewhat, but gradually it deteriorated until he was rarely on time. Then John began to miss work altogether. His absentee rate was always a little higher than usual, but it was never really remarkable. After the move to the night shift, however, it began to climb. At first he missed work once or twice a month, but eventually it reached the point where he showed up for work less than half the time. His relationships with his coworkers were very strained. Surprisingly, the actual quality of his work (when he did it) had not suffered much over the years, though he was slower and more forgetful than before.

John's supervisor tried to be understanding. He asked John if he had any special health problems or personal issues going on, but John was nonspecific and even evasive. Finally his supervisor became exasperated and instituted the formal three-step dismissal proceedings required by the union. First John was told verbally that his job would be terminated unless he showed marked improvement in his performance. He didn't. Two weeks later he received a written warning, and two weeks after that he was suspended from work. Knowing that the next step would be the actual firing, John consulted the coordinator of his union's employee assistance program (EAP) and described his heroin addiction. The EAP coordinator contacted a residential treatment center with a four-week program and arranged to have John admitted the following Monday. He then called John's supervisor. Without any explanation, he said that John would be absent for one month and that his performance should be reevaluated one month after his return.

PERSONAL HISTORY

John grew up in a predominantly African-American working-class neighborhood in Philadelphia. His father was a moderately successful electrician who maintained steady work through one or another of the many contractors he knew. He was a long-time member of the electricians' union and had become increasingly active in union politics over the years. He died suddenly of a massive heart attack a little more than two years ago. John's mother has never worked outside the home;

she is supported by social security and a small monthly annuity from her husband's union death benefit. John is the oldest of three brothers. He attended vocational school, as did his youngest brother, who is now a plumbing contractor. The middle brother graduated from a local community college and now manages a retail clothing store in downtown Philadelphia.

John's father was a large man who was prone to alcoholic binges. Occasionally while drunk he would beat his wife or one of his sons, but usually he was good-natured and jovial. He rarely disciplined the boys for staying out late or drinking; in fact he seemed more amused than angry when one of his sons came home drunk. John's mother was a quiet, passive woman who abstained from alcohol and other drugs herself. She was often upset about her husband's drinking binges but never confronted him directly. She was alarmed when she began to notice signs of drug use in her children, but again she did little to intervene.

John began to experiment with alcohol and marijuana when he was 11 years old. These drugs were readily available at his middle school, and many of his friends were daily users. John gradually increased his use of alcohol and marijuana throughout middle school. By the time he entered high school, John drank to intoxication on most weekend nights and sometimes during the week, and he smoked marijuana an average of three or four days a week. Toward the end of middle school John and his friends began to experiment with other drugs, including amphetamines, cocaine, barbiturates, hallucinogens, and heroin. John continued to use all these substances off and on throughout high school; he most frequently abused alcohol, heroin, and to a lesser extent, marijuana.

John remembers first trying heroin when he was 15. A friend brought a small amount to a party, and he and several other friends took turns snorting the white powder. The calm feeling of euphoria was similar to the effect of marijuana but more potent; he found that heroin combined with alcohol produced an especially intense high. Over the next few years John bought and snorted ever-increasing amounts of heroin until he found it difficult to find enough money to support his habit. He then began selling heroin and other drugs to fellow students.

During this period John spent a great deal of time buying, selling, and taking heroin and other illegal drugs. On many days it was difficult to get out of bed, and sometimes he didn't go to school at all. Even when he did go, he usually spent an hour or more in the school yard talking to dealers, pushers, addicts, and friends who had dropped out. His truancy rate increased year by year, and his schoolwork suffered accordingly. Fortunately for John, he had always been an above-average student, and although his grades were dropping, he still managed to graduate on time and enter a vocational school.

The vocational school was across town, and John spent much of each day either commuting to school or at the school itself. After he completed his training, he got a job working for a heating contractor. About a year later John married Sharon, a woman he had met on the bus while he commuted to the vocational school; their first daughter, Natalie, was born about a year after that. Eighteen months later, John was hired in his current job, and soon afterward they bought a modest house in a quiet, residential neighborhood near the hospital. They had a second daughter, Cicely. During this period of time, John's heroin use remained steady at about three or four times per week, less for the high than to ward off the withdrawal effects. He still used alcohol and marijuana now and then, but for the most part he stopped taking other drugs. John felt in control of his life and his drug use.

Soon after John began at the hospital, his coworkers invited him to join them for a drink on the way home. At first he would stop for a drink once or twice a week, but this soon became a daily routine. John began to drink more and more and to linger at the bar later and later, eventually until long after his coworkers had gone home. John then began to frequent different bars. He made new friends who used marijuana, cocaine, and heroin in addition to alcohol. In this supportive atmosphere, his heroin use increased dramatically, to three, four, or more times a day. And for the first time in his life, John began to take heroin by injection.

John began injecting heroin subcutaneously (under the skin), but soon progressed to injecting it directly into a vein. With each step—from snorting to subcutaneous injection to intravenous injection—came a dramatic increase in the intensity of the euphoric experience. Sometimes John would combine the heroin with amphetamines or with cocaine in an effort to heighten the euphoria and blunt the inevitable "crash" of the withdrawal, but he didn't really like the "edge" these stimulants put on the high.

An ever-increasing part of John's days was consumed by his drug use: obtaining drugs; recovering from highs, crashes, and binges; and actually taking the drugs. He couldn't come to work until he had an injection, and he had to have another during lunch break. If he didn't have any heroin, he had to find some. He had to shoot up again in the afternoon, and often left work early for this reason. John spent most evenings buying, selling, and taking drugs. This basic pattern continued after he changed to the night shift, except that now he had most of the day to sleep and engage in his drug activities. He began going to "shooting galleries," run-down apartments or abandoned buildings where ten or more heroin users would share their highs. Needle sharing was common, as was casual, unprotected sex. In his more sober moments John realized the dangers of this risky behavior, but all caution was lost during the high. On most mornings John came home to crash before going out in the afternoon. His new schedule worked out well; he came home after Sharon and the girls were gone, and he left again before the girls got home from school. Often he didn't come home at all.

Not surprisingly, John's drug use led to severe financial problems. Since he was on an hourly wage, his absentee rate resulted in his bringing home less and less money. As his habit became more and more expensive, more of what he made went to his drug habit. Soon the family's modest savings were gone. Then he began selling items in the house: the wedding silver, the family stereo, and the VCR. When Sharon asked about these items, he said they had been stolen. Still bills went unpaid, and sometimes there wasn't enough money to buy groceries. Sharon demanded to know where all the money was going, but she never received an answer. Three years ago she had gotten a job as a secretary at the local school, but even so they couldn't keep up with their bills. They frequently borrowed money from both sets of parents, often saying that one of the girls was sick. After about a year Sharon's parents refused to lend them any more money. John then turned to his mother and siblings, and he continued to get money from his mother after she was widowed.

Eventually John began to sell drugs, mostly heroin but also some cocaine, marijuana, and speed. Usually he acted as a lookout for a dealer, but sometimes he was involved in the actual buy. He bought a 9-mm automatic on the street, which he kept loaded and took almost everywhere. He was very careless with the gun; on a couple of occasions he left it out within reach of the children. Fortunately he was rarely home when his children were awake.

Although it was John's declining work performance that directly precipitated his referral, his family had also suffered greatly over the past several years. It began gradually. John would stop off at the bar more often and come home later and later. He would miss dates he and Sharon made with friends, and he forgot promises he made to his children. For example, he once told Natalie that they would go to the zoo, but when the time came to go, he was not to be found. Sharon became increasingly frustrated and depressed by his withdrawal from her and their children, and she wanted to know where he went all the time and where he spent all his money. She suspected that he had a problem with alcohol and perhaps other drugs. She was fairly sure that he was having sex with other women and figured that he was spending some of his money supporting one or more mistresses. She yelled, begged, threatened, pleaded, and cajoled him to tell her, but her efforts failed. John even managed to turn her accusations around and put the blame on her, accusing her of being needy, suspicious, and unattractive. Often their fights ended with violence. Her relationship with her own family had become strained because of their constant borrowing, and now she felt alone and helpless. On several occasions she threatened to leave him, and a couple of times she and the girls even packed up some luggage, but she could never go through with it. Eventually she resigned herself to her existence and tried to take care of their daughters as best she could.

CONCEPTUALIZATION AND TREATMENT

DSM-III-R lists several types of disorders associated with drug use: intoxication, withdrawal, abuse, and dependence. The first two describe acute responses to a psychoactive substance; the latter two describe established patterns of drug use. Although John suffered from repeated instances of heroin, alcohol, and cannabis intoxication and heroin and alcohol withdrawal, it was his long-term drug use that brought him in for therapy, and this became the focus of treatment.

Psychoactive substance dependence refers to ongoing problems in controlling the use of a drug. The person exhibits cognitive, behavioral, and physiological symptoms related to drug use, and the person persists in using the drug despite the negative consequences associated with its use. *DSM-III-R* outlines nine criteria for diagnosing psychoactive substance dependence; a person must meet at least three of these nine to warrant a diagnosis:

1. substance taken more than the person intended
2. persistent desire or unsuccessful attempts to control use
3. much time spent acquiring or recovering from the substance
4. frequent intoxication or withdrawal symptoms
5. interrupts social, occupational, and recreational activities
6. continued use despite knowledge that use is harmful
7. marked tolerance
8. characteristic withdrawal symptoms
9. substance taken to avoid or relieve withdrawal symptoms

Furthermore, the substance dependence is categorized as mild, moderate, or severe, depending on how many criteria are met.

Psychoactive substance abuse refers to a more limited use of drugs, confined to the continued or persistent use (of at least a month's duration) of a substance despite the knowledge that it is physiologically dangerous or that it interferes with social, occupational, or recreational activities. For example, a person who is diagnosed as having cirrhosis of the liver but still drinks regularly against medical advice would warrant a diagnosis of alcohol abuse.

We see from John's history that he fulfills several of the criteria for alcohol dependence, cannabis dependence, and opioid dependence, and his treatment is aimed at these problems in combination. However, in the last few years John's heroin use has predominated and has led to extremely risky behavior. For these reasons, his therapist decided to focus their initial work on John's heroin use.

John was admitted to a 28-day residential treatment program located in a newly remodeled 25-bed ward of a downtown hospital. For reasons of confidentiality, the program is located in a different hospital than where John works. The program is voluntary; the doors are not locked, and visitors are allowed. Nevertheless, the program has some inviolate rules. Any instance of physical aggression or violence, sexual activity, or drug use (checked through periodic urine screens) results in immediate dismissal from the program. In addition, the program has a very structured daily routine, and the residents are expected to participate fully.

The staff consists of a treatment director, three full-time treatment counselors, clinical nurses, and two night staff. The staff is firm but friendly; they try to instill a sense of structure combined with an atmosphere of fairness and understanding. Staff and residents are on a first-name basis. Since about 80 percent of the staff members are in recovery themselves, they can well empathize with the residents. Still, every member of the staff is highly trained and holds a certificate as a credited alcoholism counselor (CAC).

The program begins with detoxification, which takes place during the first week or so. Yet even during the detox process, the residents are expected to participate in the highly structured treatment routine. The treatment approach is based on the Minnesota Model, so called because it is modeled after St. Mary's Rehabilitation Center in Minnesota. This approach involves three aspects: changing drug behavior, tapping emotions, and restructuring living patterns. The goal of the program is not merely to end current drug use; it is also to make drug use less likely in the future. To achieve this goal, the addict must undergo a fundamental life change. Thus, the aim of the program is to restructure the habits, routines, cognitions, attitudes, and social environments of the addicts.

Many short-term changes can be accomplished on the ward, but lasting change after graduation requires an alteration in the person's social environment. For this reason the involvement of family members and intimate friends becomes an integral part of the treatment process, and the staff tries very hard to get the addict to sign a release, usually within 24 hours of admission, that will allow these people to participate. Like most addicts, John was hesitant to get his family involved in his treatment. He was embarrassed, ashamed, and guilty over how he had been mistreating his wife and daughters. His drug use had been the source of hostility between him and his family, and the program was likely to generate even more conflict as his wife learned the extent of his drug use. This prediction proved to be accurate. Nevertheless, the staff strongly encouraged him to get his family involved, and he finally relented. Sharon was similarly hesitant, but the staff also convinced her that her participation would be beneficial, even crucial. Most residents of the treatment center eventually agree to involve their family, but despite the best efforts of the staff, some never do. Likewise, most family members do whatever they can to aid the recovery process, though some want nothing to do with the addict and flatly refuse.

For the first two weeks of treatment, John's daily routine was as follows:

7:30 wake up, get dressed, make bed
8:15 breakfast (All residents must sit in the cafeteria, including those who are not eating.)
9:15 lecture
10:15 group therapy
12:00 lunch
1:15 lecture
2:15 group therapy
4:00 supervised walk around the neighborhood
5:15 dinner
6:30 lecture
8:00 12-step meeting, often with outside speakers
9:00 homework assignments, free time (This is the only time TV is allowed.)
11:00 bedtime

During the first week John missed some of the scheduled activities because he suffered symptoms of alcohol and heroin withdrawal: a craving for more heroin and alcohol, trembling, sweating, diarrhea, racing heart, fever, insomnia, running nose, watery eyes, weakness. In fact, aside from the drug craving, John's withdrawal symptoms felt like an incredibly severe case of the flu. Most of his withdrawal symptoms subsided within a week. Although John was expected to follow the daily routine despite his symptoms, the staff made allowances here and there. John's roommate, a crack addict, had a much sharper withdrawal course. Within a few days he became depressed, irritated, and agitated; his cravings for crack were obvious and desperate. However, the staff made few allowances for him and forced him to conform to the daily schedule right from the start. The staff had learned that instilling a sense of structure is paramount to treating cocaine dependency, and it must begin immediately, despite any withdrawal reactions.

John was assigned to a therapy group with seven other addicts, and each of them seemed to be as desperate as he was. Bill and José had just lost their jobs; Hector, Steve, and Curtiss were suspended or on probation. Maggie's husband threatened to file for divorce and seek custody of their son. Joe was referred by his psychotherapist. Bill and Curtiss were longtime alcoholics. Hector was a polyabuser who had a long history of taking heroin, amphetamines, cocaine, crack, alcohol, barbiturates, and marijuana, apparently with little particular preference. The rest had also abused a number of different drugs, but their predominant dependence was crack. During the first two weeks of treatment, the group members gradually revealed their secrets. They told stories of horrible neglect, cruelty, abuse, violence, stealing, and prostitution. Most incredible of all, John realized that his story was just like their stories, if not worse. Throughout his life John had always thought that he was in control of his drug use, even during the last few months. But now John could no longer deny his addiction. For him, the self-revelation that emerged from these group sessions was the most agonizing part of his treatment. But this was just a taste of things to come.

The third week of the program is known as "family week." Members of the residents' families are asked to join the addicts in the treatment process. On Monday, Tuesday, and Wednesday, the morning activities are replaced by education classes that describe the disease model of addictions using lectures, guest speakers, and films. Instead of the usual afternoon activities, the addicts and their families engage in "fishbowl exercises." The fishbowl exercises are run like group sessions, but with two important differences. First, the families of the addicts are now in the group, along with the usual group members. To keep things down to a manageable size, usually no more than two families participate in any one exercise session. Second, the addict is placed in the center of the group, where he or she becomes the focus of the entire session (and is in the "fishbowl"). On Monday the addict must remain quiet while family members take turns describing how the addict had affected their lives. On Tuesday the family must remain quiet while the addict explains the drug use from his or her perspective.

On Monday morning John was surprised to see his mother and brothers accompany Sharon; she had not mentioned this at an earlier visit. Although everyone said they were happy to see him, their interactions were awkward and they mostly avoided eye contact.

The session began with John in the fishbowl. It was very awkward at first, and their group counselor, Rick, had to do a lot of prodding. Sharon began by saying how much she had missed John these last few years. She saw him very little, but even then he seemed to be a different person. John's mother and brothers agreed that he had changed. Sharon continued that the girls missed their daddy. Natalie in particular wanted to know what she had done to make him not love them anymore. John felt a lump in his throat and tears well in his eyes, but Sharon was just starting. She said that John was a monster to live with; he always criticized, blamed, and belittled her. They never had any conversation that wasn't a fight, and they shared very few activities. When they had sex (she looked up at his mother but then continued), it was more of a punishment than anything else. He was so impossible to be with that Sharon was glad when he started working the night shift.

John was surprised at Sharon's hostility, and he was also surprised at how much she knew about his drug use. She saw the needle marks in his arms and knew that he used heroin or cocaine. She knew that he had sold their silver, stereo, and VCR for drug money. She knew that he carried a gun and probably sold drugs. She knew that he slept with other women and wondered if he supported any mistresses. Sharon then demanded to know what she didn't know already. "Who are those men I see you with in the morning?" "How much junk do you use?" "How many women are you screwing?" Although John was supposed to be quiet, he was allowed to answer direct questions. He didn't. The therapist marked down these questions to ask John tomorrow. Finally, the session reached a crescendo.

Rick: Sharon, tell John what makes you most
angry about his behavior.

Sharon: Angry? Angry? You know what this
bastard did?

Rick: Talk to John, Sharon.

Sharon: You . . . I can't look at him. (She puts
her face in her hands and sobs openly.
She continues, looking at the floor.)
You know what the worst of it is? Do
you? It's that you made me feel like this
was all my fault. And the girls, too.
You know, Cicely never really knew
you; she thinks you were always like
this. But Natalie's old enough. She remembers how you used to be, and she
thinks it's all her fault that you treat her
like that. I just can't believe how selfish
you've been to treat us like this. I don't
know why I care about you. I've asked
myself a thousand times. I feel so weak
and stupid. I hate my life, and I hate
you for making me so miserable.

Sharon sat with her face in her hands and sobbed for another few minutes. John noticed that his mother and brothers
were also looking down and holding back tears. He didn't
bother to hold back his own.

Rick helped John up, and Maggie replaced him in the fishbowl. John didn't notice much about what was said. He was
too upset by the last half hour. He also dreaded tomorrow; he
knew that would be even worse.

He was right. This time Maggie was the first one in the
fishbowl. John watched her husband sullenly look on as she described the history of her addiction to crack. The low point came
when she described having sex with drug dealers in her own
home while her husband was at work. This was more than her
husband could bear; he simply got up and left the room.

On this glum note, John entered the fishbowl. The group members were there to provide encouragement—but also to correct any glossed-over accounts; there was no need for either. John simply and plainly narrated his long history of drug use, from middle school experimentation to his suspension from work. Sharon cried when he described his frequent casual sex, and a look of horror came over her when he described the shooting galleries. But the biggest shock of all came toward the end of his story.

Rick: John, what's the worst thing you did because of your heroin addiction?

John: I guess it was shooting that cop and the other guy. (At this, Sharon's jaw dropped.)

Rick: Did you kill them?

John: You just shoot, you know. You don't stick around to see what happens.

Rick: Is that what you feel worst about?

John: Not really, no. I never really thought about it much; I guess I never thought of much of anything except for myself. But sitting here thinking about it, I guess I feel worst about what I did to Sharon and Natalie, and Cicely too. I never thought they'd blame themselves. Hell, I never thought about them at all. I remember, after the drug bust, I came home and put the gun on the table. The girls were home from school, you know. And I just thought, "I hope one of them picks up the gun; they'll never trace *those* prints." Thank God they had enough sense not to get near it. But I mean, that's how I thought. I didn't think that they might get hurt or anything. God, how can anybody get like that? How did *I* get like that?

On Wednesday afternoon, the residents and their families made concrete plans for activities they could share that would replace the time spent in drug activities. Movies, trips to an amusement park, and other events were planned with the children, including a summer vacation. Two nights a month were set aside for a "date" with Sharon. John even agreed to attend church. And he consented to be tested for the HIV virus. Finally, John enrolled in Alcoholics Anonymous (AA) and Narcotics Anonymous (NA). For her part, pledged to support John in these changes, and she enrolled in Alanon and Naranon.

Thursday's time was devoted to a communication workshop based on the principles of Communication Theory outlined by Salvador Minuchin (1974). For most couples, the most crucial aspect of the workshop was the use of communication exercises aimed at promoting "fair fighting." John was pleased to see Maggie's husband at the workshop. Friday saw a summary of the week's events and a chance to solidify future plans. One important plan involved a future relapse. What would Sharon do if John began drinking or using any illegal drug? She was instructed to make a clear decision and to stick to it. She decided that her only choice would be a separation, and she vowed to actually go through with it.

The treatment program continued for one more week. At that point, every resident who had completed the program was given a medallion as a tangible sign of his or her effort and work. Each graduate was enrolled in a two-year aftercare "growth group," a weekly two-hour meeting that provides support to recovering addicts and their families. All graduates are invited to an annual banquet sponsored by the hospital. On most years between 600 and 800 people attend.

PROGNOSIS

It is difficult to provide a definite prognosis for John. His treatment program keeps no records on relapse rates, so it is impossible to estimate John's chances of remaining sober based on the performance of other graduates. The program does know that about 65 percent of its graduates remain in the growth group for the full two years. This does not necessarily mean that all 65 percent remain abstinent (in fact that is doubtful), nor does it necessarily mean that 35 percent have relapsed (some may have moved away—or even died). But it is a rough guess as to the number who have at least maintained the sense of responsibility required to keep up with the growth group.

Because most treatment programs are voluntary and dropout rates are so high, true relapse rates are difficult to determine. Most estimates place the one-year relapse rate at about 60 percent. Two recent European studies corroborate this figure. Sanchez-Carbonell, Cami, and Brigos (1988) reported a 49 percent 12-month relapse rate in their sample of 311 addicts drawn from 16 drug-free outpatient clinics in Spain; and Nicolosi, Molinari, Musicco, Saracco, Ziliani, and Lazzarin (1991) report a 70 percent 11-month relapse rate in a sample of 460 Italian addicts. Both studies found that most addicts who did not abstain still decreased their drug use and needle sharing.

Given these figures, chances are 60/40 that John will begin using heroin again within a year. Yet John has some advantages that work in his favor. He had the determination (or desperation) to attend drug treatment, and he was able to stay in treatment and graduate. Thus, John is one of the minority who saw the program through to completion, and this is a very good sign. John has a relatively stable and supportive family environment. John returned to work on a new shift and seems to be doing well. Most importantly, John no longer associates with his "drug friends"; instead he spends most of his free time with his family and attending meetings for AA, NA, and the growth group. Finally, John has entered his thirties, a time when most heroin users begin to reduce their drug use. Though one must always be cautious with cases of heroin addiction, John seems to have a good chance at recovery.

DISCUSSION

Many Americans consider heroin addiction to be a problem of the 1970s, and indeed, surveys of drug use among American adolescents indicate that heroin use has decreased since 1975 (e.g., Johnston, O'Malley, & Bachman, 1987). However, Kozel and Adams (1986) found a cohort and aging effect for heroin use. That is, although fewer adolescents are trying heroin, those who become addicted tend to remain addicted. In the last few years, though, some urban treatment centers, including John's, have been seeing an increase in the rate of heroin use.

In contrast, the prevalence rate for heroin use in Europe has remained relatively stable over this period. Much work has been done in Great Britain. Some researchers reported a gradual increase in heroin use from 1975 to 1982 (Ghodse, Stapleton, Edwards, & Edeh, 1987), whereas others (Peveler, Green, & Mandelbrote, 1988) found little change over this period. Grapendaal (1992) reports a cohort effect among Dutch heroin addicts. A point prevalence rate of about 3.5 to 4.5 per thousand was consistently found in samples from Oxford City (Peveler, et al.), Bristol (J. Parker, Pool, Rawle, & Gay, 1988) and Merseyside (H. Parker, Newcombe, & Bakx, 1987). That is, at any one time, between 0.35 and 0.45 percent of the population is addicted to heroin.

Heroin addicts show diverse treatment histories and patterns of use (Shaffer, Nurco, & Kinlock, 1984; Watters, Cheng, & Lorvick, 1991), but some generalizations can be made. Heroin use typically starts early. J. Parker et al. (1988) found that 92 percent of their sample was under 35 years old, with some addicts as young as 10 years old. Another British study (Sheehan, Oppenheimer, & Taylor, 1988) found that the typical heroin user had a nine-year history of heroin use with a 4-year injection history. In the United States, the rate of heroin addiction among African-Americans and Latinos is proportionately high, making up about half of all heroin users. Desmond and Maddux (1984) uncovered differences that distinguish Chicano heroin users from Caucasian and African-American addicts. For one thing, Chicanos are more likely to terminate treatment before completion. They are also more likely to get arrested and will spend more time being incarcerated. However, this group is also more likely to abstain from heroin voluntarily and will spend more time employed during their drug careers.

Medical and Behavioral Complications of Heroin Use

Prolonged use of most psychoactive substances entails some medical complication: cirrhosis of the liver for alcohol dependence, lung cancer for nicotine dependence, coronary arrest for cocaine dependence, and so on. In contrast, heroin use per se has few negative health consequences. However, the behavioral consequences of heroin use can be devastating.

First, most heroin users develop incredible tolerance, and as a result, their dose increases dramatically; some addicts take a dose over 100 times their initial dose. This need for ever-increasing amounts of heroin is complicated by the fact that illegally obtained heroin is poorly regulated, resulting in wildly varying purities. These factors contribute to a high risk of overdose. An associated complication is poisoning from impure or harmful substances used to "cut," or dilute, the heroin that is sold on the street.

Second, the relatively short pharmacological effect of heroin (about four hours) requires the addict to take the drug three, four, or more times a day. As a consequence, much of each day becomes involved in drug activity.

Third, buying the frequent, large amounts of heroin needed to support a habit requires a great deal of money, sometimes more than $100 *per day*. Since so much time is spent in drug-related activities, methods of obtaining this money usually involve drug-related crime. The experience of John's treatment center is that virtually all female heroin addicts engage in prostitution in some form or another. The same is true for women addicted to other substances, especially crack. Most male addicts turn to various forms of crime to raise money, including larceny, robbery, and drug dealing. In a study of 354 male narcotic (mostly heroin) addicts, Shaffer et al. (1984) found that, on average, 63 percent of their days included at least one crime aside from actually taking heroin. B. D. Johnson, Wish, Schmeidler, and Huizinga (1991) interviewed 1539 adolescents ranging in age from 14 to 20 years and found a high rate of felony crimes committed by heroin and cocaine addicts. Interestingly, many of these crimes seem to be a result of the drug culture; the adolescents reported that fewer than 25 percent were committed primarily to obtain money for drugs.

Finally, the drug culture poses increased risks for contracting life-threatening diseases such as hepatitis B, hepatitis delta, and AIDS. The lifestyle of the typical IV drug user includes sharing unsterilized needles and engaging in casual, unprotected sex. A study of 194 Swedish heroin users (Kall & Olin, 1990) found that 45 percent tested HIV positive. Rates of HIV infection among urban U.S. samples are generally higher; a recent survey of 687 female prostitutes who use IV drugs found an average infection rate of 74 percent across seven sites in the United States (Rosenblum et al., 1992). By 1988, HIV infection was more prevalent among IV drug users than all other risk categories combined (Centers for Disease Control, 1989). The rates of HIV and hepatitis infection among IV drug users continues to rise.

Professionals have noted several factors that contribute to this problem. Most IV drug users live in poor, violent neighborhoods where few opportunities for education exist. Prolonged drug use often leads to habitually poor judgment, resulting in risky behavior despite the known dangers. Finally, some IV drug users living a violent drug lifestyle have adopted a helpless, nihilistic attitude. Few expect to live past age 30 anyway, so they are unconcerned about contracting AIDS.

The spread of AIDS through IV drug use is becoming such a public concern that some communities have set up needle exchange programs where addicts can turn in dirty syringes for sterile ones. These controversial programs have been criticized by people who fear an increase in drug use and greater risk of needle sticks to the general population. In fact, community concerns of this sort blocked a recently proposed needle exchange program in New York City. Another problem is that addicts are hesitant to identify themselves to local authorities. Still, recently professionals have reported successful needle exchange programs in Holland (Buning, 1991) and Sweden (Christensson & Bjungberg, 1991). In neither case were the community's fears or the addicts' worries realized, and in both cases the extent of risky needle sharing was reduced, though rarely did an addict stop the risky behavior completely.

As a final note, it should be emphasized that one's environment has much to do with one's drug use. People living in stressful situations where drugs are readily available are especially at risk. Indeed, numerous studies have shown that being undereducated, unemployed, and low in socioeconomic status, and having unstable family relationships are all risk factors for developing heroin addiction. Often a change in social environment will affect the course of the addiction. For example, Grapendaal (1992) found that heroin use depends more on available money than on actual need. *DSM-III-R* mentions that the vast majority of Vietnam veterans who became addicted to opiates while in Southeast Asia stopped taking drugs upon their return home. And yet a person's physical environment is not the whole story. John had an adequate income, a steady job, and a stable family life, and still he was unable to overcome the draw of heroin. A person's social acquaintances, self-esteem, and cognitions must also be considered.

Approaches to Treatment

Treatment for opioid dependence falls into two broad classes: substitution and abstinence. Substitution programs focus on changing the behavioral complications of drug use while maintaining a modified form of drug-taking behavior. Abstinence programs are aimed at reducing the drug-taking behavior itself.

Most substitution programs involve methadone maintenance. Methadone is a synthetic narcotic that relieves the heroin withdrawal symptoms, (usually) without inducing a euphoric high. The withdrawal symptoms of methadone are somewhat less severe than those for heroin, so there is a greater chance that the addict will eventually abstain completely. Perhaps the biggest advantage of methadone is that it is administered orally, thus obviating the behavioral complications arising out of using shared or otherwise unsterilized needles.

Unfortunately, methadone maintenance carries several drawbacks. It requires a daily trip to a methadone clinic, and many addicts lack the self-discipline to keep coming. In addition, the side effects of methadone, including constipation, insomnia, and decreased sexual performance, further erode the addict's will to remain in treatment. Worst of all, when taken intravenously in relatively high doses, methadone will sometimes produce a high, and a black market has sprung up, allowing for the unregulated availability of the drug, which would seem to defeat its very purpose.

Abstinence programs attempt to eliminate drug use completely and rather abruptly ("cold turkey"). They almost always involve a highly structured setting that both supports an addict during the withdrawal and yet instills a sense of order and responsibility. Many programs try to break through the addict's characteristic denial by exposing the newly sober addict to critical and sometimes harsh feedback from the counselor, fellow addicts, and even family members. Often this becomes too much for the addict to tolerate, and many programs experience high dropout rates. But often dropping out can be minimized by instituting a clear, categorical penalty (divorce, loss of job, and so on) for failure to complete the program.

Regardless of which approach is adopted, supportive therapy is a vital component. Typically this supportive therapy includes education regarding the course of drug use and its effects. Therapy often outlines a disease model of substance dependence. Most important, therapy encourages addicts to change their social environments. Often family members are involved in therapy so that they may understand the addict more fully and set up an environment that will serve as an alternative to the old drug lifestyle. Often specific activities are assigned to provide order in the addicts' lives. Finally, clear rules for behavior are set down, and equally clear responses and penalties are formulated. Take as an example an addict who habitually beat his wife. This couple may decide that physical abuse will no longer be tolerated in the home. At the first instance of violence, the husband must see a therapist. If he fails to do so or if he commits another violent act, the wife will file for divorce. Of course, the wife must be prepared to carry through should the need arise. Although these firm rules often seem impersonal and harsh, they are just the sort of structure addicts need to help maintain a sense of order in their new lives.

How successful are these programs? As was discussed in John's prognosis, the best evidence available indicates that fewer than half of those with successful therapy experiences remain abstinent for one year. And this figure doesn't include the addicts who drop out! Clearly, substance dependence is a very persistent, irascible problem. Professionals are making progress, but there is a long way to go.

MALE ERECTILE DISORDER
Eclectic Therapy

PRESENTING COMPLAINT

Jim is a 29-year-old actor living in Santa Monica, California, a suburb of Los Angeles. He has a day job as a salesman in an electronics store. He frequently auditions for various roles in television shows and commercials, and he has had what he describes as "bit parts" in two movies. On the whole, though, he assesses his acting career as "struggling."

For the past few years, Jim has experienced intermittent sexual problems, and once in a while this will come up in conversations he has with other actors while waiting for different auditions. Last week a fellow actor he had known for some time suggested that he see a therapist for his problems and provided him with a recommendation.

At his first session Jim appeared to be somewhat hesitant and awkward. He looked off in the distance when he described himself, and he occasionally stammered and giggled nervously. After several minutes, though, he became a little more relaxed and described the precise nature of his sexual problems.

For the past three or four years, Jim suffered from what he terms "off-and-on impotence problems." Sometimes he would have trouble maintaining an erection during intercourse, and he estimated that he successfully achieved orgasm "only about half the time, maybe less." Sometimes he would achieve penetration but then lose the erection soon after. Often he would lose the erection upon attempting penetration, thus being unable to complete intercourse. Occasionally he would fail to achieve an erection altogether. These difficulties seemed to be limited to intercourse; masturbation, performed either by himself or by his sexual partner, almost always resulted in orgasm.

Jim states that his sexual problem is compounded by what he perceives to be a strong emphasis in the African-American culture on masculinity and sexual prowess. He says that the women he dates, both black and white, expect him to be a "terrific lover." He feels that his behavior is inadequate in comparison to this relatively strict standard, both in his own eyes as well as in the eyes of his partners. He says that they usually feel frustrated and hurt when he loses his erection. Most blame themselves and wonder if they are not "exciting enough" or if they "can't do it right." One partner felt so upset that she locked herself in his bathroom and cried for several hours. Most of his partners have not expressed their frustrations directly, although two or three have said that their evening with him was "a disappointment." This problem has been a considerable source of anxiety for him over the past few years.

Jim is also concerned about the effects of these problems on his sexual relationships. Because of the embarrassment and anxiety he feels as a result of his disorder, he has often felt ambivalent about initiating sexual encounters for fear that he may not be able to "perform." Jim is convinced that his impotence is the primary cause of his inability to form lasting romantic relationships, and this realization leads him to feel anxious and depressed.

PERSONAL HISTORY

Jim grew up in a working-class household in Los Angeles. He has two older brothers and a younger sister. His parents, neither of whom had finished high school, held a number of different unskilled jobs while Jim was growing up. For the past 15 years his father has been employed with the U.S. Postal Service. His mother has worked as a waitress, a store clerk, and most recently as a beautician. His brothers both work "in the neighborhood"; his sister moved to San Jose after she was married. Jim could not think of anything unusual about his childhood. He summed it up by saying that his parents were "good people; they worked hard and always had food on the table."

Jim describes himself as having been a mediocre student who "barely finished" high school. For the past several years he has held various day jobs while auditioning for acting parts and taking an occasional acting class. Because of his unstable financial situation, he has lived with different people in various places in and around Los Angeles. Usually he would move in with someone out of economic necessity. Sometimes, though, he would move in with a woman he was dating, in some cases after dating for only a few weeks. He shares his present apartment in Santa Monica with a couple he met at a recent audition. He is not sexually involved with either member of the couple.

Jim's sexual history also shows instability. He became sexually active at age 14 and describes his sex life in high school as "successful." He has had many female sexual partners since then; he estimates the total number at "around five or six a year." For the most part he meets his sexual partners while auditioning for acting parts. He describes his partners as "people in the business," (actresses, script prompters, makeup and wardrobe personnel, etc.). He and his partners typically engage in sex very early in the relationship. Jim has had "numerous" one-night stands, but usually he attempts to establish relationships with his sexual partners. Typically Jim will begin dating a partner soon after meeting her. (Sometimes, as already noted, he quickly moves in with this partner, usually for practical reasons as much as romantic ones.) Usually, though, the relationship will end abruptly only a few weeks or months after it began. He estimates that the number of times he ends the relationship is

139

about equal to the number of times his partner does. He is not now in a steady relationship.

CONCEPTUALIZATION AND TREATMENT

According to *DSM-III-R*, male erectile disorder is a sexual dysfunction characterized by either (1) a persistent or recurrent failure to attain or maintain erection until the satisfactory completion of the sexual activity or (2) a persistent lack of subjective excitement or pleasure in the sexual activity. This diagnosis is not warranted if the dysfunction occurs only during the presence of some other disorder, such as a major depressive episode. In addition, *DSM-III-R* asks clinicians to specify whether the disorder is the result of psychological causes (psychogenic), physiological causes (biogenic), or both; whether the disorder has been lifelong or was acquired after a period of normal sexual functioning; and whether the disorder is generalized to all situations or situational in nature.

Jim's primary complaint is that he loses his erection, and in some cases his sexual interest, during intercourse. This has been a cause of much anxiety and frustration for him as well as his sexual partners. His complaints seem to match the criteria for male erectile disorder very well. Clearly his dysfunction was acquired, since he has been having sex for 15 years and his symptoms began only a few years ago. His problem appears to be situational, that is, specific to intercourse; Jim is able to complete the sexual act approximately half the time and is able to masturbate to ejaculation. Given these characteristics, it is very likely that his disorder is psychogenic.

In sum, Jim's Axis I diagnosis would be of an acquired, psychogenic male erectile disorder that is specific to situations involving intercourse. However, this diagnosis only addresses the objective manifestations of Jim's disorder. Jim himself seemed to focus only on this superficial level. However, several aspects of his complaints suggest that the picture may be more complex. The underlying cause of his dysfunction seems to be that he is a disorganized, impulsive, and anxious young man who lacks self-understanding and self-discipline. These characteristics would negatively affect both his sexual performance and his sexual relationships. On a performance level, self-discipline and self-confidence are needed to carry through the sexual act, especially to the point where the partner is satisfied. Lacking this, subtle signs of a performance deficit may erode the person's sexual behavior. On an interpersonal level, a certain amount of steadfastness and trust is required to develop an awareness of the partner's wants and needs and to work through the problems that inevitably occur in relationships.

Jim appears to be a good candidate for therapy. He is young and open in his descriptions of his actions and his feelings. Although he describes his problem almost completely in behavioral terms, he is nevertheless responsive to the suggestions and dynamic interpretations of the therapist. Finally, he is not resistant to the notion of behavioral exercises, many of which involve masturbation.

The overall goal of Jim's therapy is for the therapist to act as an objective facilitator, a separate, "objective" person who can act to "spark," or regenerate, his sexual behavior. Her eclectic background would be useful in providing Jim with a foundation of explicit behavioral training combined with dynamic analysis. As this implies, the therapeutic plan for Jim operated at two levels. On a cognitive and behavioral level, Jim received information about his anatomical functioning and his disorder. He also was given instruction in different practical exercises to increase his control over his sexual performance. (These exercises are described below.) On an emotional level, the therapist treated Jim through psychoanalysis. This analysis was aimed at increasing his psychological awareness of himself and others and to put him back in touch with repressed aspects of his personality.

Since Jim initially sought a rather short-term, limited treatment for his sexual problems, therapy at first involved specific behavioral techniques and recommendations. Jim was taught the basic physiology of human sexual behavior, including a brief discussion of the four phases of the sexual response cycle (desire, excitement, orgasm, resolution). The primary value of this education was to eliminate any myths Jim may have had. For example, most men are physiologically incapable of attaining an erection immediately after ejaculation (i.e., during the resolution phase). Unaware of this, many men become anxious, because they are "impotent" after having sex. Simple information describing the physiology of the male sexual cycle will often dispel the anxieties associated with this myth.

Next, Jim was taught two specific techniques to improve his control over his erection (and thereby to improve his confidence in his sexual performance). Instructions for these techniques were given during early therapy sessions; he practiced these exercises at home.

The first of these is Seeman's exercise, also called "The Start and Stop Technique." First, the patient is to masturbate to orgasm quickly to reduce tension about achieving orgasm. The next time he masturbates, however, he is to gradually build up an erection and try to maintain it before ejaculating. Eventually the patient should be able to attain an erection, maintain it for at least 3 to 5 minutes, let the erection slowly subside, and then to repeat the excitement, maintenance, and relaxation stages several times before finally reaching orgasm. The goals of this exercise are fourfold: (1) to develop control in attaining and maintaining an erection, (2) to increase the quality of the erection (i.e., its tumescence and duration), (3) to gain control over the timing of orgasm, and (4) to increase the patient's confidence in his sexual capabilities.

The second technique is known as the Kegel exercise. In this exercise the patient repeatedly tightens and loosens the pubococcygeal muscle (the muscle in the pelvis that restricts the flow of urine, sometimes called the "love muscle"). The patient is taught to flex this muscle in two ways: by tightening and relaxing it for long durations and by rapidly flexing it for many repetitions. There are three general goals to this technique: (1) to increase muscle tone, (2) to stimulate the genital region, and (3) to increase the engorgement of blood into erectile tissue.

In addition to these physical exercises, Jim was also given specific instructions pertaining to his sexual activity. Most importantly, he was told to restrict the frequency of penetration so that he can concentrate his strength and thus make intercourse more exciting. In the therapist's words, "Intercourse is exhausting. You may want to think of other ways to have sex with your partner and save intercourse for the weekends." The therapist's second piece of advice was to delay penetration until both partners were ready. Often penetration will fail simply because the penis has not been sufficiently stimulated. Similarly, intercourse may be painful and/or uncomfortable for the partner if she is not sufficiently aroused. Intercourse is more pleasurable for both partners after sufficient foreplay.

Jim was very responsive to these suggestions. He came to therapy regularly and reported that he performed the exercises as instructed. As therapy progressed, the focus of the sessions gradually widened from his specific sexual problems to more introspective topics. A particularly important topic of discussion revolved around Jim's perceptions of the expectations of his partners. He stated that most of his partners seemed to focus almost exclusively on orgasm and that he felt a strong pressure to perform. He also complained that the majority of his sexual partners lacked any deep emotional involvement, which he felt diminished the quality of his sexual relationships with them. In general, he felt that sex was too "rushed and selfish." He suggested that the stereotype of African-American men as uncaring and macho may have contributed to this problem.

The therapist responded that if any generalizations were to be made, strong demands for sexual performance and a callous, uncaring attitude seemed more descriptive of the entertainment industry than of African-American men. In actuality, Jim's complaints seemed to reveal more about himself than about these groups. For example, if Jim had a strong need for intimacy, why did he choose to earn his living (or at least to meet sexual partners) in an industry where so many people are considered shallow and selfish? In this way Jim gradually shifted his focus from others' expectations to his own attitudes and beliefs.

The therapist then widened the focus of Jim's therapy to deal with issues that did not relate directly to sex. Jim and the therapist discussed his feelings about his acting career, his anxieties about his chances of forming satisfying romantic relationships, and his needs for intimacy, among other things. Gradually she raised issues that she felt were particularly significant for him, such as his disorganized nature, his impulsiveness, and his anxieties over becoming intimate with women. They discussed the importance of these characteristics for his sexual behavior and for his life in general. As he gained a better understanding of himself and his shortcomings, he slowly began to understand that he had walled off many aspects of his personality. For example, it was possible that his impulsive and nomadic living habits were manifestations of his refusal to acknowledge his need for intimacy and commitment, perhaps because of a deep anxiety that he would be let down. As he tackled these important issues, he very gradually uncovered these repressed parts of his personality. As he became more emotionally mature, he developed a better sense of what was missing in his life. Acknowledging these underlying needs made him more confident in his relationships and more secure in his own worth.

Jim has been in therapy for slightly over three years, and he seems to have made significant behavioral and emotional progress. After about two months of therapy Jim no longer complained about his "impotence," and the behavioral aspects of his problem for the most part were resolved. His first dynamic breakthrough came after about six months of therapy. He told the therapist that he found himself being more choosy about his sexual partners. By limiting his relationships to only those women in whom he had an emotional interest, he greatly increased his chances of developing an intimate and lasting relationship. It seems that this process paid off; for the past 15 months he has been in a steady relationship with the same partner. He has also made a great many other self-discoveries; in general, his emotional awareness of himself (and, for that matter, his girlfriend) is at a much more sophisticated level than it was when the therapy began, and he is able to better assess his (and her) sexual and emotional needs. He also feels ready to commit to a long-standing, intimate relationship. It is likely that these self-discoveries will help prevent him from developing psychological problems (manifested through anxiety, depression, or sexual dysfunctions) in the future.

PROGNOSIS

The prognosis for Jim is good. He quickly eliminated his sexual symptoms and has continued to grow emotionally. He has reduced many of his impulsive behaviors, such as moving in with a new lover after only a few weeks, and his level of anxiety about his career and his relationships has decreased. He has de veloped greater awareness of the needs of his sexual partners, and he appears to have the ability to maintain a more mature, intimate relationship. Jim is very satisfied with the gains he has made in therapy.

In general, a patient's prognosis in these sorts of cases is based on two factors: his responsiveness to therapy and his underlying emotional stability. To a large extent, those patients who are willing to accept the therapist's suggestions and to perform the behavioral exercises generally show noticeable behavioral improvement after only one or two sessions. When therapy does not prove to be effective, often it is because the patient is not in touch with his repressed feelings. Unless the patient is willing to first acknowledge these underlying issues, the chances for lasting behavioral changes are relatively low. Furthermore, patients who are less emotionally stable are generally less amenable to therapy, particularly that which involves a great deal of introspection and self-discovery.

DISCUSSION

Male erectile disorder (MED) is not uncommon. Community surveys have reported rates between 3 and 9 percent of all adult men (Ard, 1977; Frank, Anderson, & Rubenstein, 1978; Neddleblatt & Uddenberg, 1979; Shover, Evans, & von Eschenbach, 1987). MED is the most common problem of men seeking treatment for sexual problems, accounting for between 36 and 53 percent of initial complaints (Bancroft & Coles, 1976; Frank et al.; Hawton, 1982). Furthermore, the incidence of MED appears to be increasing (Spector & Carey, 1990).

An initial consideration in conducting psychologically based therapy for MED is to establish clearly that the problem at hand is truly psychogenic. One indication of a psychogenic dysfunction is a prior history of normal sexual performance. Masters and Johnson (1970) distinguished two types of erectile difficulties based on sexual histories. Males who were previously able to achieve erections and then lost this ability were considered to have a secondary difficulty (a condition frequently termed "secondary impotence"). It is likely that these men suffer from a psychogenic disorder. On the other hand, men who had never achieved a satisfactory erection are considered to have a primary difficulty (a condition termed "primary impotence") and most likely suffer from a biological condition. A more reliable indication of whether erectile dysfunction is psychogenic or biogenic is the Nocturnal Penile Tumescence Test, or NPT Test. All normal-functioning males have erections during REM (rapid eye movement) sleep. In the NPT Test, the circumferences of the base and tip of the patient's penis are measured while he sleeps. If the patient shows no sign of an erection during REM sleep, he most likely has a biogenic erectile dysfunction. If the patient does have erections, however, it is probable that his erectile dysfunction is psychogenic. Secondary erectile difficulties are much more common than primary difficulties. Masters and Johnson report that 50 percent of men seeking treatment suffer from secondary dysfunction, whereas only 8 percent experience primary dysfunction. A more recent study by Renshaw (1988) yielded similar rates: 48 percent and 3.5 percent, respectively.

MED affects men of all ages, though the incidence of this problem increases dramatically with age. Kinsey's classic studies (Kinsey, Pomeroy, & Martin, 1948; Kinsey, Pomeroy, Martin, & Gebhard, 1953) are still the most comprehensive source of data on sexual behavior, and they remain arguably the most methodologically sound of all community surveys (Spector & Carey, 1990). Kinsey and his colleagues found the prevalence of MED to be only 1 percent in men under age 35. However, this rate climbs to 25 percent of men over age 70. The prevalence rate of MED also differs according to education. Using the original Kinsey data, Gebhard and Johnson (1979) found the rate of erectile difficulties among non-college-educated men to be over 3 times the rate experienced by college-educated men.

In the past, most therapies for sexual dysfunctions employed traditional psychodynamic analysis consisting of a series of interviews with the patient conducted in the therapist's office. Specific behavioral "exercises" were not used; in fact, the patient's specific sexual complaints were seen as merely a manifestation of underlying neuroses and were dealt with only tangentially. After the rise in popularity of behavioral sex therapists (e.g., H. S. Kaplan, 1974; Masters & Johnson, 1970), sexual dysfunctions began to be treated almost exclusively with direct behavioral techniques. Currently most sex clinics offer some sort of behavioral sex therapy such as Masters and Johnson's Sensate Focus program.

An important aspect of these behavioral exercises is that they rely heavily on the cooperation of a support partner. For example, the Masters and Johnson Sensate Focus program has both partners take turns as they go through three steps of the exercise: caressing, genital stimulation, and nondemand intercourse. One shortcoming of this type of treatment is that an uncooperative or unsympathetic partner can hinder or completely obstruct the progress of both partners. Some patients lack a partner with the required emotional maturity to carry out the program; other patients, like Jim, lack any steady partner whatsoever. For these reasons behavioral exercises that require only the patient's participation are often the treatment of choice.

The eclectic therapy presented in this case combines behavioral treatments with dynamic therapy. Specific exercises are

147

seen as very useful in surmounting particular problems, especially during the early stages of therapy. Providing the patient with dynamic analysis is seen as crucial in bringing about lasting behavioral and emotional changes. Thus, it is vital for an eclectic therapist to receive training in both the behavioral techniques and psychoanalysis. As Jim's therapist states, "The patient needs to derive benefit from both the behavioral and the emotional aspects of therapy, and I can only take him as far as I've come myself."

An aspect of this case that so far has not been discussed is the sex of the therapist. For the behavioral aspects of treatment, this issue is of little consequence. Most patients feel some initial discomfort and awkwardness about discussing their problems, and this awkwardness may occur with therapists of either sex. Generally, therapists of either sex seem to be equally capable of providing instructions for behavioral exercises. However, the sex of the therapist becomes somewhat more important in discussing the dynamic issues of a case. Male and female therapists both have their advantages. Male therapists may facilitate the transference relationship and may be seen as more capable of sympathizing with the patient. Female therapists, on the other hand, are generally seen as more approachable, less threatening, and better able to provide an idea of what will satisfy the patient's partner. Generally speaking, however, this difference is relatively minor; the therapist's qualifications, experience, and talents are considered to be more important factors than gender in successful therapy.

Like Jim, many patients seeking therapy for sexual dysfunctions expect a direct, short-term behavioral therapy. When therapy begins to focus on more dynamic issues, some become uncomfortable and either quit or switch to a more purely behavioral approach. Others, though, believe they can make gains from analysis and stay in therapy long after their behavioral symptoms disappear. The prevalence of MED increases dramatically with age, but ironically, older men are generally more resistant to therapy. Perhaps because of their more traditional sexual upbringing, they are less willing to perform the different exercises, especially those involving masturbation. As a group, they also seem to be less self-aware and less amenable to self-discovery. It is possible that as sexual attitudes in society become more permissive, men will be able to face their sexual problems more openly. The increasing rate of MED as a complaint among men who seek treatment may indicate an increased willingness to confront sexual difficulties more directly. However, further research is needed to firmly establish this trend.

CHRONIC SCHIZOPHRENIA, RESIDUAL TYPE
Pharmacological Therapy with Residential Treatment

PRESENTING COMPLAINT

Jerry was detained by U.S. Army MPs when he attempted to walk through an American Army checkpoint on the East German border, ignoring the commands of several border guards. In their report the border guards stated that Jerry said "something about pursuing freedom and living off the land," but for the most part what he said was vague and incoherent. During his detention Jerry was interrogated by officers at the checkpoint. He was calm, even passive, but he seemed to be completely unaware of where he was and the situation he had gotten himself into. He appeared to be an American around 50 years old, but this could not be confirmed since he carried no passport, travel visa, or any other identifying papers. In addition, he did not tell the Army interrogators anything specific about who he was or where he was from, saying only his name and that he was from "different places over there." He reported having no present address in West Germany, no steady means of support, and no means of travel. Somewhat stupefied, the officers asked him just what he planned to do in East Germany. Jerry replied, "Oh, just wander around, here and there. Nothing much—just see stuff, you know?" Jerry was then admitted to the camp infirmary for psychiatric observation. Here he was first diagnosed as schizophrenic and admitted to a U.S. Army hospital in Coburg, West Germany, where he responded well to chlorpromazine (known by the trade name Thorazine), an antipsychotic medication. After a week on medication he became amiable and cooperative, and he was now able to tell the hospital staff some details about his identity and background. The staff eventually tracked down Jerry's parents in Munich, about 140 miles to the south. After five weeks on the ward Jerry seemed to be under control and was discharged to the custody of his parents, who reported that this was the third time Jerry had "wandered off" since he had moved to Munich the previous year. For a month Jerry's parents agonized over what to do with him. They realized they could not control him, but they refused to commit him to an institution. Finally Jerry was sent to live near an aunt in Salt Lake City, Utah.

Jerry's aunt rented a small studio apartment for him and set him up with a job at a local supermarket. On his third day at the market, he walked off the job in the middle of his shift. Jerry returned to his apartment and did not go outside for several weeks; his aunt then became responsible for doing his laundry and shopping for his groceries. One morning at two o'clock, Jerry somehow became locked out of his apartment. He began yelling and banging at the door, and after about 20 minutes he finally broke it down and went inside. After this incident (and numerous other complaints of his odd behavior by neighbors), Jerry's landlord began proceedings to evict him. Jerry's aunt promised to keep a closer eye on him and persuaded the landlord to hold off on the eviction. She then found him a part-time job as a church custodian. However, after two weeks of spotty attendance, Jerry again wandered off the job. This time, however, Jerry did not return to his apartment. After three days Jerry's aunt contacted the police and reported him missing.

Seven months later Jerry was arrested for vagrancy in a small town outside Bakersfield, California. In the meantime, his parents had returned from Europe to the Los Angeles area. The police contacted his parents, who then drove out to Bakersfield to be present at his court hearing. A psychiatric evaluation, conducted at the recommendation of the county district attorney, found Jerry to be incompetent to stand trial. With the consent of his parents, Jerry was committed to a psychiatric institution for treatment. Jerry then entered a psychiatric ward in a Veteran's Administration hospital located in a suburb of Los Angeles.

PERSONAL HISTORY

Jerry's descriptions of his past are for the most part extremely vague and lacking in content. He is unable to specify any dates, places, or events in his life. Occasionally he does provide some information, but most often this is inaccurate. For example, Jerry once reported to a hospital staff psychiatrist that he was an only child, when in fact he has an older brother. As a result, the hospital staff is forced to rely on other sources of information (his parents; his brother; his aunt; various medical, school, and military records) to provide the bulk of his background data. Although these secondary sources provided most of the basic information on the important events in Jerry's life, they could not describe his perceptions of these events or his emotional reactions to them. Sadly, this subjective information is irretrievable.

Jerry is the younger son of two in an upper-middle-class family. His father is a successful executive for a German automobile manufacturer; his mother has never been employed outside the home. According to his family and the available records, his childhood was unremarkable. He seemed to have a happy childhood and got along well with his family. He received good grades throughout school (mostly As and Bs). His parents recall that he seemed to have a successful social life in high school; he dated often and participated in football and track. After high school he enrolled at a large state university to study mechanical engineering. It is in college that his odd behavior first appeared.

Jerry's grades for his freshman year were considerably below his usual performance, averaging in the low C range. His professors, his roommate, and his neighbors in the dormitory confirmed that he was not working up to his potential; they reported that he would frequently miss lectures and assignments. He seemed unconcerned about making friends or becoming active in campus activities, and his phone calls home became more infrequent as the year progressed. During his summer break he refused to work at a job set up by his father and spent most of his time either alone in his room or wandering aimlessly around the neighborhood. When he first returned home from college, Jerry's high school friends frequently came by to see him, but he seemed uninterested in them and made no effort to maintain their friendship. Although Jerry returned to college for the fall semester, it appears that he stayed in his dormitory room for most of the term. His academic work continued to deteriorate, and he wound up failing every course. In addition to having academic difficulties, Jerry was beginning to cause serious problems in his dormitory. His roommate complained that he would spend almost all of his time in his room either sleeping or mumbling to himself. He did not do his laundry the entire semester, and he often went without bathing for stretches of up to 10 days. After eight weeks his roommate demanded to be transferred to another room. Over the winter break Jerry was informed that he would not be allowed to continue at the university because of his academic and social difficulties. After his expulsion he was no longer eligible for a student deferment from military service.

Four months after he left the university Jerry was drafted into the Army. According to his evaluation during basic training, Jerry was found to be of above-average intelligence. However, his records also show that he lacked motivation and paid poor attention to instructions. He was described as a recruit who understood orders and instructions but followed them without any particular concern over what they were or if he would execute them properly. After completing basic training, Jerry was assigned to an ambulance unit in Vietnam. Jerry's combat record was similar to his record as a recruit. He never resisted orders, but he had to be supervised constantly to ensure that he actually carried them out. He was involved in combat on several occasions and once received superficial wounds to both legs. After his combat tour Jerry was assigned to work in the motor pool of an army camp in northern Texas. His stay at this camp was unremarkable aside from the fact that he again was quite indifferent about his assignments and required constant supervision to carry them out. Finally he was discharged from the Army after his two-year hitch was completed.

After his discharge Jerry got a job working at a fast-food restaurant near Wichita Falls, Texas, but he left this job after about a month. Two weeks later he was arrested for shoplifting in Norman, Oklahoma. Apparently Jerry had attempted to walk off with several items from a grocery store. In light of his veteran status and his clean record, however, the store owner decided not to press charges. For the next several years little was heard of Jerry, and his own accounts of this time are not particularly informative. Finally Jerry was arrested for vagrancy and disorderly conduct in Omaha, Nebraska, after he repeatedly harassed passersby in a park, asking strange and incoherent questions on the order of "Where's the freedom land?" and "I want to hear freedom ring!"

During Jerry's tour of duty in Vietnam, his father was transferred to the corporate headquarters in Munich, West Germany. While in the army Jerry corresponded with his family only rarely, and they heard nothing from him for the next three years. Through Jerry's military records, the Omaha police managed to identify him and contact his parents in West Germany. At the insistence of his parents, the court agreed to release Jerry to their care, and they took him to live with them in Munich.

CONCEPTUALIZATION AND TREATMENT

The term *schizophrenia* refers to a collection of diagnostic categories characterized by the presence of severe disturbances in thought, behavior, and interpersonal relationships. These disturbances may be manifested in a number of ways, as described below. In addition, schizophrenia is an episodic disorder characterized by three distinct phases. During the *prodromal phase*, schizophrenics will show a significant deterioration of their social and cognitive functioning from a premorbid level. They tend to withdraw from social situations, neglect their duties and hygiene, have strange thoughts and emotions, and lose energy and initiative. This deterioration in functioning, called "decompensation," is usually the first sign to other people that a serious disorder is present. During the prodromal phase, other people generally describe schizophrenics as "acting differently from their usual selves."

During the *active phase*, markedly psychotic behaviors will emerge. These include delusions (organized thought systems that are based on clearly false or bizarre ideas), hallucinations (vivid but illusory perceptions, usually auditory), disorganized thought patterns, odd speech, gross incoherence, inappropriate or restricted emotional reactions, and severe abnormalities of motor movement. *DSM-III-R* categorizes schizophrenics into five subtypes based on the constellation of symptoms they exhibit during this active phase of their disorder. These subtypes are described below.

As the more florid psychotic behaviors of the active phase recede, schizophrenics enter a *residual phase*. The symptoms of this phase are very similar to those in the prodromal phase with the exception that emotional blunting (lack of emotional reactivity) and a neglect for one's duties are particularly pronounced in the residual phase. Other signs that may linger from the active phase are illogical thinking and some relatively mild delusions and hallucinations. The majority of schizophrenics display some cycling of active symptoms and residual symptoms for the rest of their lives; a complete absence of symptoms, known as *remission*, is rare.

As noted above, *DSM-III-R* distinguishes five subtypes of schizophrenia based on the particular pattern of symptoms that are exhibited during the active phase of the disorder. These five subtypes are labeled the catatonic type, disorganized type, paranoid type, undifferentiated type, and residual type.

Catatonic schizophrenia is characterized by severe disturbances in psychomotor behavior. Catatonics are frequently mute and unresponsive to the behavior of other people. They may assume rigid, passive, or otherwise bizarre postures. In some cases catatonics also show brief periods of wild, excited, and purposeless activity. One unifying quality of virtually all catatonics is that they are almost completely unresponsive to their environment.

Disorganized schizophrenics are also characterized by strange, incoherent, and often silly behavior. However, their symptoms reflect gross disturbances in their thought processes as opposed to their psychomotor processes. Their speech tends to be characterized by loose associations (unpredictably drifting from one topic to another), neologisms (made-up words others do not understand), and clanging (silly, rhyming sounds). Disorganized schizophrenics also tend to show emotions that are utterly inappropriate for their current situation, such as crying when hearing a joke. In contrast to catatonics, most disorganized schizophrenics appear to be somewhat responsive to their environment. They will answer questions, notice objects, and recall events. For most people, however, these responses are bizarre, incomprehensible, and unpredictable.

Paranoid schizophrenics are preoccupied with elaborate delusional systems, usually relating to themes of grandiosity, persecution, jealousy, and/or suspiciousness. The cast of these delusional systems typically involves divine or supernatural beings, important figures from the schizophrenic's life, or images from history or the media. Unless they are in the process of acting on their delusions, paranoid schizophrenics usually appear to act fairly normally, at least at a superficial level. As they become more involved in their strange ideation, however, the full extent of their delusional thinking becomes apparent to other people.

Undifferentiated schizophrenics either display prominent psychotic symptoms from more than one of the above categories or show symptoms that do not fit easily into any of the above categories. Thus, schizophrenia, undifferentiated type is a "garbage can" label that characterizes schizophrenics who exhibit the psychotic symptoms of an active phase but cannot be described by any of the three known subtypes.

Schizophrenics categorized as residual type have not shown a clear history of the bizarre or delusional behavior of an active phase. However, they do exhibit relatively mild signs of schizophrenia such as disrupted daily functioning, social withdrawal, blunted affect, and illogical thinking. Most residual schizophrenics have a long-standing history of more or less continuous symptoms. In some cases there is evidence of a past active phase, but the details of this behavior are not sufficiently clear to allow a diagnosis of any particular subtype. Residual schizophrenics are responsive to specific stimuli in their environment, but their lives taken as a whole generally lack meaning and coherence. They seem to have a severe deficit in many of the higher-order abilities most people take for granted, such as setting life goals, making plans, and taking on and fulfilling responsibilities.

Jerry is a 37-year-old white male, though most people report that he looks to be in his late forties or early fifties. His IQ is above average, but his life seems to have little meaning or coherence. He appears to be unconcerned about the events of his life, and he also shows little emotion in his day-to-day existence. For example, he is not at all concerned by his lack of a permanent home, a steady job, companionship, or even a reasonably consistent source of food. He habitually withdraws from social situations, frequently wandering off from his home or job without any perceptible purpose or plan. When he does engage in conversation, his speech is vague and lacking in content, as illustrated by his intake interview at the VA hospital:

Therapist: Jerry, you left Salt Lake City about seven months ago, right?

Jerry: Yeah, I guess.

Therapist: So, what did you do during that time?

Jerry: Oh, I don't know. Different things I guess.

Therapist: Like what?

Jerry: You know, this and that. Nothing special.

Therapist: Well, like what? What did you do? Did you work?

Jerry: Oh, well, I did odd jobs. You know.

Therapist: What kind of odd jobs?

Jerry: Little things here and there.

Therapist: Like what? Can you think of any particular one?

Jerry: Um, yeah. I was a janitor for a while.

Therapist: How long did you do that?

Jerry: Not long.

Therapist: What's "not long"? A few days, weeks, months?

Jerry: A few days, I guess.

Therapist: Did you get paid for that?

Jerry: No, I don't think so.

Therapist: Well, how did you get money?

Jerry: Different ways.

Therapist: What kind of different ways?

Jerry: You know, odd jobs and stuff.

Therapist: Well, tell me this. How did you eat?

Jerry: You know, garbage.

(Later)

Therapist: Of all the places you were, where did you like it best?

Jerry: Arizona, I guess.

Therapist: Why Arizona?

159

Jerry: Oh, different reasons.
Therapist: Could you name one?
Jerry: Well, it's drier there.
Therapist: Do you mean it's less humid?
Jerry: No, not really.
Therapist: Well, what then?
Jerry: The ground's drier.
Therapist: What do you mean, "The ground is drier"?
Jerry: Well, there's less dew when you wake up.
Therapist: Oh, I see.

Jerry is also characterized by an almost complete absence of any emotional reaction. His blunted affect is illustrated by the following excerpt from the same interview:

Therapist: So, you were in an ambulance unit in Vietnam?
Jerry: Uh huh.
Therapist: Did you see any combat.
Jerry: Some.
Therapist: How often?
Jerry: A couple of times.
Therapist: How many times? Once, twice?
Jerry: I don't know. Ten or twelve, maybe.
Therapist: Could you describe what it was like?
Jerry: Oh, well, you know, lots of blood and stuff. Smoke. People yelling a lot. You know.
Therapist: Were you frightened?
Jerry: I guess so.
Therapist: What did you think about?
Jerry: Different things, nothing really. I just did my job.

Recollections of combat are very traumatic for most veterans. Either they are frightened and disturbed by the memories themselves, or they are bothered by the fact that these horrible memories do *not* disturb them. Jerry does not appear to have any kind of a reaction to these memories whatsoever. He tries to answer the questions as best he can, but his answers seem strangely distant and matter-of-fact.

Jerry's social withdrawal, his blunted affect, his peculiar lack of motivation or initiative, and his vague, uninformative speech all indicate the existence of a long-standing thought disorder that appeared to first emerge in college. At a concrete level he understands his own behaviors and the behaviors of those around him, but he fails to grasp the meaning or purpose of these behaviors. This pervasive lack of comprehension and purpose, especially in the absence of any full-blown psychotic symptoms, characterizes someone suffering from schizophrenia, residual type. Since his symptoms have existed for more than two years, his residual schizophrenia is categorized as chronic. (Patients with a history of psychotic symptoms between six months and two years in duration would be categorized as sub-chronic; those with shorter histories would not be diagnosed as schizophrenic.)

Jerry's history also included references to occasional agitated outbursts, such as beating down his door and harassing people in a park. These outbursts seem to indicate the emergence of active phases of Jerry's schizophrenic disorder. By the general descriptions of these outbursts, Jerry would probably be characterized as a disorganized or paranoid schizophrenic. Unfortunately, the information available from Jerry's records is not detailed enough to accurately determine which of these labels is most appropriate, or even if the outbursts indicate an active phase at all. Since the active phases of Jerry's illness cannot be classified reliably, the appropriate diagnosis for Jerry at his most recent hospitalization is chronic schizophrenia, residual type.

As is the case for most chronic schizophrenics, Jerry's treatment is primarily pharmacological. Upon admission to the VA hospital, he was given Thorazine at a standard maintenance

161

dosage of 100 milligrams four times a day. This treatment regimen serves two purposes. First, it is intended to promote the highest possible level of Jerry's functioning by minimizing his residual symptoms. Second and perhaps more importantly, this regimen is aimed at preventing a reoccurrence of an active phase of his disorder. Since Jerry's history includes only isolated instances of psychotic behavior, his therapists are confident that this maintenance dose will be effective in warding off the reemergence of any future active phase. Patients who are presently in an active phase or who have a history of frequent decompensations generally are given higher doses.

In addition to taking medication, Jerry also participates in various therapeutic activities designed to improve his social and occupational skills. On Tuesdays and Fridays, the patients and the therapeutic staff (therapists, interns, and nurses) of Jerry's ward gather together for community meetings. To promote their sense of control and responsibility, the patients are put in charge of these meetings. One patient is chosen to be the discussion leader, and another is chosen as the secretary, who will organize the proceedings and take minutes. These biweekly community meetings allow the patients to raise issues and concerns in the presence of the entire ward and are intended to facilitate direct discussions among the patients and between the patients and staff. The primary focus of these discussions usually concerns practical issues on the ward (e.g., who is leaving or joining the ward, the policy on issuing day passes, information on field trips and events). The patients also participate in group therapy sessions. These sessions involve only a few patients at a time and are led by a single staff member. The object of these groups is to discuss interpersonal issues that are of concern to individual patients. The smaller size of these groups makes it possible for an individual patient's problems to be addressed more thoroughly and in a more open and frank manner.

Like most of the patients, Jerry was not particularly interested in participating in either group activity. After a few weeks on the ward, however, Jerry was elected as the group secretary, an activity which had several positive, though indirect, effects.

This activity forced him to interact with other patients just to organize the meetings. He also had to review the minutes of the last session prior to reading them, and he had to pay close attention during each meeting. Jerry's acceptance of these responsibilities was a positive sign.

A prime topic in group therapy was Jerry's indifference to social relationships. Jerry and his group leader set up a behavioral contract that reinforced him (through public recognition and added ward privileges) for spending time interacting with other patients and staff members. Jerry responded to this contingency almost immediately. Instead of spending most of his recreation time alone, he began to take long walks around the hospital grounds with other patients. He also became much more involved in ward outings and other special events. For example, during an observation visit by a group of graduate students, Jerry approached several students and struck up a conversation. He had a friendly attitude and was responsive to their questions, although the students found the actual content of his speech to be rambling and rather uninformative. Nevertheless, even this limited approach behavior represented a big advance for Jerry.

Another aspect of Jerry's treatment program involved limited vocational training. As patients' symptoms begin to recede and become more manageable, they are enrolled in supervised workshops run by the hospital. Here they are trained to perform unskilled tasks (washing dishes, sorting cartons, etc.). Some patients are placed into semiskilled workshops. The therapeutic importance of this training is not in learning the vocational skills per se but rather in developing the discipline needed to hold a steady job. Jerry received carpentry training and presently works in the hospital's wood finishing shop, where patients refurbish used or abandoned furniture. This furniture is then used by the hospital or sold to the public.

The next step in the program is to discharge the patients from the ward and set them up in semi-independent apartments, which are located in a complex about three miles from the hospital. Patients live in individual studio apartments and are responsible for their own food, laundry, transportation, and entertainment. The rent of the apartments is controlled, and the hospital can arrange to pay a patient's rent directly if he or she proves to be incapable of doing so. In addition, the patients are supervised by a staff member who lives in the apartment complex.

After six weeks on the ward, Jerry moved into his apartment. He works at the wood finishing shop three days a week and attends group therapy once a week. He has had no problems taking public buses to the hospital, and his attendance at work and at group therapy has remained good (around 90 percent). He seems to have no problem in performing his personal errands, such as shopping and doing his laundry. One month after moving into his apartment, Jerry's medication was reduced to 200 milligrams per day; for the past eight months he has been maintained on this relatively low dose and appears to be doing well. Jerry's only particularly noticeable symptom is his persistent disinterest in forming interpersonal relationships.

PROGNOSIS

On the whole, Jerry seems to be functioning well in his structured job and sheltered living situation. Many of his more pronounced residual symptoms, such as his inability to feed and clothe himself and his unwillingness to stay at a job, have decreased as he has developed a more steady, normal routine. In all likelihood, though, Jerry will need to continue living in a fairly sheltered environment and taking his medication to maintain these therapeutic gains and prevent a reoccurrence of his more serious psychotic symptoms. As is the case with most chronic schizophrenics, getting Jerry to continue taking his medication is the key to his prognosis. Provided he remains in his supervised apartment and continues to take his antipsychotic medication, there is little reason to believe that Jerry's level of functioning will change significantly in the foreseeable future. Although his treatment has enabled him to live somewhat independently and even to be productive, there is little chance that Jerry will ever become truly autonomous. Thus, his prognosis is poor, and the goal of treatment, like that of most chronic schizophrenics, is continued maintenance, not cure.

DISCUSSION

The schizophrenias constitute a diverse class of disorders that progress through distinct phases and manifest themselves in a variety of ways. To make matters even more complex, schizophrenics show great individual differences in their behavior patterns. Some will show residual symptoms almost continuously and will decompensate into an active phase only rarely, if ever. Some will display a single acute, psychotic episode without a reoccurrence. Still others will alternate cyclically between episodes of mild, residual symptoms and florid, psychotic behavior. Furthermore, psychiatric professionals have found it very difficult, if not impossible, to predict when a particular patient will enter an active phase. Thus, estimates of the percentage of schizophrenics who fall into each of these groups at any given time vary widely, although it is generally agreed that about 1 percent of the population will suffer some form of schizophrenia during their lifetimes (Regier et al., 1988; Robins et al., 1984).

The majority of schizophrenics exhibit residual symptoms most of the time, and these symptoms are the most commonly observed signs of the disorder. Interestingly, the public perception of schizophrenia seems to be based almost exclusively on the psychotic symptoms that emerge during the active phase of the disorder. While these bizarre and seemingly "crazy" behaviors are very vivid, they are less frequently observed than are the more mild residual symptoms. This is particularly true since the majority of schizophrenics who demonstrate severe psychotic symptoms are quickly separated from the public and brought to psychiatric wards and institutions.

Although it is clear that schizophrenia has a genetic component (Gottesman, McGuffin, & Farmer, 1987), at the present time little is known about the causes of schizophrenia (Landrine, 1989). So far, therapists have not been successful in bringing about a cure for this disorder. However, a number of antipsychotic drugs, first prescribed in the 1950s, have proved to be very effective in eliminating the overt, psychotic behavior demonstrated in the active phase. Unfortunately these drugs have had only a limited effect on patients' residual symptoms. Thus, treatment for schizophrenics is primarily through the administration of antipsychotic medication with the goal of decreasing their psychotic symptoms and controlling their residual symptoms to a point where they can function at a more manageable and productive level. Most schizophrenic patients, at least during the initial stages of their treatment, are prescribed a phenothiazine such as Thorazine because of its relatively mild side effects. If this proves ineffective, the patient may then be switched to a butyrophenone such as haloperidol (Haldol).

When prescribing antipsychotic medication, psychiatrists must keep several issues in mind. First, the dosage is carefully monitored to correspond to the patients' needs. Patients who are in the midst of an active phase are given a relatively large dose (up to 1200 milligrams per day of Thorazine, for example) to counteract their blatantly psychotic behavior. As these symptoms subside, their medication is gradually reduced to a maintenance level. Some patients will show notable improvement in their residual symptoms while at a maintenance level, and their dosage may be further reduced.

Occasionally a patient will not show any residual signs following the abatement of the psychotic symptoms. In these rare cases the patient is not likely to suffer a psychotic break in the near future and may be withdrawn from medication entirely. It is possible that the person suffers from another disorder with psychotic features, such as bipolar disorder or organic delusional syndrome.

A second consideration in prescribing antipsychotic medication is making sure the patients actually take their medication. Most patients who take antipsychotic medication suffer some side effects, including nausea, grogginess, and irritability. Without supervision, most schizophrenics discontinue their medication soon after they are released. Subsequently they slowly decompensate back to an active phase, and at this point they are readmitted for treatment and again given antipsychotic medication. This cycle of treatment and decompensation has become known as the "revolving door syndrome." This problem has become more widespread as the number of available psychiatric beds declines, limiting most facilities to short-term pharmacological treatment.

Sometimes the patients' odd cognitions in and of themselves may interfere with pharmacological treatment. One case, for example, involved a paranoid schizophrenic's delusions concerning thioridazine (Mellaril) tablets, which are either green, yellow, or pink, depending on the dosage. This patient refused to take any green pills, saying they were poisoned. As a result the staff had to make sure to keep a supply of pink Mellaril tablets available.

A third consideration is for therapists to be aware of other medications and/or drugs the patient may also be taking. The home environments of many patients, especially those in poor urban areas, commonly include alcohol and illicit drugs. Sometimes friends or family members even attempt to smuggle drugs into the psychiatric wards. As much as possible, the staff must avoid prescribing medication that may have an adverse, or even lethal, interaction with other substances.

Finally, therapists must be wary of the possible side effects of medication, particularly a condition known as tardive dyskensia, a condition of impaired motor movements and shakiness resulting from prolonged pharmacological treatment. Rittmannsberger and Schony (1986) recommend frequent reviews of medication dosages.

Despite these limitations, pharmacological therapy remains the most effective treatment for the schizophrenias. Residential programs that provide schizophrenics with a sheltered environment and family behavioral treatments that teach symptom management (Terrier, 1991) seem to provide some gains over pharmacological therapy alone. Thus, a combination of antipsychotic medication and a sheltered environment appears to be the best method now available for fostering at least a minimal level of functioning and preventing the onset of future active phases.

Jerry received a very comprehensive treatment that effectively combined pharmacological therapy and residential therapy. Jerry's treatment was atypical in that he was able to benefit from the outstanding facilities of the particular VA program he entered. The vast majority of treatment programs for schizophrenics do not possess the facilities of Jerry's VA treatment; most are short-term programs that can afford to treat only the most severely psychotic schizophrenics on a "crisis management" basis. Because of a lack of sheltered housing, patients whose overtly psychotic symptoms have subsided after a few weeks are often simply released. In many cases these schizophrenics have no steady home or family, and they just wander the streets until their next active phase emerges. For most schizophrenics, this revolving door syndrome will be a behavior pattern that will predominate the rest of their lives.

PRIMARY DEGENERATIVE DEMENTIA OF THE ALZHEIMER TYPE, SENILE ONSET
Supportive Therapy

PRESENTING COMPLAINT

Emma is a 74-year-old woman who lives alone in a small town in central Indiana. She has been widowed for six years. Her daughter and son-in-law, Susan and Bill, also live in this town and visit her several times a week.

Approximately two months ago Emma and Susan went on a shopping trip to Indianapolis. Emma seemed to enjoy the ride to the city, and she and Susan engaged in friendly, although somewhat vacuous and disorganized, conversation. When they arrived downtown, Emma became very confused. She did not know where she was or why she was there. She asked seemingly foolish questions, such as "What's the name of this place?" and "Why are you taking me here?" She became very upset and asked her daughter to take her home again. Susan was very much surprised by the extent of her mother's disorientation, and she tried to explain where they were and the purpose of the trip. Emma continued to be confused, however. Seeing little use in continuing the outing, they drove home.

When they returned to Emma's house, Susan noticed other signs that something was wrong with her mother. Emma had left her stove on, and she had also left a pan with scrambled eggs in the refrigerator. Emma could not say how long the stove had been on or when she had put the pan in the refrigerator; in fact, she had no memory of having made scrambled eggs at all. She soon became very upset and refused to answer Susan's questions. She then asked Susan to leave.

That evening Susan called to check up on her mother and ask if she was feeling ill. Emma denied having any problems and asked Susan why she might have thought so. Emma had only a vague memory of their trip that morning and no recollection whatsoever of their argument.

The next day Susan took Emma to see their family physician. He found nothing wrong with her physically, but he did notice that she appeared to remember very little about recent events and seemed somewhat disoriented during the examination. He then referred her for a more detailed neuropsychological examination at the neurology clinic of a nearby hospital. Emma was given a battery of diagnostic tests, including a CT (computerized axial tomography) scan, an EEG (electroencephalogram), and various blood tests. After analyzing the results of these tests, the neurologist found evidence of cortical atrophy and nonspecific, bilateral brain wave slowing. He was noncommittal about his diagnosis, but he mentioned the possibility of Alzheimer's disease. Susan and Bill were dissatisfied with this diagnosis and sought a second opinion. They were referred to the neurology clinic of a major hospital in Indianapolis.

PERSONAL HISTORY

Susan and Bill drove Emma to the neurology clinic in Indianapolis. Emma appeared nervous, confused, and disoriented during the initial interview with the neurologist; Susan provided the bulk of Emma's history.

Emma was born in Chicago, the daughter of Swedish immigrants who came to Illinois at the turn of the century. She was the second child of six: two boys and four girls. She had an eighth-grade education and worked as a store clerk in Chicago until her marriage when she was 22 years old. She had Susan two years later; medical complications during the birth prevented her from having any more children. When Emma was 40 years old, she took a job as a teller at a local bank. In accordance with company policy, she retired when she was 65.

Emma's medical history is unremarkable. She is described by her daughter as a "light social drinker." When she was first married, she smoked tobacco occasionally, but she then quit and has not smoked in over 40 years. She has no history of any head injury, thyroid disease, or any other serious medical problem. Fifteen years ago she had cataract surgery without any complications.

The medical history of Emma's family of origin is somewhat unclear. Her mother died about 20 years ago at the age of 81, and her father died over 50 years ago when Emma was still a teenager. Susan cannot state the cause of their deaths other than saying that Emma's mother died of "old age." Emma's husband had a history of coronary disease and died six years ago from cardiac arrest. One brother was diagnosed as having Alzheimer's disease before he passed away four years ago; her other siblings are still alive.

According to Susan, Emma suffers from "minor mood problems" involving occasional feelings of anxiety and depression. Fifteen months ago Emma was prescribed the tricyclic anti-depressant doxepin (trade name Sinequan), and she continues to take a very small maintenance dose of 30 milligrams per day. Other than this, Emma has no history of any psychiatric disorder. She takes no other medication.

When the neurologist asked Susan to describe Emma's "minor mood problems" in more detail, she replied:

Mom was fine until a couple of years ago. She had been living alone for about four years. About this time she started staying home a lot. She didn't seem to want to go out much, even to visit friends, and she started calling us less often. She seemed to get angry and irritable with other people much easier than she used to. She also starting getting confused about things—where she kept different things around the house and who she talked to, that sort of thing. This was all pretty gradual. Lately she's been very hesitant to do things on her own. It seems that I take her just about everywhere now: shopping, to the beauty parlor, to the bank. And you know about the trip to Indianapolis.

About a year ago we took her to a gerontology specialist. We told him what we had been noticing, but he didn't seem to know what was wrong. He gave her medication for her anxiety, though. She still takes it, but it doesn't seem to help much; actually she seems to be getting worse. As you know, we saw another neurologist two weeks ago, but he also didn't seem to know what was wrong.

CONCEPTUALIZATION AND TREATMENT

Emma's failing memory and increasingly frequent periods of profound disorientation suggest that she is suffering from a progressive dementia. According to *DSM-III-R*, dementia (familiarly known as "senility") is a condition marked by a significant impairment in higher cortical function. Characteristic symptoms include feelings of confusion and disorientation in familiar settings, memory loss, difficulty in maintaining concentration, impairment in one's ability to exercise good judgment and think abstractly, and an increase in irritability and aggression. In many cases there may be evidence of paranoid delusions and hallucinations, aphasia (disruptions in the ability to use or understand language), agnosia (inability to recognize familiar objects or events), and apraxia (difficulty in carrying out coordinated actions such as cooking or dressing).

Several neuropsychological tests have been developed to measure the extent of a person's dementia. One is the Blessed Test (Blessed, Tomlinson, and Roth, 1968). The Blessed Test is a 33-item questionnaire that assesses the patient's functioning in the following areas: orientation (the patient's name, the time and date, the present location), memory (place of birth, names of family members), and concentration (adding two numbers, counting backward). The patient scores one point for every question he or she cannot answer correctly. Thus, the higher the score on this test, the more extensive the cortical impairment.

Emma scored 24 on the Blessed Test. She was able to state her name and her place of birth, and she knew the names of close family members. However, she failed at tasks that made use of less personal information. She did not know the correct date, the day of the week, or the month. She could not say where she was, or even that she was in a hospital. She could not recall an address or a series of numbers given to her five minutes before (or even that they had been given to her). She was also unable to count backward. When she was asked to add 8 and 5, she appeared confused and copied these numbers over and over.

Emma's responses on this test indicate moderate to severe impairment in her cognitive abilities. This finding is not wholly surprising, considering Susan's description of her odd behavior. Another factor consistent with this result is her age. Whereas dementia is rare for persons under 50, the prevalence of this disorder increases greatly with age.

About half of all cases of dementia are of the Alzheimer type, commonly referred to as "Alzheimer's disease." This form of dementia is marked by an insidious onset and a gradual but inexorable deterioration in a multitude of intellectual abilities (Grady et al., 1988). Memory, judgment, and decision-making processes are affected, and personality changes may be noticed. Agitation and irritability are common, and paranoid delusions and hallucinations may be present. Patients experience difficulty in comprehending complex and abstract problems, but in time the ability to perform even simple tasks is impaired. Eventually the patients are no longer able to care for themselves.

Unfortunately there is no practical test to demonstrate the existence of Alzheimer's disease; the only conclusive evidence is the existence of senile plaques and neurofibrillary bundles. Unfortunately, these can be detected only by brain biopsy, which is usually conducted at autopsy. (Brain biopsy has been used for premorbid diagnosis of Alzheimer's disease, but only in extraordinary cases where there is a good possibility of finding another potentially treatable cause of dementia, such as chronic alcohol use or stroke). Without a reliable positive indicator, diagnosticians are left to rely on negative indicators; that is, they must rule out other known causes of dementia. At this point a tentative but more or less reliable *DSM-III-R* diagnosis of primary degenerative dementia of the Alzheimer type is made. When symptoms manifest themselves before age 65, the disorder is said to have a presenile onset; symptoms that emerge after age 65 indicate a senile onset. Some researchers (Barclay, Zemcov, Blass, & McDowell, 1985) argue that a presenile onset marks a more severe form of the disorder with a more malignant course, but others (Grady et al., 1987) have found no differences between patients with early and late onset.

Emma's neurologist could not identify any known cause of her symptoms. The failure to identify a specific cause of her disorder, combined with the insidious onset and the gradual but steady progression of her symptoms, led him to conclude that the chances were about 90 percent that she suffered from Alzheimer's disease.

At the present time there is no known treatment for the primary symptoms of this disorder, and therapy typically focuses on the families who must now deal with the profound burden of caring for the Alzheimer patient (Pruchno, Michaels, & Potashnik, 1990). Thus, treatment for Emma mostly comes in the form of supportive therapy for her and her family. This therapy has several purposes. First, it can inform the patient and his or her family what the disease is and what they can expect in terms of functioning. Second, this therapy can suggest several tricks to aid the patient's memory and concentration, thus prolonging his or her ability to function independently. Third, this therapy gives both the patient and the family a place to air frustrations and complaints. Last, and perhaps most important, this therapy helps the patient, and especially the family, to cope with the relentless progression of this disorder.

Immediately after Emma's diagnosis, she and Susan began meeting with a counselor from the hospital once a week. Gradually these meetings became less frequent until they were held approximately once a month. These sessions provided Emma with an empathic listener with whom she could share her doubts, fears, and frustrations. Emma also found her counselor to be a useful sounding board for her complaints, especially those concerning Susan.

The counselor also provided Emma and Susan with some specific tricks to help them cope with Emma's impaired memory and judgment. First, the counselor suggested that other people ask Emma direct recognition questions instead of recall questions. The counselor explained that often memory is aided when a person is asked to decide whether a given event had happened or not (recognition) rather than having to generate the event from memory (recall). For example, Emma found it easier to answer a question such as "Did you have eggs or cereal for breakfast?" instead of "What did you have for breakfast?" Similarly, "Was that Gladys on the phone?" was easier to answer than "Who was that on the phone?"

A second set of tricks was designed to reduce Emma's increasing confusion about her routine, everyday tasks. To help Emma remember to perform these minor chores, Susan put labels around the house. Thus, a label on Emma's nightstand reading "Take your pill" reminded her to take her medication at bedtime. Labels near the door also reminded her to lock the door and to turn off the stove. Since Emma forgot which light switches controlled certain lights, Susan labeled each switch with its target: "Hall Light," "Kitchen Light," "Porch Light," and so on. As Emma's aphasia worsened, she gradually lost her ability to recognize the words on these labels. At this point Susan, with a fair amount of ingenuity, added pictures to many of the labels.

Third, because Emma often lost her place in the middle of doing her chores or errands, she (or more often Susan) wrote out directions for various everyday tasks. For instance, the particular steps involved in doing the laundry were written out in detail and attached to the washing machine. Emma found it easier to complete these tasks if she had some concrete set of directions to refer to when she forgot her place in the sequence of steps.

An important aspect of counseling is to provide reassurance and encouragement to the families of Alzheimer patients, who often need this help as much as the patients themselves. One issue that emerges early is simply trying to accept the disease. Susan was particularly slow to acknowledge the fact that her mother had developed a gradual, terminal disease. One indication of her denial was the great discrepancy between her description of her mother's behaviors and Emma's performance on neuropsychological tests. Susan reported that Emma suffered from "getting confused" and had "minor mood problems." In contrast, Emma's Blessed Test score of 24 provides evidence of considerable cognitive impairment. Another indication of Susan's denial was her refusal to accept the findings of Emma's first neurological examination. As the neurologist stated, "I get the distinct impression that Susan just refuses to believe that her mother has Alzheimer's disease." Once she finally accepted the diagnosis of Alzheimer's disease, Susan was able to care for her mother in a more constructive way. Much of her frustration at Emma's seemingly illogical behaviors evaporated. She became more aware of the many signs of her mother's dementia, and she became more patient and caring. She was eager to set up the various memory "tricks" around Emma's home. She also made an effort to explain

Emma's condition to friends, who had been surprised by the mother's apathetic and sometimes hostile attitude. She decided to take over Emma's financial affairs as well.

PROGNOSIS

Six months after her visit to the clinic in Indianapolis, Emma was unable to recall the majority of recent events, most noticeably conversations she had had with her family or friends. She was frequently disoriented and increasingly had great difficulty linking individual actions into purposeful behaviors. One by one she gave up her friendships (usually because she failed even to recognize her friends and acquaintances), and she gradually became more irritable around her daughter.

After a year she was brought back to the neurologist in Indianapolis and given a follow-up examination. As he predicted, her deterioration was marked. She now scored 31 on the Blessed Test. She was able to provide only her name and place of birth, and she did not appear to understand most other questions.

After another year her cognitive functioning had deteriorated to the point where she was unable to care for herself. She could no longer dress or wash herself and was frequently incontinent. At this point, Susan was spending virtually all her time at her mother's home. With the encouragement of her husband and her counselor, Susan finally decided to place Emma in a nursing home. There Emma's cognitive abilities continued to deteriorate, and she died of pneumonia approximately 18 months later.

DISCUSSION

Studies conducted in various countries report that roughly 5 percent of the population over 65 years of age suffers from some form of dementia (R. L. Martin, 1989; Shibayama, Kasahara, & Kobayashi, 1986), and about half of the dementia cases are of the Alzheimer type (Brayne & Calloway, 1989; Shibayama et al.). Women are roughly twice as likely as men to suffer from the disease (A. S. Henderson, 1990; Llorca, Note, Michel, & Aunoud-Castiglioni, 1989). The prevalence of Alzheimer's disease increases exponentially with age. For example, a Canadian study (Gautrin, Froda, Tetreault, & Gauvreau, 1990) found Alzheimer Type dementia in 1 percent of those aged 65 to 74, 4 percent in those aged 75 to 84, and 10.5 percent in those aged 85 or older.

Like other forms of dementia, Alzheimer's disease is characterized by a general cerebral atrophy (wasting away), which can be identified by CT and MRI (magnetic resonance imaging) brain scans as an enlargement of the lateral ventricles, particularly the third (right) ventricle (Luxenberg et al., 1987). Another indication is lowered cortical metabolism as shown on PET (positive emission tomography) scans. However, these neurological tests are not absolute indicators of the disease. Cerebral atrophy can also occur in patients with other forms of dementia as well as in cognitively normal subjects, and many Alzheimer patients do not show these neurological abnormalities. Another non-specific finding in dementia is an EEG showing slow, diffuse patterns, but again, this may occur in subjects without Alzheimer's disease.

Many neuropsychological tests to measure dementia are also available. In addition to the Blessed Test, researchers (Haxby et al., 1990; Knopman & Ryberg, 1989; Salmon, Thal, Butters, & Heindel, 1990; Satz, van Gorp, Soper, & Mitsushima, 1987) have used the Mini Mental State Exam (MMSE) (Folstein, Folstein, & McHugh, 1975) and the Wechsler Adult Intelligence Scale, Revised (WAIS-R) (Wechsler, 1958) among others. Generally, abnormalities appear earlier in neurological scans than they do in neuropsychological tests (Haxby et al., 1990).

The course of Alzheimer's disease is one of gradual, progressive cortical deterioration. Cognitive impairments such as memory loss and disorientation become increasingly pervasive. Typically the patient also experiences increased agitation and apathy as the disorder worsens (Deutsch & Rovner, 1991). The patient may withdraw almost completely from social interactions. In severe cases the patient will experience difficulties in walking and may become bedridden. Eventually the patient may lose his or her ability to perform even the most routine task such as eating (Volicer et al., 1989) and may require constant supervision. Only a minority of the patients with Alzheimer's disease die as a direct result of their dementia; however, their prolonged illness makes them especially vulnerable to opportunistic diseases such as pneumonia that ordinarily would not be fatal. The duration of Alzheimer's disease varies widely among individuals, though there is some evidence that men succumb somewhat more quickly than women (Barclay et al., 1985; Nee et al., 1987). For any particular case, the duration of the illness depends in large measure on how alert the patient's family is to his or her condition and how quick they are to respond when medical problems arise. Generally, though, the outlook is rather bleak; Belloni-Sonzogni et al. (1989) followed a group of Alzheimer's patients in an Italian geriatric institution over four years and observed a mortality rate of 86.9 percent.

Emma's case is fairly typical. The insidious onset of her cognitive impairment, the gradual progression of her symptoms, her deepening social withdrawal and irritability, her complete loss of the ability to care for herself, and her final submission to an opportunistic disease are all sadly common.

Another typical aspect of this case was Susan's denial of her mother's disorder. Because of the insidious onset of Alzheimer's disease, few family members notice any abrupt behavioral changes. Although most detect memory impairment and disorientation, these symptoms are frequently dismissed as part of "growing old."

As a result of the obvious physiological base of the patients' symptoms and the need to rule out competing diagnoses, the diagnostic focus in these cases is almost exclusively on the medical and neurological aspects of the patients' histories. Factors that would be ignored in most psychiatric evaluations are of vital importance, and patient histories tend to be limited to past diseases, surgeries, physical traumas, medication, and psychiatric disorders. In particular, factors that may support a competing diagnosis (high blood pressure, hypothyroidism, a history of depression) are investigated closely. Little weight is given to subjective experiences; in fact, most case histories are provided by family members and not by the patients themselves. Attention is paid to personal feelings, concerns, or memories only to the extent that they may provide information about the existence or extent of the patients' dementia. Since no medical or psychological cure for this disorder is known, in most cases therapy is limited to supportive counseling for the patients and their families.

Alzheimer's disease is a profoundly disturbing and frightening experience for the patient, and taking care of someone with Alzheimer's disease is an emotionally and physically taxing responsibility, particularly if the patient is a close relative (Deutsch & Rovner, 1991; Pruchno et al., 1990). For these reasons, supportive therapy is very important, perhaps more so for the families of these patients than for the patients themselves. For many family members, the information about the nature and progression of the disease and reassurance that the patient's behavior is largely involuntary are the most valuable aspects of therapy. This knowledge often helps the family members remain patient and calm in particularly trying situations.

Another common problem involves the level of commitment and responsibility family members often take on (Pruchno et al., 1990). Some report feeling a great sense of duty to the patient (who is usually a spouse or parent) and avoid being away from him or her, even briefly, lest some unfortunate accident or mishap should occur. As the patient becomes more impaired, the caretaker finds it increasingly difficult to meet the demands of his or her own life while looking after the constant needs of the patient. Feelings of frustration and resentment are common, as are pangs of guilt. Typically the central focus of counseling at this stage of the disorder is to address these very issues. Family members are told not to let the patient's needs disrupt their own lives. If the patient degenerates to the point where constant care is necessary, they are encouraged to accept this fact and either hire a private nurse or companion, or place the patient in a nursing home. Institutionalizing a patient, particularly a spouse or parent, is a very difficult decision, and supportive therapy aids the caretakers in coming to grips with this painful issue.

BULIMIA NERVOSA
Cognitive-Behavioral Therapy

PRESENTING COMPLAINT

Jill is a 25-year-old single woman who works as a flight attendant for a major airline. After getting home from a flight late at night, Jill went out to a local convenience store and bought a half gallon of chocolate ice cream, a 1-pound box of cookies, a medium-sized frozen pizza, a loaf of French bread, and a quart of milk. When she got home, she put the pizza in the oven and waited impatiently for it to cook; everything else stayed on the table. When the pizza was just edible, she brought it out and placed it with the other food. She then lunged into the food and ate everything she bought as quickly as she could, stuffing in huge mouthfuls and dribbling milk, crumbs, and pizza sauce down her chin and on her blouse. When she finished, she ran to the bathroom, knelt in front of the toilet, thrust her hand down her throat, and vomited everything she had just eaten.

The next day Jill consulted an internist for help concerning recent periods of weakness and dizziness. After performing a routine examination, he asked her about her eating habits. Jill was extremely embarrassed and guilty about describing these to him, but she felt that if she wanted to get well, she had to tell the truth. She confessed to a long-standing pattern of uncontrollably consuming extremely large quantities of food (known as binge eating) and then vomiting this food (purging). This binge-purge pattern began years ago, but it has become more severe and more frequent since Jill began working as a flight attendant. When he asked her to describe her eating pattern in more detail, she awkwardly described last night's binge and purge. According to Jill, this was a fairly typical amount of food for a binge, which she usually finishes within 20 minutes. She almost always induces vomiting right after binge eating, usually by sticking her hand down her throat. Occasionally she has used other objects, including a popcicle stick, a spoon, and a folded electric cord.

Jill admitted that her eating behavior must appear very strange to him; it felt strange to her. But she felt she couldn't control it, especially when she was at home. She goes through this binge-purge cycle once or twice a day when she is at home; she can control herself "on the road" and only rarely binges when she is traveling. On average she estimates that she binges around four times per week. She also swallows "a handful" of laxatives (about 12 to 15) once or twice a week after binge eating. In addition she takes Lasix (a diuretic) and diet pills in an effort to lose weight.

Although it was very difficult for Jill to tell her doctor about her strange eating patterns, she felt relieved once she did. Her doctor told her that she had a disorder called "bulimia nervosa" and referred her to an eating disorders clinic. Before her appointment at the clinic, Jill read several articles about this disorder and was very relieved to find out that other women suffered from these same odd symptoms. When her therapist asked her what brought her to the clinic, she merely looked down and replied, "I have bulimia."

In the course of her initial interview, Jill admitted that she recently suffered from an episode of depression following a breakup with her boyfriend. During this depression she felt so despondent and weak that she occasionally missed work. Although she frequently had suicidal thoughts during this time and had even formulated several suicide plans, she did not make any actual suicide attempts. She reported that this episode lasted approximately a month and then seemed to lift by itself. She also reported a similar episode about two years earlier, following her withdrawal from college. She did not seek treatment for either of these episodes.

PERSONAL HISTORY

Jill is the youngest of three daughters in what she considers to be a fairly average middle-class family. When asked if her parents had any psychological or medical problems, she described her father as having a minor alcohol problem and her mother as having occasional bouts of depression. Neither parent has ever been treated professionally. Jill reports that there was some degree of conflict between her parents, but she does not feel that they were unusual in this regard. There is no history of abuse or neglect in her childhood.

Jill describes herself as having been preoccupied with her weight since she was 13 years old and has been constantly concerned about being thin ever since. At age 14 Jill reached her adult height of 5 feet 6 inches and weighed 130 pounds, which she considered to be very overweight. She dieted on and off for the next two years, but without any lasting success. When she was 16, a friend told her about self-induced vomiting. Initially she was disgusted at this idea, but nevertheless she tried this method after she overate one night. She found that the vomiting was tolerable, and she quickly adopted this method as a clever trick to diet without being hungry. In her words, "Throwing up wasn't so bad; it sure beat trying so hard not to eat." During the next year she lost over 20 pounds.

When Jill was 17, she weighed 105 pounds and felt more or less satisfied with her weight. She decided to apply for a job as a model. The modeling agency did not hire her, saying that she should try to lose more weight. Discouraged, Jill gave up on modeling and, with the encouragement of her parents, enrolled in a local private university.

In college Jill had more freedom to experiment with her eating habits. She discovered that by vomiting she could eat rather large amounts of food and still maintain her weight. Gradually her binge eating became more severe and more frequent until she was eating huge amounts of food twice daily. It was now becoming more and more difficult to hide her odd eating behavior from her roommates, and on occasion she even stole food from them. Jill recalled one particularly embarrassing incident:

> Shelley had bought a bunch of ice cream and potato chips for a party for a club she was in. Well, I couldn't stand having all that stuff around, so I just went at it. Of course I had planned to replace it all, but I didn't get around to it before she got back. Boy, was she shocked to find all that stuff gone! I felt really bad and apologized. I made up a story about how some of my friends came over and we all couldn't resist it. She didn't say anything, but I think she knew what really happened.

At this time Jill also began abusing laxatives and diuretics. As her control over her eating weakened, she also began abusing alcohol. She said that she became intoxicated and vomited at almost every party she attended. By her junior year her binge eating and her alcohol abuse began to interfere with her social life and her academic performance. She began to feel weak and ill for long stretches, and she started missing assignments. She also began staying away from her friends on campus, partly because she felt so embarrassed and ashamed about her eating. During her junior year Jill dropped out and worked as a receptionist. Relieved of the social pressures of campus life, she gradually decreased her binge eating to an average of twice a week over the next few years, and gradually her weight increased to 135 pounds. Jill described herself as being totally dissatisfied with herself at this time of her life. Upon the recommendation of a friend, she enrolled in flight attendant training school.

Jill was surprised to find that the airline had a strict weight limit for their flight attendants. Trainees who were overweight were dropped from the program, and attendants who did not make their weight target were grounded. Worried that she would be cut from the program, Jill became more weight-conscious than ever before. She frantically sought ways to lose weight, and she began binge eating and purging two or three times daily. In addition she eliminated alcohol from her diet and only ate dietary foods (vegetables, diet soda, and so forth) when she was not binge eating. After two months she had lost 20 pounds. She was now well within the airline's weight guidelines, and she also felt much better about her appearance. However, she had begun to feel weak and dizzy and was concerned that she was losing control over her eating. It was at this point that she consulted her doctor.

CONCEPTUALIZATION AND TREATMENT

As Jill herself recognized, her frequent binge eating; her use of vomiting, laxatives, and diuretics as purging agents; and her constant concern with her weight are clear indications of bulimia nervosa. Most bulimics are fully aware of the unusual nature of their behavior; many, like Jill, even know the formal diagnostic label of their disorder. Nevertheless they report feeling unable to control their odd binge-purge cycles.

Jill's history contains many social and occupational pressures that induced her to focus on her weight and appearance, particularly her job as a flight attendant. For the past 10 years bulimic eating has been an effective way for Jill to control her weight, and it seems reasonable to conclude that these factors may have contributed to her development of bulimia nervosa.

After her evaluation interview, Jill was admitted as an outpatient in the eating disorders clinic. The initial focus of therapy was to alter Jill's bulimic eating pattern. Jill's cognitive-behavioral therapy incorporated three general goals: (1) to identify the circumstances that surround her binge eating, (2) to restructure her thoughts about herself and her eating, and (3) to educate her on the risks of bulimic behavior, on meal planning and nutrition, and on an awareness of cultural standards that may contribute to her bulimic behavior.

First, Jill was instructed to keep a detailed record (which she called her "diary") of where, when, and what she ate so that she and her therapist could examine the exact conditions that were associated with her binge eating. Jill was also told to note her moods in this record to see how her emotions were associated with her bulimic behavior. Jill's record showed that she frequently binged in the late afternoon and early evening, often after a particularly long or stressful flight. Her emotional entries in her record also showed that she felt a sense of relief following her binge-purge episodes. By analyzing this record, it was evident that Jill's bulimic behavior was often used as a way to cope with stressful events in her life.

Second, Jill's distorted and illogical self-cognitions regarding her body image and self-worth were addressed using a cognitive restructuring procedure. Through confrontational, Socratic dialogues in individual therapy, Jill was taught to review her thoughts and feelings, to identify her distorted or illogical thoughts, and to adjust them. These cognitions may be brought up in therapy, or they may be taken from her record.

> **Jill:** Well, here's one from my diary. When I tried on a pair of slacks, they were too tight. I felt really fat, and I was miserable for the rest of the day. I just felt worthless.
>
> **Therapist:** Did you consider other possibilities?
>
> **Jill:** Like what?
>
> **Therapist:** Maybe the slacks shrank in the laundry. Maybe it was humid and sticky, and they just felt tight. Or maybe they were just too small to begin with.
>
> **Jill:** Sure, I guess it's possible, but I don't know. I mean, they fit before. I thought

it meant that I was getting really fat.

Therapist: OK. Let's say that you really did gain a few pounds. So what?

Jill: So what!? It shows that I have to diet even harder because I'm getting obese.

Therapist: Let's look at some of your assumptions. It sounds to me like you have no middle ground; gaining a few pounds means being obese. Do you think that's really an indication of being obese?

Jill: No, I guess not.

Therapist: It also sounds to me like you have a lot of other assumptions about gaining weight. For instance, you feel that gaining a few pounds will make you a failure, and no one will love you or accept you if you do. Is that true?

Jill: Yeah. But the airline might ground me if I get too fat. I mean, it's a real worry.

Therapist: Then maybe being a flight attendant is not the right career for you.

Jill: But I like it. I don't want to quit.

Therapist: I'm not saying you have to. All I'm saying is that you should look at what it's doing to you and maybe consider other possibilities. OK?

Jill: OK.

In addition to her individual therapy, Jill also attended group sessions. Mostly these group sessions focused on sharing experiences with other bulimics and fostering a sense of mutual support. In particular, the group members discussed the difficulty they had in controlling their binge eating, and they offered to be available if any member of the group needed support or encouragement.

The third goal of therapy was to provide Jill with information regarding various aspects of her eating disorder. First, the emotional and physical risks inherent in the binge-purge cycle (social isolation, salt and water imbalances, gastrointestinal ir-ritations, tooth decay, etc.) were described. Second, Jill was taught to plan reasonable meals for herself. She was given homework assignments that required her to research the nutri-tional value of various foods and to formulate healthy meal plans. Most importantly, she was to actually eat these meals. Third, Jill was taught to recognize our culture's expectations and norms regarding appearances and weight. In Jill's case, the norms of her airline were clear and explicit. For most bulimics, however, the expectations of our society (often conveyed through the entertainment and advertisement industries) are more subtle and difficult to identify.

Jill was treated for a total of 10 weeks. For the first two weeks her meals were planned for her. She found it difficult to follow these plans without bingeing now and then. During this time she reported vomiting eight times after meals. Still, Jill was making progress over her pretreatment rate. For the next several weeks Jill devised her own meal plans with the help of the staff. She found that having planned her own meals made it a little easier to stick to the diet. Gradually she reduced the frequency of her vomiting until she stopped completely by the seventh week. After three weeks of relatively normal eating behavior, Jill discontinued treatment. She was encouraged to follow her meal plan and to contact her therapist or a therapy group mem-ber if she felt that she was having trouble controlling her eating behavior.

PROGNOSIS

Jill's treatment appears to have been effective in altering her bulimic eating patterns. In a letter she wrote to her therapist approximately two months after she ended therapy, Jill stated that she had only binged and vomited twice since her last ses-sion. She reports eating more healthy and balanced meals (both at home and during her layovers), and she feels more energetic and active. Jill also said that she feels better about herself and her appearance, and she does not feel as "stressed" after difficult flights as she used to. In short, therapy seems to have greatly reduced the frequency of Jill's bingeing and purging, and it seems to have created enhanced feelings of self-worth that may help prevent these symptoms from reappearing in the future.

Despite Jill's obvious improvement, however, her prognosis must remain guarded. Bulimia nervosa is a persistent eating disorder, and it has proved to be very difficult to effect lasting behavioral changes in those who suffer from it. Research on treatment for bulimics has begun only recently, and the limited information that is available is not optimistic. About 50 percent of the bulimics who improve in therapy relapse within 12 months (Keller et al., 1989; Mitchell, Davis, & Goff, 1985); the majority of these relapses occur within 3 months (Mitchell et al.; Pyle et al., 1990). Thus, while Jill's therapy seems to be successful for the present, it is quite possible that she might resume her binge eating and purging patterns, perhaps as a reaction to some future stressful life event.

DISCUSSION

The specific causes of bulimia nervosa are not yet known, and there are great variations from case to case in the presenting complaints and personal histories. However, it is generally agreed that bulimics put an inordinate amount of importance on their physical appearance as a way of determining their self-esteem (Dolan Lieberman, Evans, & Lacey, 1990; C. Johnson, Tobin, & Lipkin, 1989), and this preoccupation probably contributes to their development of the disorder. For most bulimics, these cognitions usually have been evident for years. There is some evidence that certain cultural and/or occupational demands may exacerbate this behavior. Mitchell, Hatsukami, Pyle, and Eckert (1986) report that the majority of bulimics feel pressure to lose weight. Other researchers (Dolan et al., 1990; Sykes, Gross, & Subishin, 1986; Sykes, Leuser, Melia, & Gross,

1988) found the instance of bulimia to be higher in Catholic and Jewish women and in homes where there was long-standing parental conflict. A physiological theory of bulimia involves the satiety mechanism. Leitenberg, Rosen, Gross, Nudelman, and Vara (1988) suggest that persistent vomiting may disrupt normal satiety cues, thus perpetuating the binge-purge cycle. While these factors may not have necessarily caused bulimics to develop their odd eating patterns, they do appear to be involved in maintaining the disorder.

The incidence of bulimia is 10 to 20 or more times as common among females than males (Gross & Rosen, 1988; Healy, Conroy, & Walsh, 1985). Generally bulimia first emerges in junior high and becomes most prevalent in high school and college. Stein and Brinza (1988) diagnosed 2 percent of their female junior high sample and 4 percent of their female high school sample as bulimic. Other surveys of high school girls average around 4 to 5 percent. Gross and Rosen (1988) reported rates ranging from 2.2 to 7.4 percent, depending on how bulimia was defined. Dacey, Nelson, and Aikman (1990) found rates of 4.9 percent and 5.8 percent, respectively. Rates among college women ranges from 2 to 5 percent (Drewnowski, Yee, & Krahn, 1987; Hart & Ollendick, 1985; Mintz & Betz, 1988; Thelen, Mann, Pruitt, & Smith, 1987). Hart and Ollendick also surveyed working women, and they found a rate of 1 percent among this sample. There is evidence that the rate of bulimia may be dropping, though many young women remain vulnerable. C. Johnson et al. (1989) surveyed girls in one high school in 1981 and repeated the survey in 1986 and discovered a 50 percent drop in the rate of bulimia. They also found decreases in the girls' preoccupation with thinness and their dieting behavior. However, the proportion of subjects who reported poor body image remained constant.

Bulimia nervosa also occurs in foreign samples in roughly the same age proportions as in U.S. samples, though the overall rates are somewhat lower (Dolan, 1991). Samples of French adolescents of both sexes (Ledoux, Choquet, & Flament, 1991), college women from Ireland (Healy et al., 1985), and 15- to

35-year-old women in the United Kingdom (Cooper & Fairburn, 1983) reported rates of 0.7 percent, 2.8 percent, and 1.9 percent, respectively.

However, disturbed eating patterns may be much more prevalent than these figures suggest. In a sample of 682 college women surveyed by Mintz and Betz (1988), 61 percent showed some form of eating behavior problem, though only 3 percent could be classified as bulimic according to *DSM-III-R* criteria.

J. R. Martin and Wollitzer (1988) studied 277 women in a family practice setting and surveyed them regarding instances of purging (self-induced vomiting, use of laxatives, and/or fasting). They found that 21 percent engaged in some form of purging, but less than 20 percent of these purgers met *DSM-III-R* criteria for bulimia nervosa.

In a discussion of bulimia nervosa, it is important to distinguish this disorder from anorexia nervosa, another serious eating disorder. These two disorders do share many common features: their victims are primarily young females who are preoccupied with food, overly concerned with maintaining a slim figure, and have a rather distorted view of their own bodies. Despite these similarities, bulimia nervosa and anorexia nervosa are distinct disorders. Anorexia nervosa is much more rare; for example, Whitaker et al. (1990) report a rate of 0.2 percent among their sample of high school students, compared to a rate of 2.5 percent for bulimia nervosa. Anorexia nervosa is characterized by maintenance of a dangerously low body weight (at least 15 percent below the minimum normal weight), usually by a severe restriction of food intake, which usually involves a startling degree of self-control. Anorexics are consequently jeopardized by severe medical complications including malnutrition, metabolic changes, and amenorrhea (a cessation of menstrual discharge). Most anorexics deny their disorder and are unwilling to receive treatment for it unless forced to, often bodily.

In contrast, the majority of bulimics recognize that their eating behavior is abnormal. Unlike the apparent willpower of anorexics, most bulimics are unable to control their binge eating and purging. The majority are of approximately normal weight and only rarely are they in any serious medical jeopardy, though they may suffer from the physical side effects of their purging: gastrointestinal difficulties, eroded tooth enamel, electrolyte imbalances, and so forth. The primary concern for bulimics involves the social and/or psychological complications that arise from their disordered eating patterns. Their attempts to hide their disorder and their feelings of guilt and shame about their binges and purges lead many bulimics to isolate themselves from friends and family members. In J. R. Martin and Wollizer's (1988) sample of 58 purgers, only 2 percent had ever mentioned their purging to a physician, and 58 percent had never told anyone at all.

The binges described by Jill are typical of most bulimics (Hadigan, Kissileff, & Walsh, 1989; Kissileff, Walsh, Kral, & Cassidy, 1986; Rosen, Leitenberg, Fisher, & Khazam, 1986). Binge foods are usually high-caloric foods rich in complex carbohydrates (sugars and starches) and fat. Typically these foods are eaten very quickly. Binges are usually followed almost immediately by purging, usually self-induced vomiting. In fact, the goal of most binges seems not to be the binge eating but rather the inducement of the following purge.

The psychological reactions that Jill had to her eating behavior are also typical (Weiss & Ebert, 1983). Many bulimics feel guilt and shame over their uncontrolled eating behavior. Others report a feeling of "psychological numbing" or relief following the binge-purge cycle. This relief does not seem to be specific to any particular mood; bulimics have reported that their binges reduce their level of anxiety, depression, anger, and even elation. Thus, it seems that for some bulimics, their binge eating serves as a buffer that insulates them from stressful (and even pleasurable) emotional states.

Bulimia nervosa is associated with a number of other psychiatric problems (Weiss & Ebert, 1983), including substance abuse (Hatsukami, Mitchell, Eckert, & Pyle, 1986; Jonas, Gold, Sweeney, & Pottash, 1987), personality disorders (Yager, Landsverk, Edelstein, & Hyler, 1989), depression (Hertzog, 1984; Laessle, Kittl, Fichter, & Wittchen, 1987; Sykes et al., 1988) and suicide (Mitchell et al., 1986). Thus, it is important to assess a bulimic's level of psychiatric functioning on a number of measures at the initiation of treatment.

As was the case with Jill, cognitive-behavioral therapy for bulimia nervosa is usually brief, in most cases lasting less than six months. Since the primary goal of treatment is to regularize the patients' eating patterns, some treatment programs routinely hospitalize bulimics to more closely monitor and control their eating behavior. Most programs, however, begin treatment on an outpatient basis. When these patients end therapy, they are encouraged to attempt to follow a regular eating routine that includes healthy, nutritious food and a strict avoidance of any dieting. Bulimics have been found to be more susceptible to relapse if they deviate from a regularized eating schedule. Follow-up studies indicate that 65 to 75 percent of the bulimics treated with cognitive-behavioral therapy show some improvement, and about half of these patients maintain these therapy gains for at least 18 months (Keller et al., 1989; Pyle et al., 1990). Traditional psychodynamic therapy has also been utilized with this population, but with less success. However, many behavior therapists concede that bulimics with particularly chronic or persistent symptoms, especially those who are also depressed, may derive some benefit from traditional, long-term psychotherapy.

SLEEP-WAKE SCHEDULE DISORDER, DELAYED TYPE
Chronotherapy with Phototherapy

PRESENTING COMPLAINT

Erin is a 10-year-old girl who lives in an affluent section of Cincinnati. Erin has experienced great difficulty getting to sleep and waking up in the morning. She first noticed this problem several months ago, when she began to feel groggy and tired in the morning. Over the next few months she grew sleepier and less attentive at school and would not feel really awake until after lunch. Erin found it extremely hard to concentrate on what was said during her morning classes, and on several occasions she actually fell asleep in class, an experience she described as humiliating and embarrassing. Eventually she found it difficult just to get out of bed in the morning, and she soon began missing school altogether. Not surprisingly, her grades began to slide. Her parents tried everything they could think of to get her to wake up and go to school, but their encouragement, cajoling, threats, and punishments had little effect. Erin wanted to avoid school, and she resented her parents for always trying to force her to attend. She adopted what her parents called a "negative attitude," meaning that she had become very rebellious and disobedient. Erin's excessive morning sleepiness continued to interfere with her schoolwork and her attendance, and about two months ago her parents withdrew her from school completely.

During this period of time, Erin also experienced increasing difficulties in going to sleep. Again, the problem progressed gradually. Several months ago she first noticed that she didn't get drowsy in the evening like she usually did. But as time went on she fell asleep later and later. On most nights she would lie awake long after the rest of her family had gone to sleep. Sometimes she would get up and make herself a snack or watch TV, but she had to make sure that her parents were asleep. One time her father found her eating popcorn and watching videos at 2:30 in the morning and became incensed. "No wonder you can't get out of bed in the morning!" he shouted, "Get some sleep instead of wasting your time!" He then grounded her for a week. During that week Erin's parents tried to get her to fall asleep around 10:00, but her disrupted schedule persisted. Now when she can't sleep she mostly stays in her room and reads or listens to her stereo using her headphones.

For the past two months Erin has settled into the following schedule: she goes to bed along with the rest of the family, around 10:00 (weeknights) or midnight (weekends). In either case, however, she doesn't actually fall asleep until 3:00 or 4:00 in the morning. Her parents expend a great effort every morning just to get her up by 10:30, when her mother leaves for work. During the weekends she is usually not awakened, and she sleeps until noon or 1:00 in the afternoon. On occasion the father suggested giving Erin over-the-counter sleeping pills at night and stimulants in the morning, but the mother absolutely refused. Erin's mood is extremely irritable for several hours after she wakes up, but it usually improves as the day progresses. By late afternoon she is often lively and chatty with her siblings, although she remains somewhat hostile toward her parents. Around bedtime she is frequently sullen and morose.

Erin's parents believe that her sleep disturbance is merely an overt symptom signifying some deeper problem, perhaps her deep resentment of them or maybe an avoidance of school brought on by an excessive fear of failing. They brought Erin to a local child psychiatrist who specializes in family therapy for evaluation and treatment.

The child psychiatrist interviewed Erin separately from her parents. Both accounts of Erin's problems were more or less similar. The psychiatrist noted that Erin's odd sleeping pattern seemed to precede her other problems. The psychiatrist agreed with the parents that there were underlying issues of rebellion, hostility, and manipulation present, but she believed that these could be worked out later. First, she wanted to know to what extent Erin's sleep disturbance may be a problem in and of itself. To find out, she referred Erin to a sleep disorders center in a large downtown hospital for diagnostic evaluation and treatment recommendations.

When Erin and her parents arrived at the sleep disorders clinic, they were interviewed by the director, a psychiatrist who had specialized in sleep disorders for more than 15 years. His interview with the parents was similar to the one held in the child psychiatrist's office except that he went into more detail about Erin's medical history and her sleep patterns and habits, particularly those that may have contributed to her condition.

PERSONAL HISTORY

Erin is the youngest of three children. Her sister (age 17) and brother (age 14) are both in high school. Neither has any history of sleep disturbance, psychiatric illness, or significant medical problems. Both are doing very well in school. Erin's father (age 47) is a partner of a law firm; her mother (age 44) is a professor at a large university. Both parents report long histories of alcohol use but deny that this has been the source of any significant problems. In addition the mother reports a period of barbiturate abuse. Several years ago the mother voluntarily abstained from barbiturates without treatment and has remained abstinent ever since. She reports that this experience has made her hesitant to give her children hypnotics or stimulants. Otherwise, family psychiatric history is limited to a paternal aunt who appears to have suffered from major depression. This remains speculative, however, since the aunt has never been diagnosed or treated.

The marriage is described as stable and generally happy, and the family appears to get along well. It seems that the mother is the disciplinarian of the family, whereas the father tends to remain lighthearted and magnanimous. The father appears to have developed the closest emotional bond with Erin. Although there have been times when his behavior has undermined the mother's discipline, the parents report little in the way of childrearing conflicts. These issues are to be explored more thoroughly by the child psychiatrist.

For the most part, Erin's medical history is unremarkable. She had an uncomplicated birth and demonstrated normal development in her growth, speech, and intellectual functioning. Her IQ is well above average. She contracted chicken pox at age 5 and mumps at age 7. The only unusual feature of her medical history is her development of severe allergies, which first appeared at age 4 and continue to the present. Erin presently takes no medication, but she does ingest caffeine in the form of a can of cola almost every day.

Aside from her odd sleep schedule, Erin's sleep habits are quite ordinary in most ways. As far as the parents know, Erin does not exhibit any abnormal movement while sleeping, nor does she complain of frequent nightmares or any pain while asleep. Erin has never walked in her sleep, although she has talked in her sleep on occasion. However, there are a few interesting features in Erin's sleep history. Because of her nasal allergies, Erin breathes through her mouth when asleep, and sometimes she experiences labored respiration. Although Erin is a mouth breather, her mother denies that she snores.

The sleep specialist asked Erin's parents to think bac⅂ to the time a few weeks before her symptoms first appeared. Did anything cause her to stay up late for a night, or perhaps for several nights? Both parents knew what it was. Her father was involved in a big case that kept him late at the office. Usually he came home around 7:00, but for a period of about a week he didn't walk in until after midnight. He always kissed Erin good night, and when he didn't come home, she waited up for him. At first he found her asleep on the sofa. They talked a bit when he came home, but she went to sleep right away. By the end of the week, though, she was awake and chatty when he came home, and they talked until he went to bed. From that point on, she seemed to get to sleep later and later.

CONCEPTUALIZATION AND TREATMENT

Human society is filled with cues that indicate when people should wake up and go to sleep. Some cues occur naturally (e.g., sunlight, bird song, changes in temperature and humidity); others are artificial (alarm clocks, bedtime stories). But even without these cues, people would follow a sleep-wake schedule based on their own internal clocks. Virtually all animal species have natural circadian rhythms, or daily cycles, that govern various aspects of behavior. Perhaps the most fundamental of these rhythms is the sleep-wake cycle.

Most humans have a sleep-wake cycle with a period of about 25 hours. These periods vary among individuals; in rare cases the period can be as short as 12 hours or as long as 48 hours, but the vast majority tend to be around 25 hours. Having a period of 25 hours means that humans are constantly advancing their natural rhythm by about an hour to adjust their sleep to fit a 24-hour schedule. For this reason it is easier to grow accustomed to a later schedule than an earlier one. Many people have experienced this phenomenon: it is easier to stay up later than usual than it is to wake up earlier than usual; it is easier to travel west than it is to travel east. Nevertheless, most people are able to advance their daily rhythms about an hour or two as a matter of routine, and occasional delays in their schedules

201

(e.g., temporary insomnia, working late) do not pose a problem. Some people, however, find it extremely difficult to advance their internal clocks more than the usual hour. If their schedules are delayed for some reason, they will be "stuck" with an incongruity between their biological clocks and their social schedules. This appears to be what happened to Erin. When she stayed up to greet her father, she delayed her circadian rhythm by several hours. Now she is unable to advance her internal clock to meet the demands of her school schedule. In a sense, Erin is always running about six hours late.

This seems to be a straightforward case of sleep-wake schedule disorder, delayed type. (In the medical field, this condition is commonly called "delayed sleep phase syndrome.") According to *DSM-III-R, sleep-wake schedule disorder* describes a mismatch between a person's natural circadian rhythm and the schedule imposed by social conventions. The person cannot fall asleep at bedtime and consequently cannot wake up at an appropriate time. Often a sleep diary is useful to confirm a diagnosis of sleep-wake schedule disorder. Erin suffers from both bedtime insomnia and severe difficulties in waking up in the morning, a pattern that is common for people with delayed phases.

Treatment for a delayed sleep phase is ingenious in its simplicity. Since these people cannot advance their biological clocks, they are instead instructed to delay their sleep three hours every day until their circadian rhythms are back in sync with their social schedules. For Erin, the clinic director provided her parents with a detailed plan to delay her sleep three hours every day. Erin presented for treatment with a circadian rhythm that was delayed approximately six hours relative to her external schedule. After the sixth day of treatment, Erin would lose another 18 hours, which should put her in sync with her social schedule. This process is called "chronotherapy," or "time therapy."

An additional component in Erin's treatment was phototherapy ("light therapy"). Again, the approach is very basic. Erin's parents were instructed to expose her to sunlight or other bright lights after waking up in the morning. Basically, Erin is using one of the strongest natural circadian cues, light, to help her adjust her sleep period.

A third component of treatment involved the prescription of vitamin B_{12}, which some studies suggest may help normalize circadian functions. Erin was also instructed to avoid any substances that might act as a stimulant or depressant on her central nervous system. For children Erin's age, the most commonly encountered substance is caffeine found in some sodas. Iced tea and chocolate also act as stimulants, but to a lesser degree than caffeine.

Erin's medical history suggested one possible complication: apnea (a disruption in breathing while sleeping). In the most common form of apnea, obstructive apnea, the person's throat tissues become unusually relaxed during sleep. Suction created by inhalation collapses the airway, preventing air from reaching the lungs. This works in much the same way as when a paper straw collapses when saturated with liquid (which is why most straws are made of plastic). The airway is reopened only when the person wakes up and muscle tone is restored. These awakenings are short (rarely more than several seconds) and almost never remembered; nevertheless they may occur hundreds of times each night, leaving the person feeling drowsy and exhausted the next day. It is possible, albeit unlikely, that Erin's morning sleepiness is the result of apnea. It is unlikely because apnea would probably leave her tired throughout the day, and not just in the morning. Still, Erin's mouth breathing raises the possibility of apnea, which must be ruled out.

At first Erin's parents were skeptical that such a simple treatment could be effective, but it worked just as the director had promised. During the first night Erin followed her typical schedule; she went to sleep at 4:00 in the morning and woke up around 1:00 in the afternoon. But this time every light in her room was on until she went to sleep, and every shade was pulled down until she woke up. The next day she went to sleep three hours later, at 7:00, and woke up around 3:30 in the afternoon. Erin delayed her sleep phase three hours every night until she went to bed with the rest of the family at 10:00 and woke up at 7:00 in the morning. Her parents then maintained this "correct" schedule by strictly enforcing lights-out at 10:00 and an alarm and open shades at 7:00. Erin was a bit groggy for the first few mornings of her new schedule, but it was nothing like her mornings before treatment. After a few days on the new schedule, she began to wake up feeling rested and refreshed. The treatment was hardest on Erin's parents, who followed her delayed schedule themselves and took about a week after that to recover fully. For Erin, the hardest part of the treatment was giving up chocolate.

After a week on her new schedule, Erin came to the clinic to have her sleep monitored. Erin and her parents arrived at the sleep clinic in the afternoon, where they provided the director with a description of her home treatment. The family then went out for dinner, being particularly careful to have Erin avoid caffeine (cola) and chocolate, or anything else that might affect her sleep. They returned in the early evening, and Erin went through the elaborate process of being monitored. First, small electrodes (paddle-shaped insulation around a wire core) were glued to her scalp at precisely determined locations. These electrodes led to a polygraph that monitored her brain wave activity. By analyzing these brain wave patterns, sleep technicians determined when she was asleep and whether the sleep was light, moderate, deep, or REM (rapid eye movement). (Hauri, 1982, provides an excellent basic description of sleep physiology and sleep disorders.) In addition, Erin was monitored with an oximeter, a small device clipped to her ear that measured her blood's oxygen content. The technicians watched to see if her oxygen saturation dropped below 90 percent, indicating the presence of apneas. Finally, Erin was watched via an infrared camera to detect gross motor movement, somnambulism (sleep walking), nightmares, or night terrors. Collectively, these sleep activities are called "parasomnias." Any of these parasomnias may have contributed to her disrupted sleep, either by actually waking her up or by instilling anxiety that made her hesitant to fall asleep.

Lights-out was at 10:00, and Erin fell asleep at 10:14. She showed a typically healthy sleep pattern throughout the night. She woke up unaided at 6:47. Her oximeter never registered below 96 percent oxygen saturation, which combined with her lack of frequent awakenings to conclusively rule out any apnea or parasomnia. During the following day Erin's daytime sleepiness was monitored using the Multiple Sleep Latency Test (MSLT). The MSLT is a series of sleep opportunities every two hours throughout the day, at 10:00, noon, 2:00, and 4:00. At each session Erin lay quietly on a bed in a dark room for 20 minutes. People with excessive daytime sleepiness usually fall asleep early in each "nap"; normal sleepers rarely fall asleep. Sure enough, Erin showed a typical healthy pattern. She fell asleep only once, about 17 minutes into the 2:00 test. This early afternoon drowsiness is quite normal; most people show an increase in sleepiness in the middle of the day.

PROGNOSIS

The prognosis for Erin is quite good. She suffered a very straightforward case of delayed phase without any significant complications. Her response to chronotherapy was excellent. From Erin's history, it appears that she has difficulty advancing her sleep phase. In the future she must be particularly careful to maintain a strict sleeping schedule and to avoid situations that may instigate a phase delay. This will be especially relevant when she enters high school and college, where the shift from weekday to weekend sleep periods can be dramatic and may contribute to poorer school performance (Kirmil-Gray, Eagleston, Gibson, & Thoresen, 1984; Lack, 1986; Thorpy, Korman, Spielman, & Glovinsky, 1988; Wirz-Justice & Pringle, 1987). However, if she were to develop a future problem with a delayed phase, it is likely that she and/or her parents could administer chronotherapy at home.

DISCUSSION

Are sleep-wake schedule disorders common? This seemingly simple question has no simple answer. In fact, little is known about the prevalence of sleep phase disturbances. The basic difficulty is that sleep-wake schedule disorders are frequently event-generated. That is, the syndrome is brought about primarily by environmental circumstances such as rotating shift work, frequent changes of time zones, unstable living situations, the use of psychoactive stimulants or depressants, as well as other factors. Because sleep-wake disturbances are seen as resulting primarily from the situation and not the person, patients receive relatively little attention from researchers compared to their life situations. For example, Akerstedt and Torsvall (1981) studied 390 Swedish shift workers and compared those who worked on the morning, afternoon, or night shift. They also compared workers who worked only one shift with those who rotated between two or among all three shifts. Not surprisingly, they found more sleep disturbances in workers on the night shift and workers who frequently rotated shifts. In a more recent study, Alfredsson, Akerstedt, Mattsson, and Wilborg (1991) compared 197 night security guards with a national sample of 1769 daytime workers on a number of physical and mental health variables. These groups differed little on various medical dimensions, but the night security guards were 2 to 3 times as likely to suffer from sleep-wake disturbances. This was particularly problematic for workers above age 45.

Occasionally researchers have focused their attention on individual differences in the tendency to suffer from sleep-wake disorders. In a survey of 211 Australian college students, Lack (1986) found that 17 percent fit the criteria for delayed type schedule disorder. However, it must be remembered that college students are notorious for having poor sleep habits. In fact, 50 percent of Lack's sample complained of insufficient sleep. Kirmil-Gray et al. (1984) surveyed 277 ninth- and tenth-graders about their sleep quality, sleep habits, and lifestyles. About 11 percent of their sample described themselves as "poor sleepers."

Most students reported that they followed a later sleep schedule on weekends. However, the poor sleepers tended to have a greater shift between their weekday and weekend schedules. They were also more prone to frequent schedule changes from a variety of other reasons.

Although little is known about the prevalence of sleep-wake schedule disorders or the characteristics of those who suffer from them, *DSM-III-R* provides a few generalizations. Younger people are more prone to developing a delayed phase problem, whereas older people are more prone to developing a problem of advanced phase. Younger people are more resilient and are affected less by disruptions in their sleep schedules. There appears to be no sex difference in sleep-wake schedule disorders. Finally, minor sleep phase difficulties are very common, but most people are able to adjust their circadian rhythms on their own. Severe, persistent cases like Erin's appear to be very rare.

Chronotherapy is the standard behavioral treatment for delayed sleep phase problems and has been shown to affect not only a person's sleep behavior but also their underlying circadian rhythm, as measured by body temperature (Ozaki et al., 1988). Laboratory studies have also demonstrated the effectiveness of phototherapy in adjusting and maintaining the sleep phase (Lewy, Sack, & Singer, 1985; Rosenthal et al., 1990).

Differential Diagnosis

One of the initial tasks of a psychiatric professional confronted with a case of sleep phase disturbance is to distinguish a sleep-wake schedule disorder from other psychiatric disorders. Because sleep-wake schedule disorders necessarily involve insomnia or excessive daytime sleepiness, it can be especially difficult to differentiate sleep schedule problems from these two sleep disorders.

Many psychiatric conditions outside the realm of sleep disorders also have sleep phase problems as part of their symptomatic picture. One of the defining characteristics of major depression is early onset awakening. Depressed people often wake up several hours earlier than desired, at 2:00 or 3:00 in the morning, and then cannot get back to sleep again. In contrast, people who suffer anxiety disorders frequently find it difficult to initiate sleep. They might stay up until 3:00 or 4:00 in the morning before they finally fall asleep. It is important for psychiatric professionals to distinguish symptoms that result from sleep schedule problems from those that are caused by an underlying mood or anxiety disorder.

One complicating factor is that the field of sleep disorders is relatively new, and many professionals and lay people are not completely informed as to the symptomatology of the various sleep disorders. DeBeck (1990) describes a case where a man faced criminal proceedings because of his delayed sleep phase. To be sure, Erin's parents believed her delayed sleep phase was merely a symptom of some other underlying psychiatric disturbance. Fortunately for Erin, the child psychiatrist who saw her was familiar with sleep disorders and was able to make a referral to the sleep center. As a result, her delayed phase was treated quickly and relatively easily. Erin's psychiatrist noted that there are other issues to work out, most concerning her relationship with her parents. Now this therapy will not be complicated by Erin's disruptive sleep schedule.

SEPARATION ANXIETY DISORDER WITH A MAJOR DEPRESSIVE EPISODE
Psychodynamic Therapy

PRESENTING COMPLAINT

Eva is a 10-year-old fifth-grader in a middle-class suburb of Chicago. In February Eva contracted a mild case of pneumonia, which kept her home for two weeks. During this time she had the undivided attention of her mother. On the day before Eva was scheduled to return to school, she complained of severe abdominal pain. This pain was so severe that she could barely walk, let alone go to school. Eva was taken to the emergency room of the local hospital, but the physician on call could find nothing wrong with her. Still, she complained of fever (though her parents could find no indication of any), headaches, and diarrhea. She was allowed to stay home one week longer. Throughout the week Eva's complaints persisted, and her parents took her to her pediatrician three times. However, neither the parents nor the pediatrician could find any objective evidence of any physical illness; her temperature was normal, she did not cough or have any difficulty breathing, she did not go to the bathroom more than usual, and her appetite and sleep seemed good. With the recommendation of Eva's pediatrician, her parents now insisted that she return to school. Eva flatly refused. She began throwing tantrums and having "yelling matches" with her mother. She carried on for hours, complaining that she still was not feeling well and that she should not be forced to go back to school. She accused her mother of being cruel and neglectful and of wanting to get rid of her. In the mother's own words, "It's been pure bedlam ever since she got over her pneumonia and wouldn't go back to school."

Eva had always been a somewhat dependent and demanding child, but she had never acted out to any extent before. Her mother became increasingly alarmed at and frustrated with Eva's uncharacteristic behavior. Although Eva did not carry on in front of her father like she did with her mother, he nevertheless became very concerned about her refusal to go to school. After another week of refusing to go to school (making five weeks of staying at home), Eva's parents decided to contact a local psychiatrist who specialized in childhood disorders.

Eva's mother took her to her initial interview at the psychiatrist's office. The mother was asked to remain in the waiting room while Eva described how she felt about what happened during the last few weeks. Eva was unusually articulate and self-disclosing for a girl her age; she began the interview by saying, "OK. Let's start at the beginning."

From Eva's viewpoint her problem was much more involved than just refusing to go to school. At first she complained that she was still sick with a fever of "almost 100" and diarrhea that would strike twice a day on average. (The psychiatrist noted that most likely her mild diarrhea was a side effect of the medication she was still taking for her pneumonia.) She was very angry with both her mother and her pediatrician for expecting her to go back to school. She charged that they did not appreciate how sick she felt and did not take her complaints seriously. "They just don't understand me. Whatever I say is a joke. I mean, what would happen if I got *really* sick?" Her psychiatrist then asked her to describe these feelings in more detail, but Eva interrupted him, saying, "I'm not done yet!" She then went on to describe a second problem:

> My mind thinks ahead. It's like my mind gets ahead of me. Every time something good happens to me, I think ahead to the bad things that may happen afterwards. It's like a state of shock or fright. Sometimes I'm afraid my mom will get killed or the house will burn down or something. This happens at school a lot. I wish I could jump out the window and run home to help. I call it The Fright. When it happens, I mostly want to be at home where someone can take care of me.

Eva was obviously very upset by her "fright," which primarily involves her morbid preoccupations that she or her family members may develop terrible diseases or be injured or killed. Eva could not specify any particular cause for her anticipatory anxiety. She denied that anything or anyone bothers her at school; she said that she has several good friends and that her schoolwork is very easy. The only really consistent aspect of her "fright" is her strong desire to be home, a place she describes as "secure and protecting."

Eva also told her psychiatrist that she feels "sadness and madness" most of the time. She described this feeling as "crying inside" and said that she cries frequently, usually for no reason. She also said that she often wakes up around 2:00 in the morning because of her "fright" and has trouble getting back to sleep.

Suicidal ideation is quite rare in children Eva's age, and usually this topic is not discussed in therapy. However, Eva's psychiatrist thought it prudent to ask her if she had ever thought of killing herself. She said that she had wished to be dead on many occasions, and she would often tell her mother that she was going to commit suicide. She would even make fake suicide attempts. For example, two days before her interview she emptied a bottle of aspirin and left it where her mother would find it. She then locked herself in the bathroom with the faucet

211

running. She said that her mother was very frightened and pounded on the bathroom door for several minutes before Eva finally opened it. She claimed that she would never actually go through with a suicide attempt; she just wants to know that her mother cares.

Eva also reported hearing voices, which usually said terrible things. She remembers that one time the voices said that she was a very bad girl and needed to die. She said that some voices seemed to be coming from inside her head while others seemed to come from outside. Occasionally there would be an argument between the inside and outside voices. Eva was very frightened by these voices and wanted them to go away. When the therapist asked if she thought these voices were unusual, she replied, "Don't you? I think they're really weird! You know, I get nervous just talking about them."

Finally, the psychiatrist asked her if she had any problems getting along with her friends, with the other kids at school, or with her family. Eva denied any serious interpersonal problems. She apparently got along well with her friends at school, and she seemed to have fairly normal relationships with her two sisters. She said she respected and admired her father, and aside from disliking the fact that he wanted her to go back to school, she had a good relationship with him. She did, however, complain of problems with her mother. Interestingly, these problems stemmed from the fact that she and her mother were too much *alike.*

Therapist:	So, Eva, can you tell me about the troubles you have with your mother?
Eva:	She's just like me; we're exactly alike. We're both yellers and screamers, and we have screaming matches all the time.
Therapist:	Do you like your mom or do you dislike her?
Eva:	Oh, I really like her.
Therapist:	Eva, let's pretend you were giving your mom a grade on a pretend report card,

           OK? What grade would you give her?
Eva: A B. No, a B+.
Therapist: B+, OK. Why a B+?
Eva: Well, she helps me most of the time, and she's good to me, so I gave her a good grade.
Therapist: Why not an A?
Eva: Because she yells at me and jumps to too many conclusions.

PERSONAL HISTORY

Eva is part of a Protestant middle-class family. Her father is a middle-level business executive, and he appears to be responsible and concerned about Eva. He spends time with his children on weekends, but because of his busy work schedule, his interactions with them during the week are limited to dinner conversations. Her mother has never been employed outside the home; she says that she spends the majority of her time and effort taking care of her children and worrying about their welfare. Eva has two sisters, one older and one younger. Their relationships with each other seem to be fairly normal for children their age; they get into occasional arguments and shouting matches, but on the whole they get along well.

Eva's early childhood appears to be unremarkable. Her mother could think of nothing unusual about it, and her medical records show no indication of any serious or unusual injuries or illnesses. Eva's school history seemed unremarkable. At age 4 Eva enrolled in nursery school held for half a day, three days a week. Transportation to and from the nursery school was provided by a carpool organized by some of the parents. Eva's mother remembers that Eva was very reluctant to go into other parents' cars in the carpool. In kindergarten the next year, Eva took a bus to school. In contrast to her uncertainty about taking rides in strangers' cars, she apparently loved the bus rides, and until now she has had no other school-related problems.

Eva's relationships with her peers do contain some early signs of her separation anxiety, however. Since kindergarten, Eva has attended a summer day camp. Although she has always enjoyed these experiences, she has steadfastly refused to attend an overnight summer camp. Similarly, Eva avoids any overnight stays with friends. Once, in second grade, Eva was invited to a slumber party for one of her close friends. According to Eva, all of her friends were invited the party, and she "just had to go." But on the afternoon of the slumber party Eva complained of leg pains that were so severe that she could not walk. Her mother took her to an orthopedist that afternoon. The orthopedist could find nothing wrong with her legs, but to be cautious he recommended that she not attend the party. This leg pain has reemerged off and on in the past years.

The psychiatrist also interviewed Eva's parents to identify any significant aspects of their histories. Eva's mother reports that a particularly noteworthy event occurred when she was 19. She was found to be at fault in a boating accident that nearly killed her mother, and she confesses that she has felt guilty and responsible for her mother's welfare ever since. She also appears to be quite worried about her father, who has had a heart condition for many years. She says that in the back of her mind she is "constantly waiting for the phone call."

Although Eva's father appears to be very responsible and concerned for his daughter's welfare, he is personally resistant to the idea of therapy. He has met with the psychiatrist only once, and even then he seemed reluctant to disclose any information about himself. An examination of his medical records shows a history of depression in his family. When asked about this, he flatly denies any history of mental illness in his family.

CONCEPTUALIZATION AND TREATMENT

DSM-III-R defines separation anxiety disorder as a child's excessive and unwarranted fear about being apart from one or more important attachment figures, usually the mother. This anxiety must have existed for at least two weeks. This disorder can be manifested through a number of symptoms, including unrealistic worries about the welfare of the attachment figures' or one's own health, complaints of physical ailments, persistent refusals to be separated from the attachment figures, and a need to be in constant contact with the attachment figures.

Eva clearly fits the *DSM-III-R* criteria for separation anxiety disorder. For the past few weeks she has exhibited excessive anxiety about being apart from her mother. She refuses to go to school and instead expresses a strong need to stay home. She complains of numerous physical ailments (headaches, abdominal pains, leg aches) and shows excessive distress when she is separated, or even anticipates being separated, from her mother. She persistently worries about her own health should she be separated from her mother ("What if I got really sick?"), and she has excessive worries that some terrible fate will befall the people close to her. As is the case with most children her age, Eva's separation anxiety disorder is manifested primarily in her refusal to go to school.

Eva also shows symptoms of a major depressive episode. She has complained of depressed mood and a lack of interest in her usual activities. She has also complained of feelings of sadness and frustration, frequent crying, early morning awakening, various somatic complaints, mood-congruent hallucinations, and suicidal ideation. Although it is not uncommon for separation anxiety disorder to co-occur with a major depressive episode, the severity of Eva's mood disorder is somewhat unusual for a child her age. The extent of her mood disturbance and her family history of affective disorders suggest the possibility that Eva may have a genetic predisposition for depression.

Eva was diagnosed as having a separation anxiety disorder with a major depressive episode and was seen for therapy once a week at the psychiatrist's office. Her therapist formulated a relatively straightforward conceptualization of her case. Her symptoms resulted from her neurotic fear that she would be abandoned and left alone. She feared that some catastrophic event would befall her parents because this would leave them unable to care for her. As Eva has grown, she has been confronted with an increasing number of subtle demands of independence, such as slumber parties and summer camp. It is apparent that she is unable to cope with these demands.

The primary aim of Eva's treatment was to reduce the neurotic defenses that have thus far inhibited her psychosocial development. The first stage of therapy consisted of three broad, progressive steps. First, Eva's pervasive anxieties, depressed mood, hallucinations, and suicidal ideation were brought under control, in part through medication. Second, her relationship with her mother was stabilized. Third, the psychiatrist worked with Eva's mother to get her to return to school.

The second stage focused on dynamic psychotherapy, which explored her unconscious thoughts and feelings. As these were uncovered and discussed, the therapist provided her with clarifications, reinterpretations, and occasional confrontations. Throughout treatment the psychiatrist provided Eva with emotional support, primarily by reassuring her that she was loved by her parents and that their frustrations and expectations were intended to be for her own good.

The first concrete action taken by Eva's psychiatrist was to put her on the tricyclic antidepressant imipramine (known by the trade name Tofranil). This is somewhat unusual in that most children with separation anxiety disorder do not require medication; for them, therapy usually consists of a combination of family intervention and situation manipulation (putting the child in situations that require a level of independence).

Eva's initial dose of Tofranil was small. This dose was gradually increased until an appropriate blood level was achieved. This procedure provides the best chance of finding an efficacious and long-lasting dosage of medication while it minimizes its negative side effects. Since Eva was only 10 years old, it was essential to monitor her medication and her reactions to it. After two and a half weeks on Tofranil, Eva's hallucinations and suicidal ideation ceased, her anxiety lessened, and her depressive symptoms began to remit. Eva was maintained on Tofranil throughout therapy.

Another aspect of Eva's therapy involved treating her mother. Typically, both parents are treated, but Eva's father made it clear that he was unwilling to participate. The psychiatrist saw Eva's mother for several sessions. One goal of these sessions was to inform her of how she may have been unwittingly exacerbating Eva's symptoms. In particular, she was told to "just walk away" from their screaming matches. She was also told that the most effective way to get Eva to return to school was to be firm and stand her ground.

A second purpose of therapy with Eva's mother was to emphasize that Eva's fears were very sincere and were not meant to punish or irritate her parents. Eva's morbid preoccupations were not simply attempts to manipulate her parents; Eva actually feared for her own safety and for the safety of her family. These fears may not have had a logical basis, but they were real to Eva. To emphasize this point, the psychiatrist informed Eva's mother of Eva's suicidal ideation and hallucinations. Her mother quickly came to realize that Eva's anxieties were more serious and painful than she had initially thought. Similarly, Eva's frequent somatic complaints were seen not simply as childish attempts at avoiding things (although they often did produce this effect); Eva really did feel pain. In short, Eva's parents were told that her fears were painful and sincere, even if they did not have any physiological base.

Four weeks after she began therapy, Eva returned to school. Despite her prolonged absence, she had no trouble catching up on her missed schoolwork. Gradually her relationship with her mother improved; they argued less and Eva became much more obedient. With Eva's return to school, therapy now focused on more underlying dynamic issues. From this point Eva's psychotherapy was increased to twice a week.

First, Eva's fears were addressed. She was reassured that neither she nor her parents were in any actual serious danger, and that they would be available when she needed them. Eva's perceptions of her parents' demands on her, such as their insisting that she go to school and their suggesting that she attend summer camp, were also discussed. She was told to think of these expectations not as their wish to get rid of her but rather as signs that they really did care for her. They expected her to be a "big girl" who could take care of herself, and they wanted her to grow up and be successful. By and large Eva reacted favorably to these suggestions.

Second, the therapist attempted to uncover Eva's latent feelings. Like most children, Eva found it difficult to express these ideas directly, especially those that involved hostility or anxiety. As a result, dynamic therapy with Eva was conducted in a subtle and indirect manner. As the first step in this process, the therapist attempted to foster a close therapeutic alliance with her through the establishment of a nonerotic transference. As the therapeutic alliance developed, Eva's unconscious perceptions of the people in her childhood began to be expressed in her current perceptions of the therapist. By listening to her carefully and observing her closely, the therapist helped Eva understand her perceptions of the world and clarify her real experiences from her imagined ones. In the course of therapy, the therapist often attempted to have Eva "slip into" a discussion of her unconscious feelings through expressive play, where her feelings were projected onto the play situation. For example, Eva occasionally played with a dollhouse during the therapy sessions. During one session she placed a small doll next to a larger one and labeled the small one "Baby" and the larger one "Mommy." The therapist asked her what the baby was thinking. Eva replied, "The baby is very sad. She thinks that her mother is dying and that she'll be all alone." Eva's underlying cognitions were also expressed through art. During a later session Eva drew a picture of a sea star. This creature had a broken arm that appeared to be dangling from its body. In the course of describing this picture to the therapist, Eva commented that her family was like the sea star and that she was the broken appendage that was not really a part of the family. As therapy progressed, the therapist was able to uncover and reinterpret many of the direct, core issues of Eva's problem, primarily her strong fears of abandonment. Since Eva's symptoms were thought to be a result of these underlying cognitions, therapy remained focused on these central issues and made no attempt to address her school avoidance directly.

An important aspect of conducting psychotherapy with children is to relate to them from their own frame of reference." Therapists attempt to match their techniques to the cognitive level of the children they treat and to discuss issues that are important to these children. For example, when Eva's psychiatrist discussed growing up with her, he made sure to put this concept in terms that she would be able to understand. Whereas for older patients "growing up" may mean choosing a career or making life goals, for Eva "growing up" meant going to different rooms for different school subjects (instead of staying in the same home room) and having a locker of her own. As a second example, Eva's general desires and goals were given a concrete form by phrasing them as birthday wishes. So, to tap Eva's hopes for the future, her psychiatrist asked, "What would you wish for on your next birthday?" As mentioned above, abstract ratings of other people are put in the context of pretend report cards. Generally speaking, discussing topics at an abstract level usually surpasses a child's cognitive development and is less effective therapeutically.

After about six months, Eva's father suggested her antidepressant medication be discontinued. Her depressive symptoms had long since remitted, and she appeared to be making slow but steady progress in overcoming her anxiety. Moreover, the process involved in monitoring her medication was very time-consuming and expensive. To comply with her father's request, Eva was gradually withdrawn from Tofranil, but within two weeks her depressive symptoms began to reappear. Eva was then put back on a maintenance dose of Tofranil, and she continues to take this medication.

Over the next 15 months of therapy, Eva's fears of separation gradually diminished. Her morbid preoccupations were rare, and her anxieties no longer interfered with her behavior. At this point Eva discontinued therapy. She still exhibited some mild residual signs of her disorder, such as a refusal to sleep over at friends' houses and a resistance to attending a full-time summer camp. However, most of her more incapacitating anxieties had long since remitted. Although her psychiatrist felt that Eva could have benefited from an additional year or so of therapy, the family's finances were such that continuing therapy was considered impractical, especially considering that only relatively small gains in functioning were anticipated.

PROGNOSIS

Eva made good progress in her 15 months of therapy; nevertheless, there are reasons to classify her prognosis as guarded. First, she has a family history of depression and has shown a reasonably full major depressive episode by age 10. Although she responded well to imipramine, a brief interruption in her medication resulted in a rapid reemergence of her symptoms. Taken together, this information indicates that Eva may have a genetic predisposition toward depression. In all likelihood she will remain vulnerable to depression throughout her life, and her medication must continue to be carefully monitored.

A second cause for concern is that Eva's symptoms have not remitted completely; she continues to show subtle signs that her disorder is persisting. In particular she continues to be apprehensive about being away from home for more than a few hours at a time; overnight outings are still out of the question. It remains to be seen whether Eva's subtle symptoms will continue to fade gradually or whether they will develop into a lifelong pattern of dependency.

In short, Eva has made substantial progress in therapy. The combination of antidepressant medication and dynamic psychotherapy appears to have been very effective in reducing her defensive anxieties. Generally speaking, the prognosis for children with separation anxiety disorder is good. However, as is the case with Eva, the anxieties of most children with this disorder persist in some form, and it is not uncommon for these children to show some mild symptoms for many years.

DISCUSSION

Eva's diagnosis was straightforward. Her pervasive fears clearly indicated a childhood anxiety disorder. Eva's symptomatology was very typical; school refusal, a fear of leaving loved ones for any extended period, morbid preoccupations, and somatic complaints are very common among children with separation anxiety disorder (Last, 1991). Other children with this diagnosis show symptoms that were not manifested by Eva. Some have great difficulty in falling asleep without the major attachment figures. They may demand to sleep in their parents' bed, or if this is not allowed, they may sleep by their parents' door. Many complain of frequent nightmares involving their morbid ideation. Some cannot stand to be separated from their attachment figures for even small periods of time. They either cling to them most of the day or constantly follow them around, a behavior pattern known as "shadowing."

Separation anxiety disorder is relatively common, affecting an estimated 2.4 percent of the childhood population (Bowen, Offord, & Boyle, 1990). In formulating Eva's diagnosis, it is important to consider the possibility that her refusal to attend school may indicate a school phobia (Last, Francis, et al., 1987; Perugi et al., 1988). Her therapist was careful to probe her attitudes regarding school. Her lack of academic problems and her generally good relationships with her peers are indications that school is not a negative experience for her. Thus, her school avoidance appears to be only a by-product of her separation anxiety and not a problem in and of itself.

An interesting aspect of this case is that Eva also suffered from a major depressive episode. Her sadness, suicidal ideation, sleep disturbance (especially the early morning awakening, of which her parents were apparently unaware), and frequent somatic complaints all support this additional diagnosis. The fact that she described hearing voices may be taken by some as evidence of a psychotic disorder such as childhood schizophrenia. However, these auditory hallucinations were wholly consistent with her depressed mood, and did not exist in the absence of other depressive symptoms. In general, mood-congruent hallucinations that occur within the context of an affective disorder are usually taken to be secondary to the mood disorder and not an indication of a psychotic disorder. Furthermore, Eva reported feeling frightened by these voices, and she realized that they were very odd. The fact that her hallucinations were not ego-syntonic (that is, they were not liked or accepted by Eva) provides additional evidence that a diagnosis of a psychotic disorder is in all likelihood secondary to her mood disorder.

Early Signs of Separation Anxiety Disorder
Many parents report some sort of subtle cues that foreshadow their children's separation anxiety disorder. Some children seem shy with strangers, and some seem hesitant about leaving their parents. Other children are afraid of the dark, monsters, odd creatures, or large, fierce animals. Some children are very demanding, whereas others are overly compliant and obedient. The majority of these *post hoc* signs, however, are not at all unusual for all children, regardless of whether they will develop separation anxiety disorder, another problem such as overanxious disorder (Last, Hersen, et al., 1987) or depression (Bowen et al., 1990), or no disorder at all. For example, in Eva's case it seemed significant to her mother that she was leery of other drivers in her nursery school carpool. However, at that age most children are afraid of entering strange people's cars (and rightly so). Thus, it is very difficult to use parents' observations to predict which children may develop this disorder.

Another difficulty in predicting separation anxiety disorder is that its onset varies widely among different children. Patients generally begin to show symptoms fairly early in childhood (Last, Francis, et al. 1987, Last, Hersen, et al., 1987), but others show no signs of the disorder until early adulthood. Many children, like Eva, first develop their symptoms after coming down with a serious illness that forces them to rely on someone else (usually one or both parents). Many other children develop their symptoms after the death of a family member or after some other catastrophe (a car accident, damage to the home from a violent storm, and so on). Yet for others no such instigating event can be identified.

The course of this disorder also varies widely. Whereas some children will never show any evidence of a separation anxiety after their symptoms recede, others will show subtle residual signs of their excessive anxiety for many years. Many seem to recover completely and function perfectly well throughout high school, but begin to show symptoms when they are about to separate from their parents when they accept a job or go off to college, especially one that is far away from home. Other children manage to separate, but they still feel a strong need to keep in contact. These children will either come home almost every weekend or call their parents frequently, some up to several times every day. In a few cases the disorder takes a chronic course. These children never move far away from, or even out of, the family home. For them, continual contact with their parents, either by living with them, visiting them frequently, or calling them several times a day, becomes a lifelong pattern.

Because the symptoms of these children often emerge as a result of their subjective fears and not as a result of any observable trauma, it is frequently difficult for other people to recognize or understand the gravity of their anxiety. In particular, parents often have great difficulty determining just what is making their children so fearful. Many parents simply think that their children have overactive imaginations; others may accuse their children of being lazy or manipulative. Not surprisingly, as in the case of Eva, these attitudes are construed by the child as evidence of rejection, thus exacerbating the anxieties. For this reason it is important for the parents to realize that their children's anxieties are unconsciously motivated. Children with somatic complaints really *do* feel pain; those with morbid preoc-

223

cupations really *do* fear that their family will be harmed. Though these anxieties may not be logical or reasonable, they are nevertheless real to the child.

Children who develop a separation anxiety often have parents who have difficulties with separation themselves; they may be overly involved with their children, overprotective, or just overly worried. For example, during her recovery from pneumonia, Eva received her mother's "undivided attention," and each of Eva's many somatic complaints precipitated a trip to her pediatrician or the emergency room. During a session with the psychiatrist, Eva's mother admitted that she has never spent a night away from her children. From this information it seems clear that Eva's mother is overprotective and cautious. It is likely that she has some unresolved separation issues of her own. Indeed, the mother's constant guilt and fear concerning her parents' health provides evidence of her own separation anxieties. Generally speaking, children with one or both parents who display some form of anxiety disorder are at greater risk for developing separation anxiety disorder themselves (Shader, 1984). In particular, parents who have had difficulties in establishing boundaries with their own parents are more apt to have children with anxiety disorders than are parents who have not.

One interesting aspect of this disorder is the parents' decision of when to seek help for their child. Some parents have described feeling "choked" or "smothered" by the excessive demands of their children. Others become embarrassed when their child acts out excessively in public or refuses to go to school or on extended outings. Of course, what constitutes "excessive" anxiety will vary from parent to parent. Although many parents tolerate or even promote a sense of anxious dependency on the part of their children, it often comes to a point where they decide that their child has become *too* anxious. Since most children with this disorder have a long history of dependent behavior, it is often unclear to therapists why parents bring their child to therapy when they do and not sooner. This ambiguity may be especially confusing for the child, who must decide how much dependency is appropriate and how much is "too much."

Psychodynamic Treatment for Separation Anxiety Disorder

Traditionally, psychodynamic therapists hold the achievement of insight as an ultimate goal; however, the immature cognitive development of children Eva's age calls for a different objective (Chethik, 1989; A. Freud, 1926/1946; Wolman, 1972). Here the aim of therapy is to free her from her defensive inhibition and facilitate future development; there is a relatively greater focus on support and encouragement. (This is also the case for many adults who lack the cognitive maturity to truly achieve insight into their disorders.)

Psychodynamic interpretations of separation anxiety disorder focus on the morbid preoccupations of these children. Traditional psychodynamic theory has interpreted these anxieties as the children's projection of their unconscious hostile impulses against one or both parents. After the Oedipal drama these children were left with strong feelings of need and resentment toward their parents, particularly their mothers, engendering pathological mother-child relationships based on mutual hostile dependency. Since hostility toward attachment figures is unacceptable to the ego, these feelings were consequently projected onto other, less specific forces that may harm the parents (illnesses, accidents, storms, and so on). As these children mature, their hostile dependence on their mothers will interfere with their ability to cope with the increased demands of independence.

More recent psychodynamic formulations have focused on the fact that many of the parents of the children with this disorder are themselves neurotically needy and dependent. By identifying with their neurotic parents, these children may have developed particularly weak conceptions of them. Since the children's conception of their parents is so fragile, they feel especially at risk of being abandoned and left alone.

MODERATE MENTAL RETARDATION
Residential Treatment with Behavior Modification

PRESENTING COMPLAINT

Steve has dark, rather lifeless eyes. His graying hair is combed straight back and is thinning noticeably. His teeth, which have a slight yellow cast, form a pronounced overbite. He has a medium build and is about 10 pounds overweight. His posture is stooped, and he walks with an unsteady, shuffling gait. All in all, Steve gives the impression of man of about 65 to 70 in declining health.

Interactions with Steve tell a different story, however. Sometimes he mutters unintelligibly; at other times he begins conversations with loud, startling comments that are not always logical. For instance, recently Steve approached a stranger with a peculiar combination of a welcoming smile and a sideways glance. Suddenly he blurted out, "Are you the dentist?" When the surprised visitor replied that he was not, Steve followed up by shouting even more loudly, "Are you the doctor?" When the answer was again no, Steve became frustrated and impatient.

The smile had disappeared, and the sideways glance now held suspicion. "Well, what are you, then?" The stranger then explained that he was a student. He was about to say that he was applying for a summer job, but Steve interrupted him. "A student. That's nice." Steve's eyebrows had lifted, and he developed a wide grin. Still grinning, he turned around and wandered down the hall.

Steve is 52 years old. For the last four years he has lived in an intermediate care facility (ICF) run by a private agency in New York City. The ICF is a residential group home with seven bedrooms and 12 patients. Steve came to the ICF from a succession of other group residences, including family home care, city-run developmental centers, and a large state-run institution. Steve's behavior in these various facilities has generally been described as uncooperative, stubborn, and aggressive.

Steve's adjustment to the ICF was slow and difficult, and he continued to show characteristic verbal and physical aggression, argumentativeness, stubbornness, and a general attitude his counselors described as "finicky." After a year at the ICF, however, Steve had become "an integral part of the family" and showed dramatic decreases in his aggression. Although Steve generally stays to himself, there are people at the ICF who would be considered his friends: people he interacts with regularly and misses when they are absent.

In his four years at the ICF, Steve has shown a gradual deterioration in his physical health and mental functioning. Physically, his posture has become more stooped, and his gait has become unsteady. Although he has a history of violence, because of his weakness he is no longer considered a physical threat. Intellectually, Steve has become forgetful and disoriented, and he tends to speak about events in the past as if they were happening in the present. Recently he has become more suspicious, even paranoid. With increasing frequency he has conversations in his room with inanimate objects and imaginary friends. At times these conversations are quite loud and take the form of two voices yelling at each other.

PERSONAL HISTORY

Steve's parents moved to New York from Puerto Rico two years before he was born, and they returned to their native island about 25 years ago. About five years ago Steve's father died. He has very limited contact with his mother, who calls him about once every other month and sends a card when he is sick. As limited as this contact is, on most occasions it was initiated by the staff at the ICF. Steve has no family in New York aside from a paternal aunt, who used to come for occasional short visits when Steve first arrived at the ICF. His aunt showed little interest in him or in the facility, however, and gradually she saw him less and less. Steve has had no contact with any other friend or family member. As a consequence of this limited social contact, little is known of Steve's early childhood aside from what can be pieced together from school reports and the records of his various residential placements.

Steve did very poorly when he was first enrolled in the New York public school system. Steve had numerous behavioral problems throughout kindergarten and first grade, including arguments with teachers and fights with fellow students. He also had a history of starting fires. Academically he was well behind his peers and was asked to repeat the first grade. Before he did, however, he was interviewed by a school psychologist and was found to have an IQ of 48. The psychologist also noted that Steve demonstrated substantial problems in his interpersonal and self-care skills. The psychologist concluded that Steve was "mentally retarded but trainable" (which is roughly equivalent to the modern *DSM-III-R* diagnosis of moderately mentally retarded), and in light of Steve's disruptive behavior problems, he recommended that Steve be placed in a special home. Steve's parents agreed and committed him to a city-run developmental center (DC), a small institution-like residence with 30 beds. Steve was 8 years old.

The staff at the DC found Steve's behavior difficult to control and very disruptive to the other residents. At age 11 he was transferred to a state-run institution in upstate New York, where he remained until he was 40. As part of a state-mandated deinstitutionalization program known as the Willowbrook Consent Decree (see Discussion), Steve was then transferred to a city-run DC. This center offered much more contact with the staff and a relatively structured program of training in social, academic, and vocational skills, including a supervised workshop. Steve did well in his work setting, where he sorted parts for toys. However, Steve was significantly older than most of the other residents, and his social skills began to deteriorate. Steve was then transferred to a residential home setting, which is similar to foster care. Steve was under the supervision of a couple trained in dealing with developmentally disabled patients. Steve continued to attend the workshop, but his social skills continued to decline. One day at the workshop he had an argument with a counselor and broke the counselor's jaw. He was immediately removed from the residential home and placed back in the DC, where there is greater supervision. After two years he was placed in his present ICF, again as a result of the Willowbrook Consent Decree.

CONCEPTUALIZATION AND TREATMENT

Steve is diagnosed as moderately mentally retarded. The cause of Steve's mental retardation is unknown. This diagnosis has changed little in the past 30 years or so, aside from updates in terminology to be consistent with current diagnostic manuals. *DSM-III-R* describes mental retardation in terms of four levels of severity: mild, moderate, severe, and profound. *Moderate mental retardation* describes people with an IQ in the approximate range of 35 to 55. As a general rule, this group is unlikely to progress in academic subjects beyond a second-grade level, though with proper supervision they may hold unskilled or semiskilled jobs. They may be able to coordinate some self-care functions (personal hygiene, doing the laundry, etc.), but generally they cannot live independently. They require close supervision when upset or under stress. They generally adjust best in community-based group homes with moderate supervision.

Steve concurrently suffers from schizophrenia (see Case 10), which was first diagnosed while he was in the state institution. People with mental retardation are 3 to 4 times as likely to develop other mental disorders as the general population. *DSM-III-R* lists early onset schizophrenia as a possible etiologic factor in mental retardation, and it is possible that this applies in Steve's case. However, without a better description of Steve's history, it is difficult to determine whether his mental retardation preceded or resulted from his schizophrenia.

Until recently Steve had been taking trazadone (known by the trade name Desyrel) to control his psychotic behavior. But about a year ago, Steve fainted on three separate occasions, twice resulting in hospitalization. His physician has been unable to pinpoint the exact cause of the fainting spells, but he believed they resulted from imbalances in Steve's blood sodium levels. Steve has been referred for a neurological evaluation, but so far no specific cause for his fainting spells has been found. As a precaution, Steve's psychotropic medication was discontinued. Steve also has chronic hypertension. His blood pressure is monitored weekly, but he takes no medication except for occasional sleeping pills administered by the staff.

The bulk of Steve's treatment consists of behavior therapy, which is divided into three aspects. The most formal of these is a token management program of in-house active treatment goals. These goals are themselves divided into three specific categories: self-care, independent living, and academics. The treatment director oversees the treatment program for every resident. She begins with a current functional assessment covering the following areas: medications, physical functioning (mobility, hearing, etc.), financial status, legal status, developmental history, emotional development, social development, and independent living skills. Based on this assessment, she determines active treatment goals most appropriate for each resident. Self-care goals, for example, may range from grocery shopping or doing the laundry (for higher-functioning individuals) to making the bed or using utensils (for lower functioning residents). These goals are posted in the lounge to serve as a reminder for the residents and staff. They reviewed at least monthly and revised as needed.

One of Steve's current self-care goals is brushing and flossing his teeth. Although Steve has known how to brush and floss his teeth since childhood, he often does an incomplete job and sometimes forgets altogether. Every time Steve successfully completes his brushing and flossing, he is rewarded with a coin-like token, which he can trade in for after-dinner snacks or special privileges during weekend activities. Steve's primary goal for independent living is to increase his interpersonal skills. He is rewarded for engaging in conversation with another resident, showing concern for another's welfare, and most of all, controlling his temper. Steve has made the greatest improvements in this area. However, Steve has done the worst in his academics. One current goal is to correctly identify and count change from purchases, but he has made little progress. As is the case for many elderly residents, Steve's intellectual functioning continues to decline with his diminishing health. Often the treatment goal for the elderly is the maintenance of existing skills rather than the acquisition of new ones.

In addition to his in-house token management training, Steve participates in adult day programing for six hours a day, five days a week. Every weekday morning Steve joins other residents (both from his ICF and from other homes) in a modified van that serves as a small bus. For two or three hours each day, the group works at a sheltered workshop, where they sort and package combs, brushes, and hair clips. The rest of the time is spent on different group events: picnics, movies, museums, and the like. Because there is a waiting list for Steve's program and others like it, the ICF must participate in several programs to fulfill the needs of its residents.

The least formal aspect of Steve's therapy may have had the greatest impact on his behavior: the social milieu established by the ICF. Steve's ICF is a renovated duplex on a quiet, middle-class residential street of single-family and two-family homes.

The ICF is clean and well maintained; the walls are painted in bright, cheerful colors; and the furniture is new but comfortable. In addition to the seven bedrooms, which the residents decorate themselves, there are three lounges and a group kitchen. The atmosphere is open, friendly, and supportive; staff and residents are addressed by their first names. In many ways the ICF functions as a large family. Perhaps the least involved member of this family is Steve, but even he has become cooperative and involved over the past four years. The matriarch of this family is the cook, an older neighborhood woman who has been at the ICF since it opened. In addition to preparing the meals, she takes it upon herself to look out for the residents and their home by giving advice, greeting visitors, and performing other helpful tasks. A housekeeper has also been with the ICF for years, but she is less involved with the residents.

Although the atmosphere of the ICF is friendly and communal, the work is very demanding. The direct-care staff consists of a residential manager, a treatment director (in charge of coordinating the residents' treatment programs), and five to six full-time staff. Burnout is a common problem. And since the ICF can offer only relatively low salaries, turnover is high; the average staff member stays for only a year or so. Despite this rapid turnover (or perhaps because of it), the staff members are generally responsive and enthusiastic.

PROGNOSIS

The prognosis for Steve is poor, both medically and psychologically. In the past year Steve has shown significant declines in his physical health and intellectual functioning. His therapist describes him as "getting several years older each year." Sadly, these declines are expected to continue or even accelerate. His case is complicated by the fact that no psychotropic medications can be offered until the etiology of his fainting spells has been established. Even if Steve's psychotropic medication can be continued, however, it is unlikely that he will make any noticeable gains aside from a reduction in his talking to imaginary and inanimate objects.

DISCUSSION

The general prevalence of mental retardation is 3 to 5 per thousand, or about 1/3 to 1/2 percent (McLaren & Bryson, 1987). Males are somewhat more likely to develop mental retardation than females. These figures vary slightly depending on sampling and screening methods, but generally they are very consistent across different studies. Similar figures are reported in African-American samples (Grubb, 1987) and in samples from Spain (Diaz-Fernandez, 1988) and the People's Republic of China (Tao, 1988).

The causes of mental retardation are diverse and complicated. *DSM-III-R* lists five categories of known etiologic factors for mental retardation: genetic causes (fragile X syndrome, Down syndrome, Tay-Sachs disease), prenatal causes (trisomy 21 syndrome, maternal alcohol syndrome), perinatal causes (fetal malnutrition, hypoxia, premature birth, birth trauma), postnatal causes (head trauma, infection, lead poisoning), and environmental and psychological causes (severe neglect, early onset schizophrenia). Collectively, these factors account for roughly 50 to 75 percent of the cases of mental retardation; the proportion of cases for which a cause cannot be determined varies from 27 percent (McQueen, Spence, Winsor, Garner, & Pereira, 1986) to 50 percent (McLaren & Bryson, 1987). Steve fits into this latter category, although it is possible that a more thorough history would have revealed an identifiable cause.

Several studies have found that the prevalence rate of mental retardation in children is decreasing, presumably as a result of improvements in public health practices, prenatal care, and perinatal experiences (Diaz-Fernandez, 1988; McLaren & Bryson, 1987; Richardson, 1989). On the other hand, medical advances and improved standards in treatment settings have prolonged the lives of the mentally retarded (Lund, 1986; McLoughlin,

1988). Furthermore, recent moves toward deinstitutionalization have increased the visibility of mentally retarded adults in the general community. As a result of these factors, the rate of mental retardation among adults has increased dramatically in recent years (Chartock, Bukenya, & Carter, 1989).

Despite these advances in health care, mentally retarded adults are at a higher risk than the general population for a number of negative health consequences, including physical illness (Haveman & Maaskant, 1989), mental illness (Buck & Sprague, 1989; Glue, Webb, & Surgenor, 1988; McLoughlin, 1988), and premature death (Eyman, Call, & White, 1989).

For many people, the term *mentally retarded* conjures up images of children. But as this research shows, Steve may be a more typical case. (Even his history of setting fires in childhood is fairly typical; Bradford & Dimock, 1986, found that 10 percent of their sample of arsonists was mentally retarded.) As his age approaches 50, he is beginning to develop a number of medical conditions, which are adversely affecting his psychiatric treatment. Sadly, Steve's poor prognosis is shared by the majority of adults with mental retardation.

Legal Regulations Governing the Treatment of the Mentally Retarded

It can be argued that Steve's treatment over the last 44 years has been affected as much by legal regulations as by medical and psychiatric advances. Judicial and legislative mandates that set specific standards for the treatment of this population were prompted by three factors: the growing numbers of mentally retarded adults, their special psychiatric and medical needs, and the uncovering of past institutional abuses. Without doubt this policy of active intervention has raised the general standard of treatment for the mentally disabled and has enabled thousands of mentally retarded adults to move from large institutions to relatively small community residences. However, in some circumstances government regulations have complicated treatment.

As a result of the appalling conditions of abuse and neglect uncovered at the Willowbrook Psychiatric Institution on Staten

Island, New York State mandated that every institutionalized patient throughout the state be moved to a community DC, ICF, or residential home by the end of 1992. This mandate is known as the Willowbrook Consent Decree. Although it is unlikely that the goal of complete deinstitutionalization will be effected by the target date, great strides have been made in locating the developmentally disabled to community-based facilities. It is because of this mandate that Steve was moved to a developmental center, then a residential home, and finally to the ICF.

The Willowbrook Consent Decree has also engendered two parallel problems. First, where will these patients go? New York State does not have nearly enough community-based facilities to house its institutionalized population, and building new ones is extremely difficult. One factor is the cost of these residences. Property is expensive, particularly in the New York metropolitan area. Furthermore, these residences must conform to strict state and local codes. Meeting these codes complicates new construction and requires virtually all existing buildings to undergo extensive renovations. These costs are particularly difficult to bear at a time when federal support for these projects is diminishing. A hurdle even more frustrating than the costs, however, is the reaction of the communities that are to host the new facilities. Community reactions to a proposed facility are almost always negative. Community residents fear unpredictable mental patients, disturbances at all hours, and drops in property values. Their reactions range from protests and legal injunctions to outright violence. But according to the Pativan Law, a community must prove saturation (a specific patient-to-nonpatient population ratio, which varies from community to community) for developmentally disabled residences for a proposal to be denied. Rarely can a community prove saturation, and most proposed sites are approved. In the end, community fears soon prove to be unfounded, and almost all residences are accepted. In fact, many residents appreciate having an abandoned property renovated and having someone up at all hours to keep an eye on the neighborhood. Nevertheless, the legal fees and delays resulting from the community's initial reaction tend to escalate costs.

A second problem resulting from the state-mandated deinstitutionalization is trying to decide who will be placed in the community residences. There simply aren't enough places to go around. For example, the private agency that runs Steve's ICF operates 12 residences throughout the New York metropolitan area, and each is filled to capacity. Still, the agency has 500 names on its active waiting list, and this number is expected double by 2010. But there is a further complication. Although the agency is privately run, it still depends on state funds to operate. A condition of this funding is that half of all new admissions come from government-run institutions, which is how Steve came to be placed in his ICF. As a result, the waiting list continues to grow.

AUTISTIC DISORDER
Behavior Modification

PRESENTING COMPLAINT

Tommy is a cute 5-year-old boy with straight brown hair and bright blue eyes. Except for his slightly crooked teeth and a somewhat blank expression on his face, he looks just like any other boy his age. After watching Tommy for just a short time, however, it becomes readily apparent that he suffers from severe abnormalities that seem to affect virtually every aspect of his life: his speech, his thinking, his actions, and his relationships with others.

The first obvious sign of Tommy's psychological impairment is his speech. Except for occasional incoherent groans, Tommy is virtually mute. In the first five years of his life he has learned only a few signed words using American Sign Language (ASL). He can gesture for "more," "eat," and "toilet," the latter by signing the letter "T." He also tries to communicate by pointing at people, places, and objects, but most often the intent of these nonspecific gestures is unclear. Other than these rudimentary sounds and gestures, Tommy has no real linguistic ability.

Tommy's IQ is 48, as measured on the Wechsler Intelligence Scale for Children-Revised (WISC-R) (Wechsler, 1958). This score would categorize him as moderately retarded. However, because of his pervasive lack of communication skills and his lack of interest in testing procedures, it is difficult to assess accurately the actual extent of his cognitive impairment.

What is easier to assess is Tommy's odd behavior. Frequently Tommy will sit with his arms grasping his chest or his knees and slowly rock back and forth, all the while staring straight ahead. Tommy also engages in other forms of repetitive behavior such as pushing a toy car back and forth (often not on its wheels) and drawing page after page of parallel straight lines. It is not uncommon for these seemingly meaningless behaviors to last for four or five hours without interruption. At these times Tommy shows little emotion and seems totally engrossed in his ritualistic behavior. In the past few months, Tommy's hand has become the central focus for many of his strange behaviors. Often Tommy will suddenly stop what he is doing, hold his hand directly in front of his face, and intensely stare at it while he rotates it slowly. As he examines his hand, he sometimes emits a high-pitched squealing tone; occasionally he smiles and giggles. Usually, though, he simply stares at it. He seems to be especially interested if his hand is wet and dripping or covered with food (which is often the case at mealtimes).

In addition to these strange, repetitive behaviors, Tommy also has bursts of wild, uncontrolled activity, usually when he is upset. Sometimes he will run around the perimeter of the room with his legs pumping and his arms flailing, screaming the whole time. At other times he pounds his hands against the floor or wall in an angry, frustrated tantrum. Often when he is examining his hand he will shake it so violently that it appears that he is trying to separate it from his arm. (This sort of flailing is termed "hand flapping.") On rare occasions Tommy manages to bite his hand while flapping, usually hard enough to break the skin. In the midst of these wild behaviors Tommy appears to be genuinely upset; his face takes on a grimace and grows red, and his whole body seems tense. When he is restrained during these uncontrolled actions, he usually struggles for a few moments and then inexplicably goes about his business as if nothing ever happened, seemingly as oblivious of the person who restrained him as he is of the actions themselves.

By far the most salient aspect of Tommy's disorder, especially to his family, is his complete inability (or unwillingness) to form interpersonal relationships. During his short life Tommy has never engaged in any meaningful communication with another person, not even at the level of establishing sustained eye contact. He seems to understand that people exist, and he even reacts to them occasionally; however, he does not seem to attach any special significance to other people as fellow human beings. For the most part he treats other people like inanimate objects to be noticed, ignored, or avoided, much like most people treat large animals or pieces of furniture. Tommy appears to attach some special significance to his parents—he will look at them when they address him and will pay attention to their actions. Even this relationship is very distant, though. Perhaps the best description for his relationship with his parents is that he treats them like two strangers on a busy city street; he seems to understand that they are fellow humans and may even be temporarily interested in what they are doing, but he seems to have no particular interest in establishing any sort of meaningful relationship with them.

Tommy's parents attempted to take care of him at home, but his odd, disruptive behavior became increasingly more unmanageable.

PERSONAL HISTORY

Tommy is the younger child of two in an upper-middle-class family living in a prestigious suburb north of Milwaukee. Tommy's father is a senior vice president of a medium-sized manufacturing firm, and his mother is an associate professor at a large state university in Milwaukee. Tommy's brother, who is four years older, is successful in school and popular with his friends.

During his infancy, Tommy's mother described him as a "model baby." He was always quiet and hardly ever cried or fussed. Throughout the first two years of his life, Tommy was usually quiet and independent. However, from early on it was difficult for Tommy's parents to get his attention or make eye contact. He was unresponsive to games such as peekaboo, and he did not demonstrate any need to be held or comforted; in fact, he completely ignored his parents, his brother, and other relatives who came to visit. As mentioned above, although his parents thought these traits were somewhat peculiar, they did not worry about them at first.

When he was 2, Tommy was enrolled in day-care. At first he was considered a quiet, cooperative child, but before long his utter failure to interact socially became obvious. He spent the majority of his day silently staring off into the distance or rocking by himself in a corner. He began to show odd repetitive behavior and to throw tantrums and run around wildly. Since these behaviors began to seriously disrupt the day-care routine, Tommy was asked to leave. The day-care staff suggested that Tommy should see a specialist, but Tommy's parents were convinced that his odd behavior was something that he would eventually outgrow. They hired a private sitter to stay with him during the day, but after only eight months three sitters had already quit.

By this time Tommy had still not begun to talk, and his parents began to worry seriously about his intellectual abilities. He was taken to numerous pediatric and neurology specialists, who said that Tommy suffered from childhood autism and would need to be institutionalized. Tommy's parents realized that he needed special care but were reluctant to institutionalize him, so they hired a private pediatric nurse to stay with him. Over the next year, Tommy's disruptive behavior became more frequent and more severe. In addition, he began to flap and bite his hand. His parents and the nurse had to monitor his behavior constantly to make sure he did not cause serious injury to himself or costly damage to the house. After about a year the private nurse quit, and Tommy's mother was forced to take a semester off to look after him herself. Finally she contacted a school for autistic and emotionally disturbed children.

(*Emotionally disturbed* is a global term that describes a range of different problems, including severe shyness and withdrawal and disabling anxiety.) After being on the waiting list for approximately four months, Tommy was enrolled when a space became available.

CONCEPTUALIZATION AND TREATMENT

The staff at the special school had no difficulty diagnosing him as having autistic disorder. Autistic disorder, commonly referred to as "childhood autism," is a pervasive developmental disorder that affects almost every aspect of a child's life. The primary feature of autism, which literally means "self-ism," is the child's inability to form meaningful relationships with other people and a more or less complete withdrawal into a private world. This profound social withdrawal is usually accompanied by severe disturbances in the child's intellectual and linguistic abilities; most autistic children are mentally retarded and have very limited, if any, communication skills. In addition, autistic children are characterized by odd behaviors, typically consisting of meaningless repetitive behaviors and bursts of wild activity. Many autistic children also engage in any of a variety of self-mutilating behaviors, including hand biting, scratching and gouging, head banging, and pica—eating nonnutritive substances such as paste or feces.

Tommy clearly fits this category. Throughout his short life he has been unable to form any adequate relationship with any other person, including the other children at his day-care, his sitters, or even his parents. His intellectual skills are severely impaired, and his communication skills are virtually nonexistent. His meaningless rocking, playing, and drawing; his wild flapping; and his frequent tantrums all provide additional behavioral evidence of his autistic disorder.

Tommy was enrolled in the school for autistic and emotionally disturbed children in November. During the academic year, the school runs from 8:30 to 4:30 on weekdays. The staff consists of nonmedical personnel with doctorates or master's degrees in clinical psychology and special education. There are five full-time therapists, three part-time therapists (one occupational therapist and two speech therapists), and several volunteers from local colleges and high schools. The pupils range from 5 to 25 years of age and are drawn from the entire Milwaukee metropolitan area. The number of pupils varies; presently the school is full, with 18. Fourteen of the children are also autistic like Tommy, although none is quite so severely disturbed. The other four children are diagnosed as emotionally disturbed (ED). Like autistic children, emotionally disturbed children exhibit extreme shyness, withdrawal, and anxiety that seriously impair their social development. These children are so intimidated by interpersonal situations that their scholastic performance also suffers. However, emotionally disturbed children differ from autistic children in that they are able to perceive their social environment relatively well, and as a rule they do not exhibit the uncontrolled and bizarre symptoms of the autistic children.

Tommy's school also runs an eight-week live-in summer camp where the students are supervised for 24 hours a day. The staff at the camp consists of one staff member from the school who acts as a supervisor and six trained undergraduate counselors. The number of students who may attend camp at any one time is limited to seven. Since there is a long waiting list for this camp, the younger and more disturbed children are limited to two weeks at the camp. The older and more capable students are allowed to stay the entire eight weeks. Being the youngest and most severely disturbed child in the school, Tommy was limited to a two-week-stay during his first two summers.

Tommy's school employs a model of treatment based on behavior modification. The primary focus of the staff is not to "cure" the students but rather to teach them some basic skills that may help them to lead more independent lives. The therapists attempt to achieve this goal by carefully controlling the children's environment, particularly the level of reinforcement (and occasionally punishment) the children receive. The more formal classroom therapy (conducted in both group and individual instruction) concentrates on providing the children with opportunities to develop social and cognitive skills. Lessons in social interaction and basic hygiene are taught through less formal instruction, which is conducted just about anywhere: on the playground, in the cafeteria, and even in the bathrooms. Since therapy relies to such a great extent on controlling the children's social environments, parents are encouraged to adopt behavioral techniques at home to help maintain the changes made at school. Researchers (Howlin & Rutter, 1987) have found that instructing the parents in behavior modification techniques leads to more widespread and lasting improvements.

Group lessons take several forms; their general aim is to teach these self-absorbed students to cooperate with each other. For example, in a shared finger painting task, each child starts a picture and then exchanges pictures with another student. The children are reinforced for allowing another student to work on "their" project, and they are given special rewards for working on a project together. In another group activity, this time conducted on the playground, students are assigned to either ride on a swing or to push another student. Again, the children are reinforced for displaying cooperation and reciprocity. During these sessions the therapists have to be careful to notice whenever a student behaves appropriately and to reinforce that student as soon as possible through encouragement, hugs, and occasionally, snacks. Just as important, inappropriate or injurious behavior must be stopped immediately.

Individual therapy focuses on developing the children's cognitive and linguistic skills. For example, the therapist might employ flash cards and practice booklets to work on a student's vocabulary or basic math skills. In addition, each child meets with a speech therapist for 50 minutes every other day to practice his or her diction or, in the case of more severely disturbed children, signing. Every student is also instructed in basic vocational skills (e.g., matching wires by colors, sorting various nuts and bolts, sweeping the work area). Getting a job in a sheltered workshop is probably the only employment opportunity most of these children will ever have.

In addition to these relatively formal lessons, the staff takes every opportunity to teach the students basic life skills. During lunch the staff attempts to monitor closely the students' behavior, and students are reinforced for such things as waiting in line cooperatively, eating with others, not playing with their food, chewing their food sufficiently before swallowing, and not causing disturbances (throwing their food, taking other students' food, running or screaming). Similar practical training takes place in the bathrooms. Although being toilet trained is a requirement for admission to the school, accidents are not uncommon among the younger and more disturbed children. The students have to be carefully monitored to ensure that they perform the common steps of toileting that most people take for granted (putting the toilet seat up or down, making sure to urinate or defecate *in* the toilet and not on or around it, wiping themselves adequately, flushing the toilet, washing afterwards). The staff regards teaching the students these basic life skills to be a vital step in helping them develop a greater degree of independence.

Developing basic life skills is the primary focus of the summer camp. Students, who are called "campers," are taught to perform a variety of everyday tasks that include cleaning their room, doing their laundry, taking a shower, and preparing for bed. Each of these basic tasks is broken up into smaller, more manageable subtasks. For example, getting the campers ready for bed involves several individual components: picking up their toys and clothes, changing into their pajamas, brushing their teeth, and so forth. The other focus of the summer camp is to develop the campers' social skills by providing opportunities for interaction and reinforcing prosocial behavior. This training occurs primarily during recreational activities and at mealtimes.

The school uses a variety of reinforcers to reward appropriate behavior. First and foremost, secondary reinforcement in the form of attention, praise, encouragement, and hugs is given to every student whenever appropriate. However, since one of the primary characteristics of autistic children is a marked disinterest in interpersonal relationships, this social reinforcement is usually supplemented by more tangible rewards such as candy and snacks. As the students become accustomed to the structure of the program, their privileges (recess time, dessert at lunch) become used as reinforcements with increasing frequency. This is especially true at the summer camp, where the students' recreational activities (swimming, hiking, playing games), their participation on field trips, and even their choice of food are contingent on their behavior.

Eliminating inappropriate behavior is more difficult. Because the staff's attention and concern may serve as secondary reinforcers for inappropriate actions, these behaviors are ignored whenever possible. In this way the staff attempts to extinguish the inappropriate behaviors. Since negative behavior can be very disrupting to the other students, especially during group lessons, often this extinction process is carried out by placing the child in a separate room, which is commonly referred to as a "time-out" room. Occasionally the children are punished by scolding them or withdrawing their privileges. On some occasions they must be physically restrained by the staff to prevent injury or damage. Such an occasion arose when Tommy suddenly ran off the playground and began beating on the back of an elderly man who was walking down the sidewalk.

Occasionally a child exhibits odd behavior that demands close supervision. For example, one autistic girl had a persistent habit involving pica. She would hide in a bathroom stall until no one was around. Then she would defecate, reach down and grab her own feces, and quickly begin eating them. The staff learned to keep a close eye on her. When they noticed that she was not with the other students, they would immediately run to the nearest bathroom and most often catch her in the act. Her habit took on the air of an addiction; when she ate her own excrement, she smiled and giggled, and she became very upset when she was interrupted and restrained from eating her feces. The staff was careful to prevent this behavior and reinforce her for flushing her feces. They also (sometimes in spite of themselves) scolded her for this behavior. Over the course of four months, her pica was gradually eliminated, presumably as a result of the staff's efforts.

Tommy was extremely upset when he first came to the school. He threw frequent tantrums, about four or five per day, and spent most of his time flapping his hand or rocking quietly in a corner. Soon he became accustomed to the school routine, though, and it became possible to engage him in the daily lessons. By the holiday break in December, Tommy had grown to expect the daily routine of the school and had in fact become very distressed when it was interrupted by the vacation.

Initially the staff concentrated on eliminating Tommy's disruptive behaviors. When he threw a tantrum, the staff was careful to ignore him. If the tantrum persisted, or if it was interrupting a group lesson, Tommy was placed in the time-out room for 10 minutes or until his tantrum ended. During the next few weeks Tommy's tantrums became less and less frequent, and by the first vacation break they had virtually ceased. Tommy's parents, who were also instructed to use this extinction procedure, reported that he had virtually stopped throwing tantrums at home as well.

The staff employed a behavioral shaping technique to control Tommy's hand flapping and uncontrolled running around. When Tommy first began these actions, he was physically restrained by a staff member. Usually he would resist this restraint by squirming or shouting. If he started to calm down, however, he was given a reward. Effective reinforcements for him were M&Ms, peanuts, and apple juice. After several incidents Tommy learned to calm down merely in response to the staff's commands and requests. Now he was reinforced for stopping his disruptive behavior only if he did not need to be restrained. Later, as Tommy learned to remain quiet after calming down, his reinforcement became contingent on remaining in control for a set period of time, first 10 minutes, then 15, then 30, and so on. Tommy was gradually shifted from primary reinforcers (snacks) to secondary reinforcers such as hugs and praise. After six months, Tommy's hand flapping and uncontrolled running was reduced to its present level. Although he still performs these disruptive actions on occasion, he does so much less frequently than he used to, and he usually stops this behavior after a short warning from a staff member.

The next focus of therapy was to increase Tommy's level of social interaction. When Tommy arrived at the school, he made no effort to communicate with the staff or his fellow students. In fact, he gave them no sign of recognition other than as inanimate objects. By selectively reinforcing his cooperative play and recreation behaviors, the staff gradually got Tommy to participate with them and with the other students in group recreation projects and unstructured play activities. Tommy's change was very slow and gradual, and even after two years he still gives little indication that he regards people with any level of empathy or interpersonal understanding.

The overriding goal of Tommy's more formal lessons and his speech therapy is to increase his vocabulary. After more than two years of intensive individual and group therapy, Tommy's vocabulary has increased from 2 words to slightly over 100. Throughout the first year, Tommy refused to make any attempt at verbal communication. As a result, most of his speech training consisted of teaching him the ASL sign for various objects and concepts in his world (e.g., "teacher," "hungry," "outside"). During the training sessions, Tommy was asked to make various signs demonstrated by the speech therapist or shown on cue cards and was given primary reinforcers for doing so. During his second year, Tommy began to verbalize the words he was learning. As was the case with his other training, Tommy was selectively reinforced for making closer and closer approximations to the words' actual sounds. Although his articulation is very poor and the majority of his speech is incomprehensible to most people, his willingness to verbalize some of this thoughts represents a great advancement in his communication skills.

During summer camp Tommy's training concentrated on more basic life skills, particularly his eating behavior and his personal hygiene. When Tommy arrived at camp, he did not use eating utensils. Furthermore, he was an unusually impatient and sloppy eater; his place at the cafeteria table was always marked by a large amount of spilled food. Occasionally he would throw relatively large food items (pieces of bread, sausage links, and so forth) around the cafeteria, often hitting other campers or staff members. Since most of his lunches at school consisted of sandwiches and treats, the extent to which he lacked proper eating skills was not readily apparent until his arrival at camp. By using his dessert or favorite foods as rewards, Tommy was taught to eat with utensils and to keep the majority of his food on his tray. After two weeks of carefully monitoring his eating, Tommy by and large stopped throwing food and began to use a spoon; after a month he began to use a fork, albeit sporadically. Unfortunately, his eating habits were not otherwise affected by his camp experiences.

Another aspect of Tommy's disorder that was not fully appreciated until he arrived at camp was his need to have order, predictability, and routine in his everyday life. For example, part of Tommy's training took place in the shower, where he was taught to wash himself thoroughly as part of his hygiene training. It soon became clear that Tommy had a set ritual when he washed himself: left foot first, then left leg, then left side, then left arm, and so on. If he performed this washing ritual out of sequence or forgot a step, he would become very upset and would insist on repeating the entire ritual. It was not uncommon for Tommy to spend over two hours in the shower, with the counselor standing with him in the shower the entire time. In an attempt to get Tommy to give up this ritual, the counselors scheduled his showers directly before his most preferred activities, swimming and hiking. Although his showers became somewhat shorter, his shower ritual did not change significantly. On several occasions he forsook his favorite activities because of this ritual. Tommy's second stay as a camper similarly had little effect on his shower ritual. Apparently, it was more important for Tommy to complete his ritualistic behavior than to participate in his favorite recreation events.

PROGNOSIS

After over two years at the school (including two camp sessions), Tommy has made some limited improvement. His vocabulary has increased to over 100 words, and he is beginning to develop his speech skills, but he still has a long way to go. Tommy is also capable of performing some simple addition problems. For the most part, though, the progress in his communication and academic skills has been very slow, and his IQ has not changed significantly. Tommy's most noticeable change is a reduction in his disruptive behaviors. His temper tantrums for the most part have stopped, and the amount of time he spends flapping his hand and running around wildly has been greatly reduced. In short, he is generally calmer in most situations and much easier to control. In addition, he is more cooperative during games and when working on recreation projects. Still, the staff and Tommy's parents get the impression that his cooperation is merely in response to their expectations; he doesn't seem to be particularly interested in forming relationships with others. Tommy still spends the majority of his free time absently playing with his favorite toys, staring at his hand, or just rocking quietly. The overall prognosis for Tommy is poor. It is unlikely that he will ever be able to establish anything resembling a normal relationship with another person, nor is it probable that he will be able to live with any degree of independence.

In general, the prognosis for children with autistic disorder is discouraging. Some of the less disturbed children may eventually be able to live relatively independently in a supervised apartment or halfway house and may hold down steady jobs in a sheltered work environment. A rare few will recover completely. A reliable, although rough, indicator of a child's prognosis is his or her attainment of speech skills. By and large, children who have developed recognizable speech by the age of 5 will be able to benefit most from therapy and have the greatest chance of eventually living on their own (Chung, Luk, & Lee,

1990; Gillberg, 1990a). Most of the more severely disturbed children, however, will probably require professional care for the rest of their lives.

DISCUSSION

The prevalence of autism is a subject of some controversy. Epidemiologic studies conducted in a number of countries around the world over the past quarter century (e.g., Burd, Fisher, & Kerbeshian, 1987; Gillberg, 1984; Lotter, 1966, Ritvo et al., 1989; Treffert, 1970) reported a very low prevalence rate, ranging from 0.012 to 0.04 percent. Some recent studies, however, have reported rates around 0.10 percent (e.g., Bryson, Clark, & Smith, 1988; Gillberg, 1990b), and others double this latter figure to a rate of 0.21 percent (Wing & Gould, 1979; Suriyama & Abe, 1986). This last figure is *17 times* higher than the figure provided by Burd et al.

Many factors contribute to this confusing situation, including demographic differences and unusual immigration patterns (Gillberg, 1990a) and methodological differences (Ritvo et al., 1989; Gillberg, 1990a). However, the greatest contributor seems to be inconsistencies in defining autism. Before *DSM-III* was published in 1980, researchers' conceptions of autism were to some extent idiosyncratic. The *DSM-III* definition was fairly narrow and restricted the diagnosis to children who exhibited most of the classical symptoms of autism before the age of 30 months. *DSM-III-R* (1987) did away with the age restriction, which may have been a factor that inflated rates in some very recent surveys. A more important factor is that some European researchers (Gillberg, 1990a; Wing, 1981) have begun to adopt a more broadly defined notion of autism that includes less severe symptomatology. The narrow conception of autism and the more broadly defined view are known as the Kanner syndrome and the Asperger syndrome, respectively. Whether the field adopts this dual conception of autism remains to be seen.

Researchers tend to show more agreement on the demographic characteristics of autistic children. Boys tend to outnumber girls roughly 3 to 1 (Bryson et al., 1988; Gillberg, 1990b; Lord, Schlopler, & Revicki, 1982; Ritvo et al., 1989; Steinhauser, Göbel, Breinlinger, & Wohlleben, 1986). Interestingly, autistic girls consistently score lower on IQ tests than do autistic boys (Lord et al., 1982; Ritvo et al.; Tsai, Stewart, & August, 1981). In other words, girls are less likely to develop autism, but when they do, it is accompanied by more profound intellectual impairment. Overall, between 65 and 85 percent of autistic children have an IQ below 70 and are thus defined as mentally retarded (Rutter, 1983; Gillberg, 1990a).

Researchers have associated autism with a wide variety of neurological and biological problems, which has led to a bewildering array of suggested causes for the disorder, including genetics (Bolton & Rutter, 1990; Krishnamurthy & Joshi, 1989), fragile X syndrome (Wahlström, Gillberg, Gustavson, & Holmgren, 1986), phenylketonuria (PKU) (Friedman, 1969), and lactic acidosis (Coleman & Blass, 1985), to name just a few. It is generally recognized that autism is a complex disorder with multiple underlying etiologies (Edelman, 1987).

Most researchers dismiss psychogenic theories of autism. Early psychodynamic theorists (Bettleheim, 1967; Kanner, 1943) attributed the development of this disorder to the child's reaction to cold, unfeeling parents. These parents, often called "emotional refrigerators," were typically very successful professionals who were seen as either too intellectual or too busy to establish an adequate emotional relationship with their infants. On the surface Tommy's parents, both successful professionals, seem to fit this pattern. However, recent epidemiologic surveys (Chung et al., 1990; Ritvo et al., 1989; Steinhauser et al., 1986) have failed to find any differences between parents of autistic children and parents of normal children in terms of their socioeconomic status, occupation, race, religion, or any other demographic variable. It is probable that the preponderance of autism among wealthy, educated families simply reflected the fact that these families were most likely to seek sophisticated treatment for their children. As the disorder has become more widely recognized, this artifact has diminished. Nevertheless, psychogenic theories of childhood autism still retain some popularity. Unfortunately, the primary effect of these theories is to intensify the hardships and frustrations of parents of autistic children by inducing feelings of guilt and failure. In contrast, biomedical theories of autism do not blame the parents for their children's misfortunes, and their value may lie as much in helping to alleviate the guilt and despair of these parents as in providing a framework to conceptualize this disorder.

In the small number of cases where PKU and lactic acidosis are identified soon after birth, special diets can prevent the onset of autism. Otherwise, no effective cure for autism exists at the present time. Careful behavior modification has shown some notable improvements in fostering living skills (Howlin & Rutter, 1987; Lovaas, 1987), but the gains from this therapy tend to be limited. Early successes reported with fenfluramine (known by the trade name Ritalin) have not been demonstrated in recent, methodologically rigorous studies (Campbell, 1988; du Verglass, Banks, & Guyer, 1988; Ekman, Miranda-Linné, Gillberg, Carle, & Wetterberg, 1989). Treatment for autism remains, at best, a long, difficult, and frustrating process. In all likelihood, effective therapy must involve multiple modalities (Gillberg, 1990a).

Isolated but widely publicized cases have reported idiot savants (literally "wise idiots"), autistic people who possess some extraordinarily well-developed ability, usually in the area of mathematical calculation or the manipulation of spatial forms. For example, Dustin Hoffman won an Oscar for his portrayal of an idiot savant in the popular film *Rainman*. Such cases do occur in real life. Daniel, a 16-year-old student at Tommy's school, could mentally add, subtract, multiply, and even divide 10-digit numbers. He also knew virtually every statistic available for every player who was ever a member of the Green Bay Packers (round drafted into the pros; number of tackles; rushing, receiving, and passing yardage). In his book *The Man Who Mistook His Wife for a Hat, and Other Clinical Tales*, Oliver Sacks (1985) describes the case of an autistic girl who was able to draw beautiful sketches of horses, roosters, and other animals with uncanny sophistication. Two aspects of this phenomenon deserve mention. First, idiot savants are extremely rare and make up but a tiny fraction all autistic cases. Second, the abilities of these autistics is usually limited to a narrow range of talents that are rarely of any practical use. For example, despite Daniel's impressive abilities at mental arithmetic, he could not make change for a dollar. If anything, the unique abilities of idiot savants seem to emphasize the differences between them and most other children and may actually serve to exacerbate the social isolation so characteristic of this disorder.

Finally, it is important to note that the behaviors of autistic children, both their wild and disruptive actions and their persistent rejection of social attachments, are very taxing for the people who must deal with them on a regular basis, mostly their parents and the therapeutic staff. At Tommy's school the staff often joked that the eight-hour school days—and especially the eight-week summer camp—were more therapeutic for the parents than for the students, and in all likelihood this was true. Treating autistic children is a grueling process with few rewards, and many professionals lose motivation in the face of the slow progress of their students. During Tommy's first two years at the school, for example, two full-time staff members quit, and there was constant turnover in the student volunteer program. The summer camp counselors were especially prone to burnout. Although none of the camp counselors (all psychology and special education majors) quit during either summer camp session, none returned for a second year and only 1 of the 12 decided to pursue a career in mental health. Of course, parents of autistic children do not have the option to quit; their choice is to persevere or to institutionalize their child.

REFERENCES

Abelson, J. L., Glitz, D., Cameron, O. G., Lee, M. A., Bronzo, M., & Curtis, G. C. (1991). Blunted growth hormone response to clonidine in patients with generalized anxiety disorder. *Archives of General Psychiatry, 48,* 157-162.

Adler, D. A., Drake, R. E., & Teague, G. B. (1990). Clinicians' practices in personality assessment: Does gender influence the use of *DSM-III* Axis II? *Comprehensive Psychiatry, 31,* 125-133.

Akerstedt, T., & Torsvall, L. (1981). Shift work: Shift-dependent well-being and individual differences. *Ergonomics, 24,* 265-273.

Akhtar, S., Byrne, J. P., & Doghramji, K. (1986). The demographic profile of borderline personality disorder. *Journal of Clinical Psychiatry, 47,* 196-198.

Alfredsson, L., Akerstedt, T., Mattsson, M., & Wilborg, B. (1991). Self-reported health and well-being amongst night security guards: A comparison with the working population. *Ergonomics, 34,* 522-530.

American Psychiatric Association. (1980). *Diagnostic and statistical manual of mental disorders (DSM-III)* (3rd ed.). Washington, DC: Author.

American Psychiatric Association. (1987). *Diagnostic and statistical manual of mental disorders (DSM-III-R)* (3rd ed. rev.). Washington, DC: Author.

Ard, B. N. (1977). Sex in lasting marriages: A longitudinal study. *Journal of Sex Research, 13,* 274-285.

Baer, L., Jenike, M. A., Ricciardi, J. N., Holland, A. D., Seymour, R. J., Minichiello, W. E., & Buttolph, M. L. (1990). Standardized assessment of personality disorders in obsessive-compulsive disorder. *Archives of General Psychiatry, 47,* 826-830.

Bancroft, J., & Coles, L. (1976). Three years' experience in a sexual problems clinic. *British Medical Journal, 1,* 1575-1577.

Baptista, T., & Novua, D. (1989). Evaluation of the diagnosis of schizophrenia in the first decade of operation of the inpatient psychiatric unit of Merida, Venezuela (1974-1983). *Research Communications in Psychology, Psychiatry, and Behavior, 14,* 99-112.

Barclay, L. L., Zemcov, A., Blass, J. P., & McDowell, F. H. (1985). Factors associated with duration of survival in Alzheimer's disease. *Biological Psychiatry, 20,* 86-93.

Barner-Rassmussen, P. (1986). Suicide in psychiatric patients in Denmark, 1971-1981: II. Hospital utilization and risk groups. *Acta Psychiatrica Scandinavica, 73,* 449-455.

Belloni-Sonzogni, A., Tissot, A., Tettamanti, M., Frattura, L., & Spagnoli, A. (1989). Mortality of demented patients in a geriatric institution. *Archives of Gerontology and Geriatrics, 9,* 193-197.

Berg, C. Z., Whitaker, A., Davies, M., Flament, M. F., & Rapoport, J. (1988). The survey form of the Leyton Obsessional Inventory—Child version: Norms from an epidemiological study. *Journal of the American Academy of Child and Adolescent Psychiatry, 27,* 759-763.

Bettleheim, B. (1967). *The empty fortress.* New York: Free Press.

Bland, R. C., Orn, H., & Newman, S. C. (1988). Lifetime prevalence of psychiatric disorders in Edmonton. *Acta Psychiatrica Scandinavica, 77*(Suppl. 338), 24-32.

Blazer, D. G., Hughes, D. C., & George, L. K. (1987). The epidemiology of depression in an elderly community population. *Gerontologist, 27,* 281-287.

Blessed, G., Tomlinson, B., & Roth, H. (1968). The association between quantitative measures of dementia and of senile change in the cerebral grey matter of elderly subjects. *British Journal of Psychiatry, 114,* 797-811.

Bliss, E. L. (1984). A symptom profile of patients with multiple personalities, including MMPI results. *Journal of Nervous and Mental Disease, 172,* 197-201.

Block, J. H., Gjerde, P. F., & Block, J. H. (1991). Personality antecedents of depressive tendencies in 18-year-olds: A prospective study. *Journal of Personality and Social Psychology, 60,* 726-738.

Bolton, P., & Rutter, M. (1990). Genetic influences in autism. *International Review of Psychiatry, 2,* 67-80.

Bowen, R. C., Offord, D. R., & Boyle, M. H. (1990). The prevalence of overanxious disorder and separation anxiety disorder: Results from the Ontario Child Health Study. *Journal of the American Academy of Child and Adolescent Psychiatry, 29,* 753-758.

Boyd, H. I., & Weissman, M. M. (1981). Epidemiology of affective disorders. *Archives of General Psychiatry, 38,* 1039-1046.

Bradford, J., & Dimock, J. (1986). A comparative study of adolescents and adults who willfully set fires. *Psychiatric Journal of the University of Ottawa, 11,* 228-234.

Brayne, C., & Calloway, P. (1989). An epidemiological study of dementia in a rural population of elderly women. *British Journal of Psychiatry, 155,* 214-219.

Brown, F. W., Golding, J. M., & Smith, G. R. (1990). Psychiatric comorbidity in primary care somatization disorder. *Psychosomatic Medicine, 52,* 445-451.

Bryson, S. E., Clark, B. S., & Smith, I. M. (1988). First report of a Canadian epidemiological study of autistic syndromes. *Journal of Child Psychology and Psychiatry, 29,* 433-445.

Buck, J. A., & Sprague, R. L. (1989). Psychotropic medication of mentally retarded residents in community long-term care facilities. *American Journal on Mental Retardation, 93,* 618-623.

Burd, L., Fisher, W., & Kerbeshian, J. (1987). A prevalence study of pervasive developmental disorders in North Dakota. *Journal of the American Academy of Child and Adolescent Psychiatry, 26,* 700-703.

Burke, K. C., Burke, J. D., Rae, D. S., and Regier, D. A. (1991). Comparing age at onset of major depression and other psychiatric disorders by birth cohorts in five U.S. community populations. *Archives of General Psychiatry, 48,* 789-795.

Campbell, M. (1988). Annotation: Fenfluramine treatment of autism. *Journal of Child Psychology and Psychiatry, 29,* 1-10.

Centers for Disease Control (1989). Acquired immunodeficiency syndrome associated with intravenous drug use. *Morbidity and Mortality Weekly Report, 38,* 165-170.

Chartock, P., Bukenya, T., & Carter, R. (1989). *Findings of the survey of services for older New Yorkers with developmental disabilities.* New York: New York City Task Force on Aging and Developmental Disabilities.

Chethik, M. (1989). *Techniques of child therapy: Psychodynamic strategies.* New York: Guilford.

Chung, S. Y., Luk, S. L., & Lee, P. W. H. (1990). A follow-up study of infantile autism in Hong Kong. *Journal of Autism and Developmental Disorders, 20,* 221-232.

Cohen, S., Khan, A., & Cox, G. (1989). Demographic and clinical features predictive of recovery in acute mania. *Journal of Nervous and Mental Disease, 177,* 638-642.

Coleman, M., & Blass, J. P. (1985). Autism and lactic acidosis. *Journal of Autism and Developmental Disorders, 15,* 1-8.

Conte, H. R., Plutchik, R., Karasu, T. B., & Jerrett, I. (1980). A self-report borderline scale: Discriminative validity and preliminary norms. *Journal of Nervous and Mental Disease, 168,* 428-435.

Coons, P. M., Bowman, E. S., & Milstein, V. (1988). Multiple personality disorder: A clinical investigation of 50 cases. *Journal of Nervous and Mental Disease, 176,* 519-527.

Coons, P. M., & Milstein, V. (1986). Psychosexual disturbances in multiple personality: Characteristics, etiology, and treatment. *Journal of Clinical Psychiatry, 47,* 106-110.

Cooper, P. J., & Fairburn, C. G. (1983). Binge-eating and self-induced vomiting in the community: A preliminary study. *British Journal of Psychiatry, 142,* 139-144.

Dacey, C. M., Nelson, W. M., & Aikman, K. G. (1990). Prevalency rate and personality comparisons of bulimic and normal adolescents. *Child Psychiatry and Human Development, 20,* 243-251.

Dahl, A. A. (1985). Diagnosis of the borderline disorders. *Psychopathology, 18,* 18-28.

Davanloo, H. (1988). The technique of unlocking the unconscious. Part 1. *International Journal of Short-term Psychotherapy, 3,* 99-121.

DeBeck, T. W. (1990). Delayed sleep phase syndrome: Criminal offense in the military? *Military Medicine, 155,* 14-15.

Desmond, D. P., & Maddux, J. F. (1984). Mexican-American heroin addicts. *American Journal of Drug and Alcohol Abuse, 10,* 317-346.

Deutsch, L. H., & Rovner, B. W. (1991). Agitation and other non-cognitive abnormalities in Alzheimer's disease. *Psychiatric Clinics of North America, 14,* 341-351.

Dewald, P. A. (1982). Psychoanalytic perspectives on resistance. In P. L. Wachtel (Ed.), *Resistance: Psychodynamic and behavioral approaches* (pp. 45-68). New York: Plenum Press.

Diaz-Fernandez, F. (1988). Descriptive epidemiology of registered mentally retarded persons in Galicia (Northwest Spain). *American Journal on Mental Retardation, 92,* 385-392.

Dolan, B. (1991). Cross-cultural aspects of anorexia nervosa and bulimia: A review. *International Journal of Eating Disorders, 10,* 67-79.

Dolan, B. M., Lieberman, S., Evans, C., & Lacey, J. H. (1990). Family features associated with normal body weight bulimia. *International Journal of Eating Disorders, 9,* 639-647.

Downing, R. W., & Rickels, K. (1985). Early treatment response in anxious outpatients treated with diazepam. *Acta Psychiatrica Scandinavica, 72,* 522-528.

Drewnowski, A., Yee, D. K., & Krahn, D. D. (1987). Bulimia in college women: Incidence and recovery rates. *American Journal of Psychiatry, 145,* 753-755.

du Verglass, G., Banks, S. R., & Guyer, K. E. (1988). Clinical effects of fenfluramine on children with autism: A review of the research. *Journal of Autism and Developmental Disorders, 18,* 297-308.

Dwyer, J. T., & DeLong, G. R. (1987). A family history study of twenty probands with childhood manic-depressive illness. *Journal of the American Academy of Child and Adolescent Psychiatry, 26,* 176-180.

Edell, W. S. (1984). The Borderline Syndrome Index: Clinical validity and utility. *Journal of Nervous and Mental Disease, 172,* 254-263.

Edelman, G. (1987). *Neural darwinism: The theory of neuronal group selection.* New York: Basic Books.

Ekman, G., Miranda-Linné, F., Gillberg, C., Carle, M, & Wetterberg, L. (1989). Fenfluramine treatment of 20 autistic children. *Journal of Autism and Developmental Disorders, 19,* 511-532.

Escobar, J. I., Karno, M., Burnam, A., Hough, R. L., & Golding, J. (1988). Distribution of major mental disorders in a U.S. metropolis. *Acta Psychiatrica Scandinavica, 78*(Suppl. 344), 45-53.

Esman, A. H., Dechillo, N., & Moughan, V. (1985). "Hidden" eating disorders in female patients. *American Journal of Psychiatry, 143,* 803.

Eyman, R. K., Call, T. L., & White, J. F. (1989). Mortality of elderly mentally retarded persons in California. *Journal of Applied Gerontology, 8,* 203-215.

Faravelli, C., Degl'Innocenti, B. G., & Giardinelli, L. (1989). Epidemiology of anxiety disorders in Florence. *Acta Psychiatrica Scandinavica, 79,* 308-312.

Fieve, R. R., Go, R., Dunner, D. L., & Elston, R. (1984). Search for biological/genetic markers in a long-term epidemiological and morbid risk study of affective disorders. *Journal of Psychiatric Research, 18,* 425-445.

Flamert, M. F., Whitaker, A., Rapoport, J. L., Davies, M., Berg, C. Z., Kalikow, K., & Sceery, W. (1988). Obsessive-compulsive disorder in adolescence: An epidemiological study. *Journal of the American Academy of Child and Adolescent Psychiatry, 27,* 764-771.

Folstein, M. F., Folstein, S. E., & McHugh, P. R. (1975). "Mini-mental State": A practical method for grading the cognitive state of patients for the clinician. *Journal of Psychiatric Research, 12,* 189-198.

Ford, M. R., & Widiger, T. A. (1989). Sex bias in the diagnosis of histrionic and antisocial personality disorders. *Journal of Consulting and Clinical Psychology, 57,* 301-305.

Frank, E., & Anderson, B. P. (1987). Psychiatric disorders in rape victims: Past history and current symptomatology. *Comprehensive Psychiatry, 28,* 77-82.

Frank, E., Anderson, C., & Rubenstein, D. (1978). Frequency of sexual dysfunction in "normal" couples. *New England Journal of Medicine, 299,* 111-115.

Frankel, F. H. (1990). Hypnotizability and dissociation. *American Journal of Psychiatry, 147,* 823-829.

Freud, A. (1946). Introduction to the technique of the analysis of children. In N. Proctor-Gregg (Trans.), *Psychoanalytic techniques for children* (pp. 1-126). London: Imago. (Original lecture presented 1926)

Freud, S. (1958). The dynamics of transference. In J. Strachey (Ed. and Trans.), *The standard edition of the complete psychological works of Sigmund Freud* (Vol. 12, pp. 99-108). London: Hogarth Press. (Original work published 1912)

Friedman, E. (1969). The autistic syndrome and phenylketonuria. *Schizophrenia, 1,* 249-261.

Gautrin, D., Froda, S., Tetreault, H., & Gauvreau, D. (1990). Canadian projections of cases suffering from Alzheimer's disease and senile dementia of the Alzheimer type over the period 1986-2031. *Canadian Journal of Psychiatry, 35*, 162-165.

Gebhard, P. H., & Johnson, A. B. (1979). *The Kinsey data: Marginal tabulations of the 1938-1963 interviews conducted by the Institute for Sexual Research.* Philadelphia: Saunders.

Gershon, E. S., Hamovit, J., Guroff, J. J., Dibble, E., Leckman, J. F., Sceery, W., Targum, S. D., Nurnberger, J. I., Goldin, L. R., & Bunney, W. E. (1982). A family study of schizoaffective, bipolar I, bipolar II, unipolar, and normal control probands. *Archives of General Psychiatry, 39*, 1157-1167.

Ghodse, A. H., Stapleton, J., Edwards, G., & Edeh, J. (1987). Monitoring changing patterns of drug dependence in accident and emergency departments. *Drug and Alcohol Dependence, 19*, 265-269.

Gillberg, C. (1984). Infantile autism and other childhood psychoses in a Swedish urban region: Epidemiological aspects. *Journal of Child Psychology and Psychiatry, 25*, 35-43.

Gillberg, C. (1990a). Autism and pervasive developmental disorders. *Journal of Child Psychology and Psychiatry, 31*, 99-119.

Gillberg, C. (1990b). What is autism? *International Review of Psychiatry, 2*, 61-66.

Glue, P., Webb, O. J., & Surgenor, L. (1988). Psychopathology in adult mentally handicapped hospital patients. *Australian and New Zealand Journal of Psychiatry, 22*, 312-315.

Goldring, N., & Fieve, R. R. (1984). Attempted suicide in manic-depressive disorder. *American Journal of Psychotherapy, 38*, 373-383.

Goodman, W. K., Price, L. H., Rasmussen, S. A., Mazure, C., Delgado, P., Heninger, G. R., & Charney, D. S. (1989). The Yale-Brown Obsessive-Compulsive Scale: II. Validity. *Archives of General Psychiatry, 46*, 1012-1016.

Goodman, W. K., Price, L. H., Rasmussen, S. A., Mazure, C., Fleischmann, R. L., Hill, C. H., Heninger, G. R., & Charney, D. S. (1989). The Yale-Brown Obsessive Compulsive Scale: I. Development, use, and reliability. *Archives of General Psychiatry, 46,* 1006-1011.

Gorman, J. M. (1987). Generalized anxiety disorders. *Modern Problems of Pharmacopsychiatry, 22,* 127-140.

Gottesman, I. I., McGuffin, P., & Farmer, A. E. (1987). Clinical genetics as clues to the "real" genetics of schizophrenia. *Schizophrenia Bulletin, 13,* 23-47.

Grady, C. L., Haxby, J. V., Horwitz, B., Berg, G., & Rapoport, S. I. (1987). Neuropsychological and cerebral metabolic function in early vs late onset dementia of the Alzheimer type. *Neuropsychologia, 25,* 807-816.

Grady, C. L., Haxby, J. V., Horwitz, B., Sundaram, M., Berg, G., Schapiro, M., Friedland, R. P., & Rapoport, S. I. (1988). Longitudinal study of the early neuropsychological and cerebral metabolic changes in dementia of the Alzheimer type. *Journal of Clinical and Experimental Neuropsychology, 10,* 576-596.

Grapendaal, M. (1992). Cutting their coat according to their cloth: Economic behavior of Amsterdam opiate users. *International Journal of Addictions, 27,* 487-501.

Greenberg, D. (1984). Are religious compulsions religious or compulsive: A phenomenological study. *American Journal of Psychotherapy, 38,* 524-532.

Greenberg, R. P., & Bornstein, R. F. (1988a). The dependent personality: I. Risk for physical disorders. *Journal of Personality Disorders, 2,* 126-135.

Greenberg, R. P., & Bornstein, R. F. (1988b). The dependent personality: II. Risk for psychological disorders. *Journal of Personality Disorders, 2,* 136-143.

Greenson, R. R. (1967). *The technique and practice of psychoanalysis* (Vol. 1). New York: International Universities Press.

Gross, J., & Rosen, J. C. (1988). Bulimia in adolescents: Prevalence and psychosocial correlates. *International Journal of Eating Disorders, 7,* 51-61.

Grubb, H. J. (1987). Intelligence at the low end of the curve: Where are the racial differences? *Journal of Black Psychology, 14*, 25-34.

Gunderson, J. G., Kolb, J. E., & Austin, V. (1981). The Diagnostic Interview for Borderlines (DIB). *American Journal of Psychiatry, 138*, 896-903.

Gunderson, J. G., & Zanarini, M. C. (1987). Current overview of the borderline diagnosis. *Journal of Clinical Psychiatry, 48*(Suppl.), 5-11.

Hadigan, C. M., Kissileff, H. R., & Walsh, B. T. (1989). Patterns of food selection during meals in women with bulimia. *American Journal of Clinical Nutrition, 50*, 759-766.

Hart, K. J., & Ollendick, T. H. (1985). Prevalence of bulimia in working and university women. *American Journal of Psychiatry, 142*, 851-854.

Hatsukami, D. K., Mitchell, J. E., Eckert, E. D., & Pyle, R. L. (1986). Characteristics of patients with bulimia only, bulimia with affective disorder, and bulimia with substance abuse problems. *Addictive Behaviors, 11*, 399-406.

Hauri, P. (1982). *The sleep disorders.* Kalamazoo, MI: Upjohn.

Haveman, M. J., & Maaskant, M. A. (1989). Defining fragility of the elderly severly mentally handicapped according to mortality risk, morbidity, motor handicaps, and social functioning. *Journal of Mental Deficiency Research, 33*, 389-397.

Hawton, K. (1982). The behavioral treatment of sexual dysfunction. *British Journal of Psychiatry, 140*, 94-101.

Haxby, J. V., Grady, C. L., Koss, E., Horwitz, B., Heston, L., Schapiro, M., Friedland, R. P., & Rapoport, S. I. (1990). Longitudinal study of cerebral metabolic asymmetries and associated neuropsychological patterns in early dementia of the Alzheimer type. *Archives of Neurology, 47*, 753-760.

Healy, K., Conroy, R. M., & Walsh, N. (1985). The prevalence of binge-eating and bulimia in 1063 college students. *Journal of Psychiatric Research, 19*, 161-166.

Henderson, A. S. (1990). The social psychiatry of later life. *British Journal of Psychiatry, 156*, 645-653.

Henderson, J. G., & Pollard, C. A. (1988). Three types of obsessive-compulsive disorder in a community sample. *Journal of Clinical Psychology, 44*, 747-752.

Hertzog, D. (1984). Are anorexic and bulimic patients depressed? *American Journal of Psychiatry, 141*, 1594-1597.

Hollifield, M., Katon, W., Spain, D., & Pule, L. (1990). Anxiety and depression in a village in Lesotho, Africa: A comparison with the United States. *British Journal of Psychiatry, 156*, 343-350.

Howlin, P., & Rutter, M. (1978). *Treatment of autistic children.* London: Wiley.

Inman, D. J., Bascue, L. O., & Skoloda, T. (1985). Identification of borderline personality disorders among substance abuse in-patients. *Journal of Substance Abuse Treatment, 2*, 229-232.

Jacobs, J., & Glasser, B. (1984). Manic depression and suicide. *Case Analysis, 2*, 5-19.

Jacobs, S., Hansen, F., Kasl, S., Ostfeld, A., Berkman, L., & Kim, K. (1990). Anxiety disorders during acute bereavement: Risk and risk factors. *Journal of Clinical Psychiatry, 51*, 269-274.

Jacobs, S., & Kim, K. (1990). Psychiatric complications of bereavement. *Psychiataric Annals, 20*, 314-317.

Johnson, B. D., Wish, E. D., Schmeider, J., & Huizinga, D., (1991). Concentration of delinquent offending: Serious drug involvement and high delinquency rates. *Journal of Drug Issues, 21*, 205-229.

Johnson, C., Tobin, D. L., & Lipkin, J. (1989). Epidemiologic changes in bulimic behavior among female adolescents over a five-year period. *International Journal of Eating Disorders, 8*, 647-655.

Johnston, L. D., O'Malley, P. M., & Bachman, J. G. (1987). Psychotherapeutic, licit, and illicit use of drugs among adolescents: An epidemiological perspective. *Journal of Adolescent Health Care, 8*, 36-51.

Jonas, J. M., Gold, M. S., Sweeney, D., & Pottash, A. L. (1987). Eating disorders and cocaine abuse: A survey of 259 cocaine abusers. *Journal of Clinical Psychiatry, 48*, 47-50.

Jonsdottir-Baldursson, T., & Horvath, P. (1987). Borderline personality-disordered alcoholics in Iceland: Descriptions on demographic, clinical, and MMPI variables. *Journal of Consulting and Clinical Psychology, 55,* 738-741.

Kall, K. I., & Olin, R. G. (1990). HIV status and changes in risk behaviour among intravenous drug users in Stockholm, 1987-1988. *AIDS, 4,* 153-157.

Kanner, L. (1943). Autistic disturbances of effective content. *Nervous Child, 2,* 217-240.

Kaplan, H. S. (1974). *The new sex therapy.* New York: Bruner-Mazel.

Kaplan, M. (1983). A woman's view of *DSM-III. American Psychologist, 38,* 786-792.

Karno, M., Golding, J. M., Burnam, M. A., Hough, R. L., Escobar, J. T., Wells, K. M., & Boyer, R. (1989). Anxiety disorders among Mexican-Americans and non-Hispanic whites in Los Angeles. *Journal of Nervous and Mental Disease, 177,* 202-209.

Karno, M., Golding, J. M., Sorenson, S. B., & Burnam, M. A. (1988). The epidemiology of obsessive-compulsive disorder in five U.S. communities. *Archives of General Psychiatry, 45,* 1094-1099.

Kashani, J. H., Carlson, G. A., Beck, N. C., Hoeper, E. W., Corcoran, C. M., McAllister, J. A., Fallahi, C., Rosenberg, T. K., & Reid, J. C. (1987). Depression, depressive symptoms, and depressed mood among a community sample of adolescents. *American Journal of Psychiatry, 144,* 931-934.

Kass, F., Spitzer, R. L., & Williams, J. B. (1983). An empirical study of the issue of sex bias in the diagnostic criteria of *DSM-III* Axis II personality disorders. *American Psychologist, 38,* 799-801.

Keller, M. B., Herzog, D. B., Lavori, P. W., Ott, I. L., Bradburn, I. S., & Mahoney, E. M. (1989). High rates of chronicity and rapidity of relapse in patients with bulimia nervosa and depression. *Archives of General Psychiatry, 46,* 480-481.

Kendler, K. B., Silberg, J. L., Neale, M. C., Kessler, R. C., Heath, A. C., & Eaves, L. S. (1991). The family history method: Whose psychiatric history is measured? *American Journal of Psychiatry, 148*, 1501-1504.

Kinsey, A. C., Pomeroy, W. B., & Martin, C. (1948). *Sexual behavior in the human male.* Philadelphia: Saunders.

Kinsey, A. C., Pomeroy, W. B., Martin, C., & Gebhard, P. (1953). *Sexual behavior in the human female.* Philadelphia: Saunders.

Kirmil-Gray, K., Eagleston, J. R., Gibson, E., & Thoresen, C. E. (1984). Sleep disturbance in adolescence: Sleep quality, sleep habits, beliefs about sleep, and daytime functioning. *Journal of Youth and Adolescence, 13*, 375-384.

Kissileff, H. R., Walsh, B. T., Kral, J. G., & Cassidy, S. M. (1986). Laboratory studies of eating behavior in women with bulimia. *Physiological Behavior, 38*, 563-570.

Klein, D. N., Clark, D. C., Dansky, L., & Margolis, E. T. (1988). Dysthymia in the offspring of parents with primary unipolar affective disorder. *Journal of Abnormal Psychology, 97*, 265-274.

Klein, D. N., Depue, R. A., & Slater, J. F. (1985). Cyclothymia in the adolescent offspring of parents with bipolar affective disorder. *Journal of Abnormal Psychology, 94*, 115-127.

Klein, D. N., Taylor, E. B., Dickstein, S., & Harding, K. (1988a). The early-late onset distinction in *DSM-III-R* dysthymia. *Journal of Affective Disorders, 14*, 25-33.

Klein, D. N., Taylor, E. B., Dickstein, S., & Harding, K. (1988b). Primary early-onset dysthymia: Comparison with primary nonbipolar nonchronic major depression on demographic, clinical, familial, personality, and socioenvironmental characteristics and short-term outcome. *Journal of Abnormal Psychology, 97*, 387-398.

Klein, D. N., Taylor, E. B., Harding, K., & Dickstein, S. (1988). Double depression and episodic major depression: Demographic, clinical, familial, personality, and socioenvironmental characteristics and short-term outcome. *American Journal of Psychiatry, 145*, 1226-1231.

Kluft, R. P. (1984). Aspects of the treatment of multiple personality disorder. *Psychiatric Annals, 14,* 51-55.

Kluft, R. P. (1987). First-rank symptoms as a diagnostic clue to multiple personality. *American Journal of Psychiatry, 144,* 293-298.

Knopman, D. S., & Ryberg, S. (1989). A verbal memory test with high predictive accuracy for dementia of the Alzheimer type. *Archives of Neurology, 46,* 141-145.

Kocsis, J. H., & Frances, A. J. (1987). A critical discussion of *DSM-III* dysthymic disorder. *American Journal of Psychiatry, 144,* 1534-1542.

Kohut, H. (1977). *The restoration of the self.* New York: International Universities Press.

Kovacs, M., Paulauskas, S., Gastonis, C., & Richards, C. (1988). Depressive disorders in childhood: III. A longitudinal study of comorbidity with and risk for conduct disorders. *Journal of Affective Disorders, 15,* 205-217.

Kozel, N. J., & Adams, E. H. (1986). Epidemiology of drug abuse: An overview. *Science, 234,* 970-974.

Kragh-Sorensen, P., Holm, P., Fynboe, C., Schaumburg, E., Andersen, B., Bech, P., & Pichard, J. (1990). Bromazepam in generalized anxiety: Randomized, multi-practice comparisons with both chlorprothixene and placebo. *Psychopharmacology, 100,* 383-386.

Kramer, M., German, P. S., Anthony, J. C., von Kopff, M., & Skinner, E. A. (1986). Patterns of mental disorders among the elderly residents of Eastern Baltimore. *Journal of the American Geriatrics Society, 33,* 236-245.

Krishnamurthy, K., & Joshi, M. R. (1989). The syndrome of infantile autism in siblings. *Child Psychiatry Quarterly, 22,* 107-114.

Kroll, J. (1988). *The challenge of the borderline patient: Competency in diagnosis and treatment.* New York: Norton.

Kullgren, G. (1987). An empirical comparison of three different borderline concepts. *Acta Psychiatrica Scandinavica, 76,* 246-255.

Kunjukrishnan, R., & Bradford, J. M. (1988). Schizophrenia and major affective disorder: Forensic psychiatric issues. *Canadian Journal of Psychiatry, 33,* 723-733.

Lack, L. C. (1986). Delayed sleep and sleep loss in university students. *Journal of American College Health, 35,* 105-110.

Laessle, R. G., Kittl, S., Fichter, M. M., & Wittchen, H. U. (1987). Major affective disorder in anorexia nervosa and bulimia: A descriptive diagnostic study. *British Journal of Psychiatry, 151,* 785-789.

Landrine, H. (1989). The social class-schizophrenia relationship: A different approach and new hypotheses. *Journal of Social and Clinical Psychology, 8,* 288-303.

Last, C. G. (1991). Somatic complaints in anxiety disordered children. *Journal of Anxiety Disorders, 5,* 125-138.

Last, C. G., Francis, G., Hersen, M., Kazdin, A. E., & Strauss, C. C. (1987). Separation anxiety and school phobia: A comparison using *DSM-III* criteria. *American Journal of Psychiatry, 144,* 653-657.

Last, C. G., Hersen, M., Kazdin, A. E., Finkelstein, R., & Strauss, C. C. (1987). Comparison of DSM-III separation anxiety and overanxious disorders: Demographic characteristics and patterns of comorbidity. *Journal of the American Academy of Child and Adolescent Psychiatry, 26,* 527-531.

Ledoux, S., Choquet, M., & Flament, M. (1991). Eating disorders among adolescents in an unselected French population. *International Journal of Eating Disorders, 10,* 81-89.

Leitenberg, H., Rosen, J. C., Gross, J. Nudelman, S., & Vara, L. S. (1988). Exposure plus response prevention treatment of bulimia nervosa. *Journal of Consulting and Clinical Psychology, 56,* 535-541.

Lewinsohn, P. M., Rhode, P., Seely, J. R., and Hops, H. (1991). Comorbidity of unipolar depression: I. Major depression with dysthymia. *Journal of Abnormal Psychology, 100,* 205-213.

Lewy, A. J., Sack, R. L., & Singer, C. M. (1985). Immediate and delayed effects of bright light on human melatonin production: Shifting "dawn" and "dusk" shifts the dim light melatonin onlet (DLMO). *Annals of the New York Academy of Sciences, 453,* 253-259.

Llorca, M., Note, Y. D., Michel, B., & Aunoud-Castiglioni, R. (1989). Behavioral strategies in taking charge of patients with Alzheimer-type dementia. *Psychologie Medicale, 21,* 628-632.

Lord, C., Schopler, E., & Revicki, D. (1982). Sex differences in autism. *Journal of Autism and Developmental Disorders, 12,* 317-330.

Lotter, V. (1966). Epidemiology of autistic conditions in young children: I. Prevalence. *Social Psychiatry, 1,* 124-137.

Lovaas, O. I. (1987). Behavioral treatment and normal educational and intellectual functioning in young autistic children. *Journal of Consulting and Clinical Psychology, 55,* 3-9.

Lund, J. (1986). Treatment of psychiatric morbidity in the mentally retarded adult. *Acta Psychiatrica Scandinavica, 73,* 429-436.

Luxenberg, J. S., Haxby, J. V., Creasey, H., Sundaram, M., & Rapoport, S. I. (1987). Rate of ventricular enlargement in dementia of the Alzheimer type correlates with rate of neuropsychological deterioration. *Neurology, 37,* 1135-1140.

Mahler, M. S. (1968). *On human symbiosis and the vicissitudes of individuation.* New York: International Universities Press.

Marks, I. M. (1986). Epidemiology of anxiety. *Social Psychiatry, 21,* 167-171.

Marquez, C., Taintor, Z., & Schwartz, M. A. (1985). Diagnosis of manic depressive illness in blacks. *Comprehensive Psychiatry, 26,* 337-341.

Martin, J. R., & Wollitzer, A. O. (1988). The prevalence, secrecy, and psychology of purging in a family practice setting. *International Journal of Eating Disorders, 7,* 515-519.

Martin, R. L. (1989). Update on dementia of the Alzheimer type. *Hospital and Community Psychiatry, 40,* 593-604.

Masters, W., & Johnson, V. (1970). *Human sexual inadequacy.* Boston: Little Brown.

McLaren, J., & Bryson, S. E. (1987). Review of recent epidemiological studies of mental retardation: Prevalence, associated disorders, and etiology. *American Journal on Mental Retardation, 92,* 243-254.

McLoughlin, I. J. (1988). A study of mortality experiences in a mental-handicap hospital. *British Journal of Psychiatry, 153,* 645-649.

McQueen, P. C., Spence, M. W., Winsor, E. J. T., Garner, J. B., & Pereira, L. H. (1986). Causal origins of major mental handicap in the Canadian Maritime provinces. *Developmental Medicine and Child Neurology, 28,* 697-707.

Mezzich, J. E., Fabrega, H., & Coffman, G. A. (1987). Multiaxial characterization of depressive patients. *Journal of Nervous and Mental Disease, 175,* 339-346.

Miller, S. D., Blackburn, T., Scholes, G., White, G. L., & Mamalis, N. (1991). Optical differences in multiple personality disorder: A second look. *Journal of Nervous and Mental Disease, 179,* 132-135.

Mintz, L. B., & Betz, N. E. (1988). Prevalence and correlates of eating disordered behaviors among undergraduate women. *Journal of Counseling Psychology, 35,* 463-471.

Minuchin, S. (1974). *Families and family therapy.* Cambridge, MA: Harvard University Press.

Mitchell, J. E., Davis, L., & Goff, C. (1985). The process of relapse in patients with bulimia. *International Journal of Eating Disorders, 4,* 457-463.

Mitchell, J. E., Hatsukami, D. K., Pyle, R. L., & Eckert, E. D. (1986). The bulimia syndrome: Course of the illness and associated problems. *Comprehensive Psychiatry, 27,* 165-170.

Myers, J. K., Weissman, M. M., & Tischler, G. W. (1984). Six-month prevalence of psychiatric disorders in three communities. *Archives of General Psychiatry, 41,* 959-967.

Nace, E. P., Saxon, J. J., & Shore, N. (1983). A comparison of borderline and nonborderline alcoholic patients. *Archives of General Psychiatry, 40,* 54-56.

Nee, L. E., Eldridge, R., Sunderland, T., Thomas, C. B., Thompson, K. E., Weingartner, H., Weiss, H., Julian, C., & Cohen, R. (1987). Dementia of the Alzheimer type: Clinical and family study of 22 twin pairs. *Neurology, 37,* 359-363.

Nettlebladt, P., & Uddenberg, N. (1979). Sexual dysfunction and sexual satisfaction in 58 married Swedish men. *Journal of Psychosomatic Research, 23,* 141-147.

Nicolosi, A., Molinari, S., Musicco, M., Saracco, A., Ziliani, N, & Lazzarin, A. (1991). Positive modification of injecting behavior among intravenous heroin users from Milan and northern Italy, 1987-1989. *British Journal of Addiction, 86,* 91-102.

O'Connell, R. A., Mayo, J. A., Flatow, L., Cuthbertson, B., & O'Brien, B. E. (1991). Outcome of bipolar disorder on long-term treatment with lithium. *British Journal of Psychiatry, 159,* 123-129.

Ozaki, N., Iwata, T., Itoh, A., Kogawa, S., Ohta, T., Okada, T., & Kasahara, Y. (1988). Body temperature monitoring in subjects with delayed sleep phase syndrome. *Neuropsychobiology, 20,* 174-177.

Pardes, H., Kaufman, C. A., Pincus, H. A., & West, A. (1989). Genetics and psychiatry: Past discoveries, current dilemmas, and future directions. *American Journal of Psychiatry, 146,* 435-443.

Parker, H., Newcombe, R., & Bakx, K. (1987). The new heroin users: Prevalence and characteristics in Wirral, Merseyside. *British Journal of Addictions, 82,* 147-157.

Parker, J., Pool, Y., Rawle, R., & Gay, M. (1988). Monitoring problem drug use in Bristol. *British Journal of Psychiatry, 152,* 214-221.

Perugi, G., Deltito, J., Soriani, A., Musetti, L., Petracca, A., Nisita, C., Maremmani, I., & Cassano, G. B. (1988). Relationships between panic disorder and separation anxiety with school phobia. *Comprehensive Psychiatry, 29,* 98-107.

Peveler, R. C., Green, R., & Mandelbrote, B. M. (1988). Prevalence of heroin misuse in Oxford City. *British Journal of Addictions, 83,* 513-518.

Physician's Desk Reference (4th ed.). (1992). Oradell, NJ: Medical Economics Company.

Pope, H. G., & Hudson, J. I. (1989). Are eating disorders associated with borderline personality disorder? A critical review. *International Journal of Eating Disorders, 8,* 1-9.

Pruchno, R. A., Michaels, J. E., & Potashnik, S. L. (1990). Predictors of institutionalization among Alzheimer disease victims with caregiving spouses. *Journals of Gerontology, 45,* S259-S266.

Putnam, F. W., Guroff, J. J., Silberman, E. K., Barban, L., & Post, R. M. (1986). The clinical phenomenology of multiple personality disorder: Review of 100 recent cases. *Journal of Clinical Psychiatry, 47,* 285-293.

Pyle, R. L., Mitchell, J. E., Eckert, E. D., Hatsukami, D., Pomeroy, C., & Zimmerman, R. (1990). Maintenance treatment and 6-month outcome for bulimic patients who respond to initial treatment. *American Journal of Psychiatry, 147,* 871-875.

Rapoport, J. L. (1986). Childhood obsessive-compulsive disorder. *Journal of Child Psychology and Psychiatry and Allied Disciplines, 27,* 289-295.

Rasmussen, S. A. (1990, May). Recent advances in obsessive compulsive disorders. Paper presented at the Regent Hospital Grand Rounds, New York.

Rasmussen, S. A., & Eisen, J. L. (1989). Clinical features and phenomenology of obsessive-compulsive disorder. *Psychiatric Annals, 19,* 67-73.

Rasmussen, S. A., & Eisen, J. L. (1990). Epidemiology of obsessive-compulsive disorder. *Journal of Clinical Psychiatry, 51*(Suppl. 2), 10-13.

Regier, D. A., Boyd, J. H., Burke, J. D., Rae, D. S., Myers, J. K., Kramer, M., Robins, L. N., George, L. K., Karno, M., & Locke, B. Z. (1988). One-month prevalence of mental disorders in the United States: Based on five epidemiologic catchment area sites. *Archives of General Psychiatry, 45,* 977-986.

Regier, D. A., Narrow, W. E., & Rae, D. S. (1990). The epidemiology of anxiety disorders: The Epidemiologic Catchment Area (ECA) experience. *Journal of Psychiatric Research, 24*(Suppl. 2), 3-14.

Reich, J. (1987). Sex distribution of *DSM-III* personality disorders in psychiatric outpatients. *American Journal of Psychiatry, 144*, 485-488.

Reich, J. (1990a). Comparisons of males and females with *DSM-III* dependent personality disorder. *Psychiatry Research, 33*, 207-214.

Reich, J. (1990b). The relationship between *DSM-III* avoidant and dependent personality disorders. *Psychiatry Research, 34*, 281-191.

Reich, J., Noyes, R., & Troughton, E. (1987). Dependent personality disorder associated with phobic avoidance in patients with panic disorder. *American Journal of Psychiatry, 144*, 323-326.

Reich, W. (1949). *Character analysis* (3rd ed.). New York: Orgone Institute Press.

Renshaw, D. C. (1988). Profile of 2376 patients treated at Loyola Sex Clinic between 1972 and 1987. *Sexual and Marital Therapy, 3*, 111-117.

Richardson, S. A. (1989). Issues in the definition of mental retardation and the representativeness of studies. *Research in Developmental Disabilities, 10*, 285-294.

Rickels, K., Schweizer, E., Csanalosi, I., Case, W. G., & Chung, H. (1988). Long-term treatment of anxiety and risk of withdrawal: Prospective comparison of clorazepate and buspirone. *Archives of General Psychiatry, 45*, 444-450.

Rihmer, Z., Barsi, J., Arato, M., & Demeter, E. (1990). Suicide in subtypes of primary major depression. *Journal of Affective Disorders, 18*, 221-225.

Rittmannsberger, H., & Schony, W. (1986). Prevalence of tardive dyskensia in a population of long-stay schizophrenic inpatients. *Nervenartz, 57*, 116-118.

Ritvo, E. R., Freeman, B. J., Pingree, C., Mason-Brothers, A., Jorde, L., Jenson, W. R., McMahon, W. M., Petersen, P. B., Mo, A., & Ritvo, A. (1989). The UCLA-University of Utah epidemiologic survey of autism: Prevalence. *American Journal of Psychiatry, 146,* 194-199.

Robins, L. N., Helzer, J. E., Crougham, J., & Ratcliff, K. S. (1981). National Institute of Mental Health Diagnostic Interview Schedule: Its history, characteristics, and validity. *Archives of General Psychiatry, 38,* 381-389.

Robins, L. N., Helzer, J. E., Weissman, M. M., Orvaschel, H., Gruenberg, E., Burke, J. D., & Regier, D. A. (1984). Lifetime prevalence rates of specific psychiatric disorders in three sites. *Archives of General Psychiatry, 41,* 949-958.

Rosen, J. C., Leitenberg, H., Fisher, C., & Khazam, C. (1986). Binge-eating episodes in bulimia nervosa: The amount and type of food consumed. *International Journal of Eating Disorders, 5,* 255-267.

Rosenblum, L., Darrow, W., Witte, S., Cohen, J., French, J., Gill, P. S., Potterat, J., Sikes, K., Reich, R., & Hadler, S. (1992). Sexual practices in the transmission of hepatitus B virus and prevalence of hepatitus Delta virus infection in female prostitutes in the United States. *Journal of the American Medical Association, 267,* 2477-2481.

Rosenthal, N. E., Joseph-Vanderpool, J. R., Levendosky, A. A., Johnston, S. H., Allen, R., Kelly, K. A., Souetre, E., Schultz, P., & Starz, K. E. (1990). Phase-shifting effects of bright morning light as treatment for delayed sleep phase syndrome. *Sleep, 13,* 354-361.

Ross, C. A., Miller, S. D., Reagor, P., Bjornson, L., Fraser, G. A., & Anderson, G. (1990). Structured interview data on 102 cases of multiple personality disorder from four centers. *American Journal of Psychiatry, 147,* 596-601.

Ross, C. A., Norton, G. R., & Wozney, K. (1989). Multiple personality disorder: An analysis of 236 cases. *Canadian Journal of Psychiatry, 34,* 413-418.

Rutter, M. (1983). Cognitive deficits in the pathogenesis of autism. *Journal of Child Psychology and Psychiatry, 24,* 513-531.

Sacks, O. (1985). *The man who mistook his wife for a hat, and other clinical tales*. New York: Summit Books.

Salmon, D. P., Thal, L. J., Butters, N., & Heindel, W. C. (1990). Longitudinal evaluation of dementia of the Alzheimer type: A comparison of 3 standardized mental status examinations. *Neurology, 40*, 1225-1230.

Sanchez-Carbonell, J., Cami, J., & Brigos, B. (1988). Follow-up of heroin addicts in Spain (EMETYST Project): Results one year after treatment admission. *British Journal of Addiction, 83*, 1439-1448.

Satz, P., van Gorp, W. G., Soper, H. V., & Mitsushima, M. (1987). WAIS-R marker for dementia of the Alzheimer type? An empirical and statistical induction test. *Journal of Clinical and Experimental Neuropsychology, 9*, 767-774.

Scott, J. (1988). Chronic depression. *British Journal of Psychiatry, 153*, 287-297.

Shader, R. I. (1984). Epidemiologic and family studies. *Psychosomatics, 25*, 10-15.

Shaffer, J. W., Nurco, D. N., & Kinlock, T. W. (1984). A new classification of narcotic addicts based on type and extent of criminal activity. *Comprehensive Psychiatry, 25*, 315-328.

Sheehan, M., Oppenheimer, E., & Taylor, C. (1988). Who comes for treatment? Drug misusers at three London agencies. *British Journal of Addictions, 83*, 311-320.

Shekim, W. O., Asarnow, R. F., Hess, E., & Zaucha, K. (1990). A clinical and demographic profile of a sample of adults with attention deficit hyperactivity disorder, residual state. *Comprehensive Psychiatry, 31*, 416-425.

Shibayama, H., Kasahara, Y., & Kobayashi, H. (1986). Prevalence of dementia in a Japanese elderly population. *Acta Psychiatrica Scandinavica, 74*, 144-151.

Shover, L. R., Evans, R. B., & von Eschenbach, A. C. (1987). Sexual rehabilitation in a cancer center: Diagnosis and outcome in 384 consultations. *Archives of Sexual Behavior, 16*, 445-461.

Spanos, N. P., Weekes, J. R., & Bertrand, L. D. (1985). Multiple personality: A social psychological perspective. *Journal of Abnormal Psychology, 94*, 362-376.

Spector, I. P., & Carey, M. P. (1990). Incidence and prevalence of the sexual dysfunctions: A critical review of the empirical literature. *Archives of Sexual Behavior, 19,* 389-408.

Spiegel, D. (1986). Dissociating damage. *American Journal of Clinical Hypnosis, 29,* 123-131.

Spitzer, R. L., Endicott, J., & Gibbon, M. (1979). Crossing the border into borderline personality and borderline schizophrenia: The development of criteria. *Archives of General Psychiatry, 36,* 17-24.

Stein, D. M., & Brinza, S. R. (1988). Bulimia: Prevalence estimates in female junior high and high school students. *Journal of Clinical and Child Psychiatry, 18,* 206-213.

Steinhauser, H.-C., Göbel, D., Breinlinger, M., & Wohlleben, B. (1986). A community survey of infantile autism. *Journal of the American Academy of Child Psychiatry, 25,* 186-189.

Steketee, G. (1990). Personality traits and disorders in obsessive compulsives. *Journal of Anxiety Disorders, 4,* 351-364.

Stephansson, J. G., Lindal, E., Bjornsson, J. K., & Gudmundsdottir, A. (1991). Lifetime prevalence of specific mental disorders among people born in Iceland in 1931. *Acta Psychiatrica Scandinavica, 84,* 142-149.

Strean, H. S. (1985). *Resolving resistances in psychotherapy.* New York: Wiley.

Suriyama, T., & Abe, T. (1986). The prevalence of autism in Nagoya, Japan: A total population study. *Journal of Autism and Developmental Disorders, 19,* 87-96.

Swartz, M., Blazer, D., George, L., & Winfield, I. (1990). Estimating the prevalence of borderline personality disorder in the community. *Journal of Personality Disorders, 4,* 257-272.

Swartz, M. S., Blazer, D. G., George, L. K., Winfield, I., Zakaris, J., & Dye, E. (1989). Identification of borderline personality disorder with the NIMH Diagnostic Interview Schedule. *American Journal of Psychiatry, 146,* 200-205.

Sykes, D. K., Gross, M., & Subishin, S. (1986). Preliminary findings of demographic variables in patients suffering from anorexia nervosa and bulimia. *International Journal of Psychosomatics, 33,* 27-30.

Sykes, D. K., Leuser, B., Melia, M., & Gross, M. (1988). A demographic analysis of 252 patients with anorexia nervosa and bulimia. *International Journal of Psychosomatics, 35*, 5-9.

Tao, K.-T. (1988). Mentally retarded persons in the People's Republic of China: Review of epidemiological studies and services. *American Journal on Mental Retardation, 93*, 193-199.

Terrier, N. (1991). Behavioural psychotherapy and schizophrenia: The past, the present, and the future. *Behavioural Psychotherapy, 19*, 121-130.

Thelen, M. H., Mann, L. M., Pruitt, J., & Smith, M. (1987). Bulimia: Prevalence and component factors in college women. *Journal of Psychosomatic Research, 31*, 73-78.

Thorpy, M. J., Korman, E., Spielman, A. J., & Glovinsky, P. B. (1988). Delayed sleep phase syndrome in adolescents. *Journal of Adolescent Health Care, 9*, 22-27.

Treffert, D. A. (1970). Epidemiology of infantile autism. *Archives of General Psychiatry, 22*, 431-438.

Trindler, J. (1988). Subjective insomnia without objective findings: A pseudo diagnostic classification? *Psychological Bulletin, 103*, 87-94.

Trull, T. J., Widiger, T. A., & Frances, A. (1987). Covariation of criteria sets for avoidant, schizoid, and dependent personality disorders. *American Journal of Psychiatry, 144*, 767-771.

Tsai, L., Stewart, M. A., & August, G. (1981). Implication of sex differences in the familial transmission of infantile autism. *Journal of Autism and Developmental Disorders, 11*, 165-173.

Turner, T. H., Dossetor, D. R., & Bates, R. E. (1986). The early outcome of admission to an adolescent unit: A report on 100 cases. *Journal of Adolescence, 9*, 367-382.

Volicer, L., Seltzer, B., Rheaume, Y., Karner, J., Glennon, M., Riley, M. E., & Crino, P. (1989). Eating difficulties in patients with probable dementia of the Alzheimer type. *Journal of Geriatric Psychiatry and Neurology, 2*, 188-195.

Wahlström, J., Gillberg, C., Gustavson, K.-G., & Holmgren, G. (1986). Infantile autism and the fragile X syndrome: A Swedish population multicenter study. *American Journal of Medical Genetics, 23,* 403-408.

Watters, J. K., Cheng, Y.-T., & Lorvick, J. J. (1991). Drug-use profiles, race, age, and risk of HIV infection among intravenous drug users in San Francisco. *International Journal of Addictions, 26,* 1247-1261.

Wechsler, D. (1958). *The measurement and appraisal of adult intelligence* (4th ed.). Baltimore: Williams and Wilkins.

Wechsler, D. (1974). *Manual for the Wechsler Intelligence Scale for Children—Revised.* New York: Psychological Corporation.

Weeke, A., & Vaeth, M. (1986). Excess mortality of bipolar and unipolar manic-depressive patients. *Journal of Affective Disorders, 11,* 227-234.

Weiss, S. W., & Ebert, M. H. (1983). Psychological and behavioral characteristics of normal-weight bulimics and normal-weight controls. *Psychosomatic Medicine, 45,* 293-303.

Weissman, M. M. (1990). Panic and generalized anxiety: Are they separate disorders? *Journal of Psychiatric Research, 24,* 157-162.

Weissman, M. M., Leaf, P. J., Bruce, M. L., & Florio, L. (1988). The epidemiology of dysthymia in five communities: Rates, risks, comorbidity, and treatment. *American Journal of Psychiatry, 145,* 815-819.

Weissman, M. M., Leaf, P. J., Tischler, G. L., Blazer, D. G., Karno, M., Bruce, M. C., & Florio, L. P. (1988). Affective disorders in five United States communities. *Psychological Medicine, 18,* 141-153.

Weissman, M. M., & Merikangas, K. R. (1986). The epidemiology of anxiety and panic disorders: An update. *Journal of Clinical Psychiatry, 47,* 11-17.

Whitaker, A., Johnson, J., Shaffer, D., Rapoport, J., Kalikow, K., Walsh, B. T., Davies, M., & Braiman, S. (1990). Uncommon troubles in young people: Prevalence estimates of selected psychiatric disorders in a nonreferred adolescent population. *Archives of General Psychiatry, 47,* 487-496.

Wing, L., (1981). Sex ratios in early childhood autism and related conditions. *Psychiatric Research, 5,* 129-137.

Wing, L., & Gould, J. (1979). Severe impairments of social interaction and associated abnormalities in children: Epidemiology and classification. *Journal of Autism and Developmental Disorders, 9,* 129-137.

Winokur, G., & Crowe, R. R. (1983). Bipolar illness: The sex-polarity effect in affectively ill family members. *Archives of General Psychiatry, 40,* 57-58.

Wirz-Justice, A., & Pringle, C. (1987). The non-entrained life of a young gentleman at Oxford. *Sleep, 10,* 57-61.

Wolman, B. B. (Ed.). (1972). *Handbook of child psychoanalysis: Research, theory, and practice.* New York:VanNostrand Reinhold.

Wu, J. C., Buchsbaum, M. S., Hershey, T. G., Hazlett, E., Sicotte, N., & Johnson, J. C. (1991). PET in generalized anxiety disorder. *Biological Psychiatry, 29,* 1181-1199.

Yager, J., Landsverk, J., Edelstein, C. K., & Hyler, S. E. (1989). Screening for Axis II personality disorders in women with bulimic eating disorders. *Psychosomatics, 30,* 255-262.

Zetin, M. (1990). Obsessive-compulsive disorder. *Stress Medicine, 6,* 311-321.